THE NEW GENERATION OF ACTING TEACHERS

Eva Mekler is the author of books and articles in both theater and psychology. Her theater books include *Contemporary Scenes for Student Actors* (Penguin) and *The Actor's Scenebook* and *The Actor's Scenebook, Vol. II* (both from Bantam). She has also been an actress, appearing in Broadway, off-Broadway, and off-off-Broadway productions. Her adaptation into a play of Anton Chekhov's novella, "The Duel," was produced in an off-off-Broadway production. In 1985 she taught acting and directed productions at the Usdan Center for the Creative and Performing Arts. She herself has studied acting both in New York and at the London Academy of Music and Dramatic Arts (LAMDA).

In psychology, Ms. Mekler has written the book *Bringing Up a Moral Child* (Addison-Wesley) and various articles, including "How to Raise a Moral Child," in the March 1986 issue of *Working Mother*. She has a master's degree in psychology from New York University.

The NEW GENERATION of ACTING TEACHERS

—————— ❦ ——————

by Eva Mekler

PENGUIN BOOKS

PENGUIN BOOKS
Viking Penguin Inc., 40 West 23rd Street,
New York, New York 10010, U.S.A.
Penguin Books Ltd, 27 Wrights Lane, London
W8 5TZ (Publishing & Editorial), and Harmondsworth,
Middlesex, England (Distribution & Warehouse)
Penguin Books Australia Ltd, Ringwood,
Victoria, Australia
Penguin Books Canada Limited, 2801 John Street,
Markham, Ontario, Canada L3R 1B4
Penguin Books (N.Z.) Ltd, 182–190 Wairau Road,
Auckland 10, New Zealand

First published in Penguin Books 1987
Published simultaneously in Canada

LIBRARY OF CONGRESS CATALOGING IN PUBLICATION DATA
Mekler, Eva.
The new generation of acting teachers.
1. Acting teachers—United States—Interviews.
I. Title.
PN2078.U6M4   1987   792'.028'0922   87-7015
ISBN 0 14 00.8898 9

Printed in
the United States of America by
R. R. Donnelley & Sons Company, Harrisonburg, Virginia
Set in Electra and Windsor Light
Designed by Victoria Hartman

for Michael

Contents

Preface

When the Moscow Art Theater toured the United States in 1923 it seized the imagination of an entire generation of actors. The new naturalism that these Russian actors brought to the stage presented a sharp contrast to the melodramatic acting style that had dominated the American stage for so many years. Very quickly a group of young actors adopted the techniques of Konstantin Stanislavsky, the originator of the system of training that promoted this new style. These artists became the first generation of American acting teachers. Among them were such names as Lee Strasberg, Stella Adler, Harold Clurman, and Sandy Meisner—soon to be followed by Elia Kazan, Uta Hagen, and Bobby Lewis, among others. These were the founders of the modern American approach to the craft of acting.

In the years that followed, these teachers left an indelible mark on three generations of actors and acting teachers. Some of these instructors combined careers in acting and directing; some formed theater companies and began to direct workshops where both professional and amateur actors could acquire the new techniques, which were rooted in an emotional reality that often astounded and sometimes perplexed audiences.

Although the predominant acting style today in film and on stage is still referred to as the American method, it is now being taught by a new generation of acting teachers. Most of them studied with the early proponents and interpreters of Stanislavsky. Some basically continue this tradition with slight alterations and additions, while others developed procedures of their own that differ radically from the training they received. As a result, a new group of important teachers has emerged who collectively train thousands of students every year. Some teach in their own professional workshops in New York and Los Angeles, and some teach in the major university theater programs such as Juilliard, Yale, and Northwestern. Their students have become some of our most prominent theater, TV, and film stars. Some of these instructors are private coaches to today's best-known actors as well as continuing to train beginners. This group constitutes a new and different influence on the art of acting.

My goal was to present the work of some of these teachers in their own words. Although they are a new influence, many have been teaching for more than thirty years. I was particularly interested in the procedures they developed themselves and how their work today resembles and differs from the approaches of their own teachers. I also wanted to know about their basic philosophies of theater, acting, and the actor's process, and how these led them to explore new procedures with their students. Since the advent of television new demands have been placed on the working actor. I wanted to know what these teachers believed today's actors needed to learn in order to meet the demands and challenge of TV and regional theater as well as film and stage.

Today's acting teachers are still concerned with teaching their students techniques that promote the spontaneity of the moment, help them develop a character, and arouse authentic emotion and expressive physical and vocal behavior. They all share a new concern as well—to help students acquire the technical skill needed to play classical theater. This is crucial since the number of commercial productions has dwindled, and today's actor must look to the classical repertoire of the regional theater for work. The increase in classical productions—Shaw, Molière, Restoration comedy—has brought with it different demands on the actor's skill. This new focus is also both a result of the influence of British acting on the American theatrical community and a reaction against some of the limitations of Method acting as it was taught in the 1950s and 1960s.

The purpose of this book is twofold: to provide actors and teachers across the country with a sourcebook of new procedures and to create a document on the evolution of the actor's craft. Although the names of these teachers are well known to professional actors and to the more experienced students, it is difficult for students to get information on what these teachers actually do. I hope the interviews will provide readers with information on the specific techniques used by individual teachers so that they can evaluate different approaches in the light of their own needs. Since most teachers have expressed their dismay over the lack of opportunity to share their work and are eager to learn what their colleagues in different parts of the country are teaching, I hope these interviews will not only be informative, but will also promote a sense of community in their collective commitment to the artistic process. I have found that despite differences in background and approaches to the craft of acting, these contemporary teachers are all committed to an ongoing exploration of the acting process and share a common goal: to provide actors with a structure that, once acquired, will permit them to harness that elusive quality we call inspiration.

ON THE
EAST COAST

Michael Howard

Michael Howard has been active professionally as an actor, director, and teacher for more than thirty years. During the past eight years he has been teaching full-time and he recently expanded his studio to include teachers from other disciplines because of what he perceives as a growing need for actors to work in a wide variety of theatrical styles.

Mr. Howard has directed on Broadway for the Theatre Guild, among other producers, and was a pioneer of the off-Broadway movement. He directed in Atlanta for four years and was the founder of the Alliance Theatre, in which capacity he directed the landmark production of King Arthur, the Dryden–Purcell Masque, which opened the Atlanta Cultural Center in 1968.

Mr. Howard taught and directed at the Juilliard School drama division for eight years, at the Yale School of Drama with Robert Brustein, and at Boston University, where he was a visiting associate professor.

He is a graduate of the Neighborhood Playhouse, is a member of the Ensemble Studio Theatre, and has been a member of The Actors Studio since its inception. Married to the voice teacher Betty Howard, he has two sons in the entertainment industry.

How did you get started in teaching acting?

I started as an actor and supported myself, as all actors must, with various jobs as my children were growing up. I was performing in a summer stock company and was asked to come back the following year as a director. That was in Woodstock, New York. Very soon after that some actor friends, several of whom were from the Neighborhood Playhouse, where I had been a student, suggested we form a class, and I was asked to lead it. I really enjoyed it. It was small at first—seven, eight people.

At about that same time the High School of Performing Arts was organized by some dedicated educators at the Board of Education. They invited some professionals—Sidney Lumet and myself among them—to help form the program and teach there part-time. It was, and probably still is, a good part-time job for actors. Good for the kids, too.

All the while you were still pursing a career as an actor?

Yes. I was both acting and directing in regional theaters, summer stock, off Broadway . . . places like the Greenwich Mews Theatre and New Stages. This was in the mid-1950s. The Greenwich Mews was a very influential off-Broadway theater. It was one of the very first theaters to cast interracially—without regard to color. Also, in 1954 I directed *Land Beyond the River* by Lofton Mitchell, the first play in New York by a black writer to deal with the civil rights movement.

Even earlier, New Stages was organized by a large group of actors and directors, each of whom contributed $100, I think, to buy an abandoned movie house on Bleecker Street and turn it into a theater. It's now the Circle in the Square Theatre. We did some first productions of Sartre plays in this country—plays like *The Victors*, *The Respectful Prostitute*—and first productions of plays of Barrie Stavis. It was a very good theater.

In what ways has your early training influenced your teaching?

Well, you see, I kept on training all during the early years of my teaching. I am an early member of The Actors Studio and I studied with Lee privately. He was a great influence on me, as was Sandy Meisner at the Neighborhood Playhouse.

All my training was influential. Even before Lee and Sandy there was a wonderful man—David Danzig, I think his name was. I was only fourteen years old, but I still remember him. He was a member of The Group Theatre and had a job as a counselor in a camp I went to. He gave us some exercises from his work with The Group Theatre.

You knew you were interested in acting when you were fourteen years old?

Yes. That was the summer that I knew absolutely, clearly and unequivocally. David gave me a gibberish improvisation and I heard my own "voice" for the first time. When I threw away the real words and used gibberish, I was able to speak to another person, a young woman, clearly, deeply, personally, and openly for the first time— on or off stage. It was a startling experience. From then on I began to pursue acting actively, so that I was working professionally by the time I was seventeen.

Do you use gibberish as an exercise in your classes?

Yes, I do indeed. I use all the things that I found valuable in my own acting and directing life. Gibberish is a wonderful way to help an actor become more expressive, to communicate using all of himself. For example, in a scene an actor might find it easy to say "I love you" because the words do it for him. But if he can only use nonsense sounds, it forces him to use his body more expressively and his voice becomes more colorful in his attempt to make his feelings clear and to communicate with his partner. It also forces the actors to tune into each other more carefully since they can't rely on words but have to look for meaning in sounds and body language.

Is there anything from your early training that you have discarded, that you have come, through experience, to feel is not useful?

No. There are things that I use less because I think they are less important or have been overemphasized. Occasionally I will get an actor who would benefit from a particular exercise, let's say an

Affective Memory Exercise, which I do not give everyone. I can give it individually if I feel it will be useful to a specific actor. There are exercises that I may not use for years at a time which suddenly seem most useful to solve a particular acting problem.

You mentioned that you have discarded nothing from your early training but that there are some techniques you emphasize more than others. What are they?

Techniques to develop muscular relaxation, enhance the ability to concentrate, and extend the imaginative capabilities are all techniques that I emphasize. For instance, many actors lack a developed imagination. Their sense of reality is often very flat or earthbound . . . limited. Actors working for long periods of time in soap operas, for example, will use only a certain part of themselves, a certain melodramatic reality with which they have become comfortable. In soap operas, the unexpected and illuminating imaginative leap is not encouraged. How could it be, with practically no rehearsal, the day-after-day repetition, and the mechanical problems? So the good professional actor, in most of today's theater and television, has never had much stretching of the imaginative vocabulary.

Naturally, there are innumerable exercises to help solve this technical problem—for instance, what's called the metaphor exercise—that is, an exercise in which a simile or metaphor is treated literally. Instead of giving an actor the sensory problem of height, he is given the simile "I feel as if I'm on top of the world." Then, instead of looking for a feeling, he begins to develop that experience literally—the slight curve under his feet, the rush of air, the visual things, the acrophobia perhaps, the danger certainly, a sense of power. So out of a nonliteral, nonrealistic experience, the actor develops physical and emotional behavior. Unexpected feelings emerge. An acceptance of the reality of the place occurs.

How do you begin to work with a student?

When a new person comes to work with me, even when I've seen him or her work professionally, I always have that student start with a prepared monologue, after which I lead the actor through some muscular relaxation exercises. I don't think you can learn very much about an actor in a short monologue, so the rest of the ten or fifteen minutes we work together is for me to begin to discover . . . to find out as much as I can about this person with whom I am going to work. I begin by helping the actor exist in the moment without cover, without involuntary movement—to be aware of how his body is responding, to be conscious of his breathing, and to try to be conscious of muscular tension as it becomes evident. To take in, to receive and send no message—in a word, to be neutral. It's not easy. We have so much involuntary body language. We send messages: "I'm OK," "This is fun," "You can't intimidate me," "I hate this." It can be quite revealing, the ease or difficulty with which an actor accomplishes this exercise.

The next part of this first work varies. I might have him sing and skip around the room, sometimes dance—that is, I want to hear musical sound produced and I want to see the body move through space. Sometimes I will ask the actor to transform himself slowly into an animal, sometimes into himself as a child. I ask him to repeat the text with different kinds of adjustments that I suggest to him. Sometimes I ask for another monologue that might be more useful to work with. Sometimes I ask him to sing the monologue instead of speaking it. I'm learning about him. I don't believe I have anything to teach the actor until I know him.

If I wonder about the actor's expressiveness, his range, I might ask him to do the monologue as a nineteenth-century actor in a large theater. I might ask another actor to make the adjustment that he is a stand-up comic and that the monologue text is his routine. I give him an entrance, I announce him, I ask the class to take part. I want to know about his sense of humor. I remind him that these are games, and that he shouldn't take himself too seriously. These exercises can be very exhilarating and sometimes very painful for an actor who is covered or protected. The simple act of holding out his arms to the class can make all the defenses drop away. So when it's over I know a great deal more about this person, and the actor is on the way to being integrated into the class.

How do you help an actor experience more of the moment-to-moment life of a character?

Most of my work with the actor, in the early stages at any rate, is involved with that particular problem—helping the actor deepen the experience of the here and now. I see it as a beginning, an essential base for the actor's work.

First the actor must see the value of being in danger. It is the opposite of comfortable, the opposite of safe. The actor must have something at stake, something on the line. Risk and danger are the lifeblood of the theater. The actor must say, "Let me put myself out there in front of them with no shield, no security blanket."

For this I do what's called an unrehearsed scene exercise. It's structured as follows:

Two actors choose a scene—and that's the last they see of each other or talk to each other until they move onto the stage in class. No discussion, no plan—nothing to make it easier, not even little things like "Which side are you entering from?" or "Will you bring the prop?" Each learns the scene by rote—no choices, no character decisions, rote. When they arrive I give them the set of the previous scene to work on. Now this is very difficult to describe. It's actually a very structured exercise. One wants, as always in the theater, freedom within structure. First, they must be reminded of the large number of specific realities that surround the actor—the reality of the stage set, the brightness of the lights, the traffic going by, the colleagues watching, the text itself, and, most important, the discomfort, the games, the provocative behavior of the other actor. Each of these realities must be explored at any one moment and become the whole focus of the scene, pursued until it no longer interests. The text continues and sometimes the text itself is the strongest reality.

The actors are often confused until they actually begin and I help them moment to moment to explore all the realities. Then it usually is a very liberating, creative experience.

Do you do this unrehearsed scene as the character or as yourself?

No. You do not use the character's given circumstances, only the most basic element of relationship—let's say a mother and son—and only the most basic circumstances of the situation: a mother who has summoned her son to her bedchamber. No other choices, no other elements coming from the play.

There is another exercise, an improvisation that in a different way encourages the actor's responsiveness—in this case, to the partner. In this improvisation I send one actor out of the room and the other actor is given a full set of circumstances, including a strong objective. The other actor, having heard none of the situation, enters relaxed, available, and with no circumstances—an empty vessel ready to be filled. He is neither old nor young, neither male nor female, neither eighteenth nor twentieth century, neither human nor animal. He will discover everything from the other actor—from what he says and how he says it, from how he relates physically to him, from how the actor has arranged the set, even from the amount of clothes he has taken off or put on. The work is not passive. Tests, probes should be made. By relating physically in an overt way, by speaking in a very formal or familiar manner, one gets back information as to the appropriateness of the behavior.

The moment the actor receives some sense of his gender or relationship or the place he's in, he begins immediately to act on it (male or female, old or young, and so forth). If he discovers a moment later that he was wrong, the actor drops what he has begun to create and works on what now, in fact, seems true. Questions are not allowed: How did I get here? When did I call you? All of the evaluating is done internally—no living off the self-consciousness, the not knowing.

Little by little he drops and picks up, drops and picks up, until he finds that he is on the right track, developing the character, relationship, the situation as the evidence becomes clear to him. When the actor feels he has all the circumstances he is free to resolve the situation in any way that seems logical.

In this exercise the connection between the two actors becomes very focused. They are connected in ways that are not only verbal. They understand things without knowing where the understanding came from. They suddenly know, and they are never quite sure how they found out. I'll ask, "What made you realize you were nine years old and a girl in this improvisation?" And the actor will say, "I don't know exactly. Maybe it was the way he touched my hair and spoke about my friends." It's important to point out that the actor who does know the circumstances does not consciously either help or hinder his partner. He simply behaves logically within the circumstances.

What about character work? What techniques do you give your students to develop a character who is very different from themselves? How do you have them start?

All the work of the actor is character work. Creating a character starts with the self. The work begins internally and grows outward. Those good actors who find it useful to start externally—with a moustache of a piece of cotton in the upper lip—I believe simply know themselves well enough to say "I work better behind a mask. Let me have this little disguise that changes me visually, and then the inner reality will flourish."

It is foolish to say to an actor, "Use yourself in this part," or, for that matter, "Don't use yourself in this part." Which self are they speaking of? I know there are many Michael Howards and, of course, some of them are very public and in use 70 or 80% of the time. But there are many others, some right below the surface and some deeply buried. The work of the actor is to become familiar with all the Michaels. To know where they hide, and to have them available is one of the roads of actor training. So the actor has to be selective about which self he brings to work on the play.

As the early rehearsals develop, the actor sometimes may confront elements of the character, either physical or emotional, that he cannot find in himself. It's at that point that the actor must have tools to continue to develop elements of character. For instance, the use of an animal in developing character behavior can be extremely valuable, particularly for the actor who has done animal exercises. It's useful for the actor to go to the zoo, choose an animal suited to his character, and study it in every detail, muscularly. The actor then can make choices as to what elements of the behavior of the animal will be useful.

Sensory work, the creation of a particular event by trying to re-experience specific sensory detail, can radically alter the way a character performs simple tasks. To sit in an anteroom as if you were being rained on, to walk as if there were ten-pound weights on your shoes, creates specific behavior.

Michael Chekhov's work with psychological gestures is useful, and so is work with physical centers, body language, and so on. Specific ways of adjusting to objects create character. One woman will handle a sable coat as if it's an old woolen blanket, another woman will handle a woolen blanket as if it's a silk shawl. Charlie Chaplin playing a bank teller in *Monsieur Verdoux* turns the pages of the phone book the way he counts in his teller's cage.

Are there specific exercises you do to help actors prepare for film and TV?

If a new student tells me he or she is only interested in film or TV, I dissuade that person from taking my class. I am only interested in helping to develop actors who are interested in all mediums.

Is it different? My opinion is that what can be learned in a class about the differences between film, TV, and stage acting are inconsequential. The mechanical things that a good actor has to learn about camera, sound, and movement are minor and are learnable by a well-trained actor who knows his instrument in a very short time. And then there are things that the great movie actors have learned over a period of many years in front of the camera that are not teachable.

Are there any techniques or approaches to acting that you feel are destructive?

I think any approach can be destructive because it's not *what* is taught, but *how* it's taught. Of course, there are some techniques that are silly or useless, but in the main I think what is dangerous is people who don't know what they are doing. They could teach anything and it would be dangerous.

There are teachers who use so-called psychological techniques and encourage actors to reveal their personal lives in the name of their art. Do you see that as useful?

Reveal literally? No. That can be destructive. Actors have to choose very carefully with whom they work. I think that the line between an acting class and psychotherapy is very delicate. It is very important that a teacher recognize that line.

I am told therapy, especially Gestalt, has taken a great deal from experimentation in acting classes. Certainly it's the other way around as well. Acting exercises to expand and develop the emotional vocabulary of the actor, to put him in touch with his feelings, are an important part of the work in an acting class.

How do you recommend that actors work with directors?

I tell them that they have to prepare themselves to work with dreadful directors, and that they should assume there will be times when they will get no help. They have to develop a way of working that leaves them open, available, and responsive to good directors and, at the same time, able to work on their own with bad ones.

An actor must have the tools to create whatever is demanded of him, either by a director or himself, and he must not abandon his own artistic integrity by abdicating responsibility for the final work. The actor who complains that "the director made me do it—I hate it" is not doing his job.

How do you advise beginning actors to start working on a script?

I would say there is no way for everybody to begin the work on a play. I believe that. I am against training actors to do it in one particular way. Perhaps we should give them three or four days to begin work and let them choose. But I am not against the following because, of course, young actors need the security of knowing they have a way to begin. Of course, in five years they'll find their own way.

The script should be read three times. The first time as if you were reading a novel. It should be read for pleasure, for the story line. The second time for relationships: who likes who, who is hinting at what, who needs whom. It's important that you not stop when your character shows up. Forget who you're playing. If anything, be more attentive to the other people. You want the play to reach the intuitive response the way a good story does when you have nothing at stake. You want the play to influence you unconsciously and establish roots in you that are not intellectual. So, just read it. Don't stop. Don't try to be professional. Don't try to be an actor. Connections will be made that you are not aware of.

Now read it again. Make two lists: one of what all the other characters say about you, and the other what you say about yourself. Make accurate notes on given circumstances other than dramatic reality. The objective reality at this stage is more important: the time of day, month, hot, cold. The author consciously and unconsciously buries all kinds of raw material in the body of the play on which the actor will base all of the later work.

Then I suggest that you don't do too much homework before you meet with the other actors and begin to rehearse. Whatever thoughts and ideas you have formed from your reading, allow them to lie there. Just begin to live off and take from what is happening with the other actors. It's at this point that choices of objective and of physical action are made. The first thing I remember Sandy Meisner at the Neighborhood Playhouse saying is "Acting is doing." That's still the best definition.

What do you feel is the most common problem facing actors today?

Lack of work. Getting seen. Getting an agent. The 3,000 miles that separate Los Angeles and New York. The same problems that have existed for the last fifty years. And then there's the problem of fads—fashion in acting styles. I suppose that it's inevitable that actors, anxious to work, find themselves, perhaps unwittingly, "acting in the style of" whoever is most successful in the movies or on television. What is less acceptable are the teachers who spring up espousing this current method or that current method. I think it's a danger because creative work becomes swamped with concern for methodology. Actors are therefore cut off and not open to the joyfulness and sense of creativity in acting or the potential in themselves as actors. They are looking for a strong rule: teach me so that I can have a sense of security about how I should do it.

Do today's actors approach their work differently from their predecessors?

In my generation I would say that when you were done studying at, for instance, the Neighborhood Playhouse, that was the end of your training. Now actors recognize that that's a beginning. There has been a stronger sense of the need to go on training and developing, like a singer or dancer. Actors are more prone to see their work in a professional class as a necessary complement to their work for an audience. They recognize now that it's a question of continuing their development. After all, there are children who can act wonderfully, with spontaneity and freshness, but it takes a very long time to fulfill your potential, to master the art of acting.

Do you want to mention some of the people who have trained with you?

If you mean some of the famous ones, some who have been fortunate enough to become stars—I don't. I know that it's interesting and makes good reading, but it's really not relevant to what I do. There are actors who have studied with me in companies spread across the country, off Broadway and on Broadway and in the movies. There are also a goodly number who, sadly, gave up—and then, of course, there are those who haven't and should have.

What do you feel has been your main contribution as a teacher?

Myself. My person. My love of actors. My unwillingness to let them violate themselves. My rage when they use themselves badly and my passion when they use themselves well. That translates itself into technical things like demanding that I not be satisfied with small realities. I want an actor who can do Shakespeare and Odets. I don't believe that it has to be one or the other. I encourage the actor to take chances, live dangerously, make the effort, and be willing to fall on his face. That's very exciting and I think I encourage that stretch, that reaching.

What are your feelings about English actors?

I'm bored, frankly, with elements of the theater community crying out against English actors taking jobs from American actors on the one hand, and other elements of the theater community weeping that the English do it better, and that we can't do it at all. Odious! It's the kind of generalizing that is only useful at cocktail parties. English actors are not better than American actors and vice versa. Just because there's some truth in the idea that our culture has at times been more spontaneous, more immediate, more alive, and the English culture more responsive to words, to text, to the past, to history, doesn't mean we can't use words or they lack spontaneity. Good actors can do both and there are wonderful actors on both sides. And I want to see them all working here! And I want our people to work there in the classics so the English will find out how wonderfully we can do them.

What advice would you give to someone who is just starting out in his or her career?

Well, I tell you, I'm an enthusiast. I love the theater. I have two sons and I encouraged them to consider a career in the theater. I have friends who left the theater to pursue other careers, and most have regretted it.

I think actors are extraordinarily generous people. And when they are committed and accomplished, what they give is themselves. What actors are about is sharing. They are saying to an audience, "This is a piece of me. I hope you'll find it illuminating. Through this character you are getting *me*." It's a generous act and it's very dangerous. Most people say, in one way or another, "I'm not going to let you see me because I don't trust you. You can't have it. I'm hiding it."

When the work of a painter, composer, or writer is finally evaluated by the public, the artist can be off somewhere having a beer or taking a walk in the woods. The performer is out there every night. It's an act of such courage. It's life-affirming to say, "I'm going to risk it again."

When I'm asked by an actor whether he or she should continue in the struggle, or by a young person whether he should begin a career, I tell that person what everybody else says who's been around for a while: how hard it is, how difficult it is to make a living, how little recognition he or she can expect—all the verities. And then I tell that person that if he or she can grow to enjoy the danger, relish the combat that is the day-to-day life of the actor, and most of all develop deep personal satisfaction in the art of acting—the exhilaration of solving an intractable craft problem, the astonishment of two actors suddenly released from themselves and totally in tune with each other, riding the same wave—if the actor can develop an obsession for those technical moments of fulfillment, and put recognition and applause on a back burner with a low flame, where they belong—then I say, have at it.

Nicholas Levitin

William Esper

William Esper has had an acting studio in New York since 1965. For the past eight years he has also headed the MFA and BFA professional actor training programs at the Mason Gross School of the Arts at Rutgers University. A graduate of the Neighborhood Playhouse, where he studied with Sanford Meisner and Martha Graham, Mr. Esper underwent teacher training with Sanford Meisner and subsequently worked with him for many years, becoming a leading exponent of Mr. Meisner's technique. He is also a former director of the Company Lab at Circle Repertory Company in New York, and has been a guest artist and directed productions at Canada's Banff Festival, the St. Nicholas Theatre Company in Chicago, and the WPA Theatre and Circle Rep in New York.

Mr. Esper believes that the "real contact between actors comes when they listen to what they are saying to each other, and then respond truthfully from themselves, from their own point of view." He subscribes to Sanford Meisner's principle that what an actor does doesn't depend on him, but on what the other actor does to him. He believes that this is the foundation from which all acting training should begin.

How did you get started teaching acting?

My own background is with Sanford Meisner. I went to the Neighborhood Playhouse and studied with him, and I finished just before he went out to California to become head of talent for Twentieth Century-Fox. He got very disenchanted and came back to New York to found the American Musical and Dramatic Academy, which still exists today, but in a very different form. While Meisner was there it had a fantastic faculty. That was about twenty-three years ago. Things got shaky at AMDA and Sandy went back to the Neighborhood Playhouse. I went with him and stayed until 1977.

What I teach is based on what I learned from Sandy Meisner during the seventeen years I worked with him. He was a brilliant teacher, a brilliant theater man. He had three important attributes: a tremendous sense of truth, an inventive way of working with actors, and a great feeling and love for theatricality. In that way his temperament was different from Strasberg's. He was closer to Stella Adler, but I think much more technically precise than she. He was wonderful at process. It was really from him that I learned how important it is for actors to be taken through a specific series of steps, one at a time, and how each step is the basis for the next so that what an actor did yesterday becomes the foundation for what he does today. In this way the actor has a process for constantly developing and evolving his work. It's not scattered. It's a very particular method based on improvisation that is tremendously helpful.

I don't think of myself as an acting teacher in that I don't really give acting classes. I undertake the training of professional actors and I'm a specialist in actor training, not just somebody who conducts a class to give actors some helpful hints on how to improve their next performance. I'm not focused on that. I think that the only things that are teachable are fundamental principles, because every time an actor has a problem in a performance it always comes back to one of those principles: either he's not listening or he doesn't know why he's there or he doesn't understand the relationship between himself and the other person or he's acting his emotions and not really leaving himself alone.

The moment an actor starts to work he has the problem of what to do about the text because the text can easily corrupt him. If someone can memorize lines and talk, you might think that he is acting when, in fact, he may be doing nothing more than saying lines. So in order to get clear about what happens in acting, it's a good idea to get rid of the text temporarily. That means improvising. But improvising brings its own difficulties. The moment you take the text away from an actor he'll start writing dialogue himself. So often a lot of improvisation work is not very helpful to the actor because he starts making up dialogue or ad libbing his way through a situation. Instead of being *in* the situation, he's thinking of what to say. That's not helpful because when you play a part you don't have to think of what to say. You know your lines. Someone has written them for you, you have memorized them, and they are right there. You don't have to make up your own dialogue.

I base my first year's work on Meisner's form of improvisation. We start with his Repetition Exercise. Two actors stand on stage facing each other. One says something—makes an observation about the other. It may be about what the other actor is wearing or something else that catches his interest. Then his partner repeats everything he hears the other say. For example, one student may say to another, "That's a very nice green shirt." If that makes the actor wearing the green shirt feel good, he might say, "That's a very nice green shirt" back, but it will be colored by his good feelings. Repeating everything creates a dialogue substitute because the other person is always giving you your line. You hear what the other person says and that's your line. You repeat it from your point of view, keep repeating the same word or sentence, and only change what you say or how you say it when you feel the impulse to do so.

What do you mean by "point of view"?

How you feel at that *moment.* That's a very important issue in the development of an acting artist. It's vital, and that is a major area of work in the first year of training. A lot of people who come to study acting are very disconnected from themselves even though they may have acted a lot. They tend to be depersonalized and they don't know how to respond subjectively, from themselves. That's not good for an artist because the raw material an artist works with is how *he* feels about everything. Ultimately, every moment in a performance is made up of how the actor feels about that moment. But before an actor can get to that he has to get closely attuned to his own personal feelings about everything under the sun.

How would you summarize the purpose and goal of the Repetition Exercise?

The first thing this exercise does is help actors learn how to listen. That's the bottom line in acting. You have to start by listening, and through listening comes the beginning of contact. The beginning of real contact between actors comes when they really listen to what they are saying to each other, and then really respond truthfully from themselves, from their own point of view. Because they have to repeat everything, they've got to listen or they can't do the exercise. So it forces them into contact immediately and into really listening to each other.

The Repetition Exercise is not a complete exercise in itself. It is the beginning of the work. It lays the groundwork for what is eventually a very sophisticated kind of improvisational exercise that ultimately trains the actor to do and live truthfully under imaginary circumstances. It does several things immediately: it forces the actor to listen, forces him to put his attention on the other actor and off himself; and teaches him to work impulsively and spontaneously and to be able to respond emotionally and not intellectually.

Without spontaneity acting is like soup without salt: it's stale, flat, and completely unprofitable. Plus an actor will never develop an attractive personality because spontaneity has an awful lot to do with stage charm—if you have some charm to begin with. Just as in life, people who are not spontaneous are very boring. Those who are spontaneous are very charming. It's a delightful trait. And only when you're spontaneous does the real person begin to emerge, not the person you think you are, but the one you really are. You have to do a lot of work tricking the actor into being spontaneous so you can see who he really is and give him a chance to find himself. The truth of someone is in his spontaneous responses, not his edited ones.

How does the Repetition Exercise progress?

The next step in the Repetition Exercise can only be described as a kind of Ping-Pong game of impulses in which actors are bouncing spontaneous impulses off each other. Again, there are two actors on stage facing each other and one starts with a personal observation about the other; for instance, "You have a pretty sweater on." The two actors may initially repeat that sentence thirty times to each other. Then something will happen inside one of them—an impulse to change will occur from the sheer repetitiveness of this sentence— and it will produce an impulse in one actor to change. He may say, "All right, so I've got a pretty sweater on. So what? Okay, okay!" Meaning, that's enough of that sentence. Through this exercise actors begin to learn how to sense an impulse and act on it. The actor's repetition of the sentence always adjusts to the truthfulness of his impulse. If it means that he has to change the words in the repetition in order to keep his answer an honest one, he does that.

The next step in this exercise has to do with behavior. The actor starts responding not just to the words being said but also to the behavior of the other person. Now it is no longer a question of what the person is saying, but what he means. One actor may say to his partner, "Gee, that's a nice sweater." His partner may answer, "Well, I'm sorry you don't like it," because the first actor's intonation made him feel that he didn't really like the sweater. As students become more sensitized and hear more of what is really being said, they change the sentence being repeated more frequently and become more aware of what is happening in the other person's behavior. As they become more responsive, the repetition gradually becomes more flexible. Then you may have two students repeating sentences to each other that will change after every three or four repetitions.

So now you have the actor working off his partner's behavior and things begin to pop up in the repetition that are a response to behavior, like, "What are you laughing about?" or "Why are you getting so serious?" Now they are in very close contact, and they work harder to hear not just what they are saying, but what they mean. When they begin the Repetition Exercise their exchanges may go back and fourth twenty times before something happens to make a change in the words. As they keep working it gets more and more flexible so that a change in the sentence they are repeating will occur with more frequency. Eventually the repetition falls away altogether and the actors work directly off each other's subtext in each moment. At this point it's important that all excess verbalizations come out of the exercise.

You see, the tendency that actors have is to make conversation, and that will interfere with their emotionality because they can't think and feel at the same time. An actor has to be rooted in his feelings. The least important aspect of an actor's instrument is his mind. It's much more important that he have an understanding heart, an ability to empathize with other human beings, an ability to respond with his feelings, not with his head. That's what makes an actor.

A lot of great actors can't articulate or communicate how they do it, and they would make terrible teachers. I understand that Alfred Lunt was like that. He was a great actor, but when he directed he couldn't communicate. He would only know how to show you how he would do it himself. Teaching is a special gift. Not only do you need an insight into what is going on in a talented person, but you need the ability to articulate it so that someone else can understand it.

After about four or five classes of using the Repetition Exercise I introduce a task called an Independent Activity. This is an addition to the Repetition Exercise. A good Independent Activity has to have three elements: it has to be difficult to execute; there has to be a concrete, specific, and ultimately personal reason the actor is doing it; and it has to have reasonable immediacy—which means that the actor says to himself, "What is the least amount of time in which I would reasonably be able to complete this task?" All of this is, of course, imaginary, but must be taken as a reality.

Students do this kind of concrete task with concrete objects while they are doing the Repetition Exercise. One student may be mending a broken plate, fixing a clock, copying a drawing, making something out of clay—some task that is very difficult and complicated to do so that it forces the actor to use every drop of his concentration in order to complete it. The actor is forced to deepen his concentration on the object, which ties up his conscious mind so that he can't think about anything else except the activity in which he is engaged. At the same time, he has to keep responding repetitively to each moment that comes from his partner.

You now have one actor struggling with a mound of clay or trying to mend a broken clock while he is responding to his partner's sentence, both the way it's said and what is being said. And how a sentence is repeated is influenced by the person's behavior as he works on his Independent Activity, and his partner is responding moment by moment to the behavior created in the other actor by his task.

Then I introduce a time limit. I tell the student who is working on the Independent Activity that he has to complete the task while he is engaged in the Repetition Exercise within a certain amount of time; i.e., to fix the clock in an hour. This adds urgency.

One of the most important things that the Independent Activity brings to the actor's attention is the whole question of justification. *Why* is it important that I fix this clock within an hour? This is a major area in the training of the actor and one that I think is not fully understood in a lot of the training that goes on. It isn't until the actor asks himself why he is doing this that his creativity begins to operate. Here you begin to tap into the real use of the actor's imagination. This is another important part of the training because all of the training is based on the use of the dramatic imagination.

A good Independent Activity has an element of struggle in it. Now you have an actor trying to get this damn thing done, whatever it is, and, without the actor even knowing it, he's upset. The emotion that comes out of that has a wonderful quality because it's not just a question of getting the actor to come alive. Everybody wants an emotionally alive actor. The emotion has a wonderful quality because the actor has not become "emotion conscious." One of the worst things that can happen to an actor is for him to become an emotionally self-conscious actor who concentrates on what he is feeling and tries to manufacture the feeling. That's no good. He must be involved in what he is *doing*. And if he knows why he's doing it and the reason has meaning for him, he will come to a full emotional life.

This brings us back to the important notion of justification. This is where wish fulfillment or fantasies come into the training because now the actor who is engaged in the Independent Activity has to endow the object with something important to him. Perhaps he decides that if he repairs this clock he can sell it for a lot of money and then go on a vacation to the Bahamas. He brings that desire into the work. It must be a total fantasy, but at the same time have *real* meaning for him as a person.

Now we begin to get into the actor's wants and desires. The actor has to make his need to complete the Independent Activity stronger and stronger. Let's say an actress wants to finish making a clay pot because she wants to sell it in order to buy a terrific cocktail dress that she knows is going to make her look like a million bucks. Or an actor may want the money to go see his dying father. Students have to come up with justifications for completing the Independent Activity that are more and more personal and urgent.

While the actor continues the exercise I give another actor—one who doesn't have an Independent Activity—a simple objective to carry out with respect to the actor in the exercise. For instance, he wants to borrow fifty dollars. And I have him come to the door while his partner is engaged in his urgent Independent Activity.

How is this carried out within the Repetition Exercise?

Let's say one actor has a simple objective, to come to the door, and he knocks playfully—dum di di dum dum, dum dum. The actor opening the door will use that knock as a point of departure. He might say, "What are you kidding around for?" Or if he can't get a sentence from the knock, he might use some behavior that he observes, like "Gee, you look cold." There is never manufactured dialogue. The dialogue in these improvisations (which incorporate the Repetition Exercise) always has to come from an actor's personal response to what exists in the moment. And the exercise or improvisation can go in a lot of different directions.

At this point in the training I hammer home an important principle of Sandy Meisner, one that is at the core of his work: what you do doesn't depend on you, but on what the other actor does to you. You can't do anything unless the other actor does something to make you do it. This means that the objective must be left alone, and all the actor's concentration must be focused on the other fellow's behavior and how he feels about it moment by moment. It is terribly important that the actor play off what exists in each moment and not begin to manipulate himself because of the objective. Later the objective is activated by emotional preparations.

How do you bring the Repetition Exercise into scene work?

The first scene a student works on is always a simple conflict scene. I assign scenes to students that are usually from terrible plays like *Tomorrow the World* or *On Whitman Avenue*. The scenes are based on a simple conflict with two opposing points of view.

Then the actors memorize a scene by rote. In the first year of training we memorize all the text we work on by rote. The purpose is to focus the actor's whole attention on what his acting partner is doing and not on remembering his lines.

When students do a scene, they have not worked out any moments. The interpretation of the scene is a result of two actors working off each other's behavior, out of their moment-to-moment behavior. I don't want them to do the scene. I want them to let the scene do them. All a student may know about the scene is where he is and why he is there. He will eventually learn about his relationships. Then he works off his acting partner spontaneously. This ability to improvise with a memorized text is crucial. You have to develop a strong feel for this in the actor. There is a great deal of work in our theater today for which an ability to improvise with the text is vital.

This ability is the basis for cold readings. And it's also the key to television and film work, where improvisation, not rehearsal, is important. Rehearsal is a theater concept, and you can't train an actor to work only in the theater.

When a student is working on a scene, instead of answering what his acting partner says or expressing what he feels is being said, he must answer using the words of the text he has memorized so he doesn't have to think about what to say. He already has the lines. The lines are now used instead of repetition but in the same way. The point is that the student has to answer before he adjusts himself or thinks about the line of dialogue, so that he is responding from a spontaneous impulse. This is where the teacher has to have a good eye to catch it and say, "You see, in this moment you didn't pick up on your impulse."

That's what I mean by "improvising" in a scene with the text. The student is working off his spontaneous impulses all the time and the text is coming to the surface off his impulses. He is responding in the moment using the text but, at this stage, he doesn't consider if it's right for the character or if it's right for the play. For the time being, the student ignores these considerations because he is trying to establish a way to work from himself and with himself. A good actor adjusts his text to his subtext, what's really going on inside him. You have to break the actor's conventional response to text. Most actors tend to be conventional about text and have to be broken of that habit. I try to rid them of that conventionality. At this point I don't want the actor to try to solve the interpretive problems of the scene. That comes later.

The next step in the training is learning Emotional Preparations.

Is that different from prior circumstances?

Yes, in a way. It's the way the actor relates himself emotionally to the prior circumstances. Let's say the actor is doing a scene and ten lines into the scene his stage wife says to him, "What are you so happy about?" His line is, "Honey, you are looking at the new vice president of the Crocketsville National Bank." The audience then thinks, "So that's why the actor was so happy." Emotional Preparation is what the actor does offstage to bring himself alive so that he is emotionally related to his prior circumstances when he comes to the *first* moment, the moment of his entrance.

How do you teach students to do Emotional Preparations?

Through daydreaming. We daydream in life when something

triggers it, and we drift off spontaneously. It isn't a question of imagining something, but of actually daydreaming about it, which means living out a scenario. The actor has to go into that drifty condition because it is then that the conscious mind relaxes and the unconscious starts to open up.

One of the things that the actor has to learn is the difference between daydreaming about something and thinking about it. There's a difference between thinking about making love to someone and daydreaming that you are doing it. Daydreaming is much more evocative.

How is daydreaming used in Emotional Preparation?

I tell a student to sit down quietly and give himself a topic and start to daydream about it. For instance, I might say, "You're emperor of the world," or "You're a star," or "You're going to die," or "Daydream about the worst thing in the world that could happen to you." It's very freeing for an actor to do this because he is not locked into what has actually happened to him. I feel very strongly about that. It isn't a question of what did happen, but what *might* happen, what *could* be—not the most frightening or wonderful thing that did happen to you, but what could happen. Once an actor says what could be, he can start to daydream.

What instruction do you give students to help them develop this facility?

I start by telling the actor to relax and I may give him a topic to start from, but then he has to let it go if other associations come up. Let's say a daydream starts about an agent who has rejected you. Then it goes to a policeman beating up a bum and you find yourself getting into the middle of it, getting into a fight with the policeman. This kind of daydream may come to the surface in someone who is very sensitive to authority. The policeman may suddenly change into your father, with you having an argument with him. And then you come to and you are in a rage, and that's when you come on stage if that's what you need to fulfill the circumstances of that particular scene. Of course it takes a very long time for the actor to use it with confidence. It is one of the most delicate areas in acting and one that demands great vigilance from the teacher so that the actor does not end up acting his emotion.

How is this different from an Affective Memory?

Affective Memory means going back to a past experience, and I think it has a lot of problems. First of all, you have to teach the actor to do an Affective Memory. You don't have to teach anyone how to daydream. Next, you often run into a lot of resistance with an Affective Memory because the actor may not want to go back to it. It also makes acting a very dreary thing. You can't keep going back to re-create your mother's funeral for thirty years. That's not healthy, it's not good for the actor. And you don't need to do it either, because when your mother died it created an area of sensitivity to loss in you and that's what you need—that area of sensitivity. Then any daydream that plays on loss, losing something precious to you, is going to emotionalize you. And when you get tired of one daydream, you can invent another. Your mother's funeral will wear out as a source of emotionality after a while, but you can invent a million daydreams.

You know there are just so many emotions that human beings are capable of: fear, anger, pain, joy, humiliation. And joy is joy is joy, and pain is pain is pain. It doesn't matter where it originates because once it's alive in the actor it's easy to relate it to the circumstances of the scene.

Do you encourage students to reveal their daydreams as part of the process of learning how to do it?

No. They never divulge their daydreams. They never share them. Daydreams are too personal. First of all, to talk about them is not going to be helpful to the actor. One man's daydream is another man's bore. Second, daydreams come out of the unconscious, so they are often very crude and ugly. People will often daydream things that they would never do in real life, things they would never act out. If the actor reveals those things, he starts to worry about what people will think about him. As long as the daydream brings the actor to life, it doesn't matter where he got if from. As long as he is alive when he walks out on stage, nobody cares where it came from. Then, of course, he must leave his emotion alone and respond fully and openly to whatever his partner's behavior means to him. The danger is that the actor will try to hold on to his emotion.

What is the next stage of the training?

Next we work on improvisations and scenes that have prior given circumstances and require Emotional Preparations. Now we are at another level. Students are working off each other in a very intense emotional way and we bring in emotional relationships. For example, we will do an improvisation in which a woman is home and opens the door to the man who walked off and left her when she was pregnant two years ago.

Next I set up circumstances in an improvisation that are common to both students. In the above example, the man might be coming back because he realizes that he was a fool, that the woman he went off with was a real bitch, and that he truly loved the one he left. This is a whole other level from those earlier simple improvisations when an actor's objective might be simply to borrow a car to go on a date. In this way the actor is learning how to live truthfully under imaginary circumstances, and he is ready to work on more demanding scenes.

During the whole first year of Meisner's work students are developing a truthful instrument and it all has to do with straight acting, the actor being himself in the imaginary world, working with his real responses to what is happening. The actor is the character. Students are substituting themselves for the character. There is no character work at all during the first year. That comes later.

At the end of the first year you have an actor who is very good at being himself and has a strong sense of who he is, a strong sense of truth, and a good ability to live truthfully in the imaginary world. He is able to promote real spontaneity in himself and will act off his real impulses all the time. He can't help working off other people's behavior because he is so sensitized and has done it so much and he is always working with his *real* feelings. You have an actor who has a developed imagination and can invent very personal justifications to make himself do almost anything under the sun. He knows how to work with objectives and leave them alone and how to focus on the other person and work off him or her, always adjusting the text to what's happening at the moment between him and the other person, and not the other way around. You have an actor who is able to take a text and improvise it, identify the prior circumstances very quickly, ask himself, "How do I or the character feel about them?" or "How do I think the character feels about them? What does the text tell me about what the character feels about them?" Then he can create, push the button and find the emotional life in himself, connect himself with it emotionally, and then walk into contact, absolutely relaxed, leave himself alone and live it out off the other person from unanticipated moment to unanticipated moment. If you looked at the scene being played you would swear it was real life. That's what you have at the end of the first year.

How do you help students develop a character?

We begin the second year's training by using the improvisational technique and asking the student to play himself but to pick one addition to his behavior, such as a limp, a speech impediment, a dialect—one element that is different from himself. At this point he is not using a text, just improvising situations. Now it's the actor still being himself but with the addition of a lisp or a sprained ankle, etc. That allows us to begin to work on the physical or sensory adjustments of a character. And we begin to do sensory work on heat and cold. I've also begun to experiment with exercises where the actor will take a point of view that is not his own.

Could you describe that?

For instance, I set up an improvisational situation in which one person owes another a lot of money and hasn't paid it back. The one who owes money may take the point of view that it's only money, how can this other guy possibly get upset over something as insignificant as $1,000? And anyway, if I had it, I would lend it— but I don't have it. I can't pay it back. I'd have to get a job to do that, and he couldn't possibly want me to do that. That situation gets the actor to take on a point of view that isn't his. That's a very important ingredient in acting and in character work. A person who has that kind of point of view about owing money is a specific kind of character.

The criterion for choosing a point of view is that it has to be something that is humanly true, that is life as it is lived by most people (not eccentric or crazy people). You may have a character who believes that stealing is not wrong, or one who gets upset over losing a small amount of money. They can both be characters.

Character work is very complicated. There are a number of ways to create a character. One way is out of the emotional life: a happy woman is a character; a depressed man is a character. An interesting question to ask about a character is what his or her point of view about life is. Some characters view life as an endless party; others have a very tragic sense of life. Thus a character may be dominated by a particular emotional life that will color his responses. I am teaching the actor to play the emotional line of a character—so that everything is adjusted to the dominant thing that is going on inside the person. We will do that through the exercise work and take it into scenes like the scene in *Two for the Seesaw* in which Gittel has the ulcer attack. The character of Gittel has a physical adjustment. She has ulcers and is in pain. It's also a very good teaching tool for an actor to adjust all dialogue to the physical and emotional pain of the character. And if you throw in a dialect, you have a complete character.

Do you use animal exercises for character work?

Sometimes, but it's important for the student to understand that he is not doing a literal animal, but a human being who has the characteristics of that animal. He is not a bear, but bearlike. It's dangerous to have students work on animals literally.

In animal work it's the behavior that counts. Camels are wonderful when you want to play a snobbish character because they really seem to be looking down at the world. Squirrels are good when you need to play someone who is very anxious. Certain kinds of dogs are good. In fact, when you get into style, you might say that style comes out of the theatricality of your ideas. I once directed the letter-writing scene from *The Country Wife* with the two actors playing a bulldog and a poodle. It worked very well because the actors' qualities were right for the choices. I had another actor do the same scene and he used the image of an old Model T Ford for the male character and that worked well also. The more upset he became, the more he huffed and puffed like an old car. Now that's very theatrical.

But I'm getting ahead of myself. When an actor works on character he has to work on making specific choices. That's the heart of the character work: making choices. There is a scene from a play called *Timelimit* in which a fellow comes in to be interrogated who has had a terrible experience the day before, one that was very painful for him. An actor might choose to enter the room as if it could be booby-trapped. He would then enter in a certain way and, using that choice, capture all the wariness and suspiciousness of that character.

In the first year of training students never really pick actions because they follow the principle, "I don't do anything except what the other actor makes me do"; therefore they do everything. But once the actor starts to work with interpretation he has to be more conscious of what he is doing; he has to be able to translate text into choices—things to do, actions.

What do you mean by actions?

To tell a joke is an action, to teach somebody, to flirt, to introduce oneself, to give somebody an order. A great deal of the second year of training is spent developing the students' understanding of actions, intentions, and objectives. The other part is learning that although most human beings do the same things, what distinguishes one from another is how he or she does it. For instance, a priest and a gangster may both give warnings to a person. The difference is in how they give that warning.

What's really interesting is when a priest gives a warning the way a gangster would and vice versa.

Exactly. Then you get unexpected behavior and it becomes interesting for an actor to play a priest like a gangster and a gangster like a priest. Whenever an actor can find a way to go against the text, he or she can make a big impression.

Do you recommend that students do that?

Sure. Good actors will always find things to act that are not in the text. You never really want to play the text. That's the point, to my mind. That's the point of Strasberg's sensory work: you never play the text. You play the heat and the cold or the ice cream you were eating.

And I don't believe you can go into period work until you've created a very sound, solid, truthful actor. If you do it before that, you'll have a disaster. It's like juggling. It's okay to juggle three balls, but then you have to juggle, four, five, six. You have to work your way up to that.

It's difficult to do period work in New York studios because I'm not in the position to impose voice, speech, and movement on the actor. Even though I have colleagues I've worked with for a long time and I implore students to work with them, they are not all going to do it. At Rutgers I can.

Do you follow the same course of training at Rutgers?

For the first two years at Rutgers the training is the same process as my private classes. But on the MFA level, the whole third year is devoted to style. I start with Victorian–Edwardian plays—Shaw and Wilde because they are more accessible. Then I move on to Restoration and Molière and Shakespeare.

You encourage your students to use the circumstances of the character. Do you ever encourage them to substitute events from their personal lives?

I don't believe in substitutions. I'm against them because they divide an actor. Substitutions are what gave Method acting a bad name. You get two actors on stage and they are not relating to each other; they are trying to see someone else in each other's faces because they are working on substitutions. You get very absent-minded behavior that way, as if someone isn't quite there. When an actor uses substitutions, he must always find his own personal justifications for what he is doing and he will very seldom find that they agree with the text.

But you said justification involves using something from your own experience that is similar to that of the character you are playing.

I do teach actors to personalize, and most legitimate teachers will. Personalizations are those personal examples that an actor will use to illuminate some aspect of his performance. In the example I gave of an actor using a booby trap, that's an "as if." The actor is making a comparison between something in the scene that is not very well understood and something he does understand.

Do you give students these "as if" situations, or do you ask them to find them for themselves?

I ask them to ask themselves, "What is my personalization for this moment? What is this like?"

Personalizations can be drawn from the actor's own life. If an actress is playing a scene in which her husband leaves her, it might occur to her that it's just like the time when she was eight years old and her father left and she watched him go out the door. It's the same thing. But the important thing to understand is that once the actor gets the personalization he or she must take the behavior from it and throw the personalization away. She can't stand there thinking about her father leaving. Once she's found that for herself it's like a nut. The meat of the nut is the behavior and she extracts it and throws the shell away. In a substitution the actor goes onstage with it and tries to hang on to it.

One of the big keys is the question of meaning. I never train the actor to think literally, but essentially. It's never the facts; it's what they mean to him. It's not a question of what is true, but of the association of the meaning. For example, let's say I'm working on a scene in which I get a big promotion at work. Perhaps I can't personally relate to the kind of work that the character does, but I can relate to achievement, and that promotion is achievement. Then I can make my own associations with that because achievement is achievement is achievement. Once I make my personal associations they give living meaning to the text.

Another aspect of interpretive work in the second year is the problem of homework. How does the actor do it? He sits down with the script and daydreams through it. If he wants to take an hour to daydream around one moment, he takes that hour to explore it fully, find its meaning for him in terms of his own associations. It is very private and subjective work and if done correctly results in a kind of conditioning.

I remember when Paul Sorvino was in *That Championship*

Season. That play has a problem in it. The first act ends right after Sorvino breaks the news to his friend that he's had an affair with his wife. The other fellow grabs a gun, points it at him, and says "I'm going to kill you." Then the curtain comes down for intermission, and when it comes up again it picks up where it left off. That's a real acting problem because the actor has to stay in the moment during the ten-minute intermission so that he can walk back on stage and still feel the same fear of dying. When I talked to Paul about it he said that at the beginning of the run of the play he used to spend the entire intermission preparing to keep himself emotionally alive. After a while he became so conditioned that all he'd have to do was walk out in the dark and the emotion came up. He was conditioned. It was just there. That's what homework does. It's like doing a preparation over and over again until the emotion becomes so connected with the moment that it comes up by itself.

Stanislavsky said that the actor rehearses to make habits. First he decides what habits he wants to have, then he rehearses to acquire them, which means conditioning himself by doing it repeatedly until it's a habit. Then the whole performance becomes a habit. In the last phase of rehearsal you make all the habits beautiful. Ultimately, acting is also an aesthetic consideration. It has to look aesthetically pleasing. That's why someone pushing to summon up an emotion is not agreeable to watch on the stage. It's not aesthetic and it's not moving. It has to look as if it has just happened without any work showing.

Are there any areas in which you differ from Meisner in your teaching?

I owe a tremendous debt to him. I find that by and large everything I learned from him enables me to do everything I want to do with the actor. I differ from him not so much in methodology as in classroom atmosphere. I think I am very good at creating an atmosphere of freedom. I agree that there has to be discipline and a great sense of purpose, but you also have to keep a climate of freedom so that actors can feel free to make mistakes and be willing to take risks.

At the same time you have to maintain a standard so that the *best* student can say, "I have contended with it and met it and I feel as if I have really done something because I measured up to that standard. I know that this is the top so I can be confident that if I please Bill Esper or any other reputable teacher, I've got some genuine level of competence."

I also differ from Meisner in my serious concern with period and style. He was very interested in them and wonderfully good at period and style, but he didn't devote himself to them in the way I have. I've spent eight years working constantly in that area. My feeling has been that they are the most important frontier for American actors. Putting together the real American-based Stanislavsky work to make a truthful actor and the ability to find a vivid theatrical way to express that inner reality—that's the whole ball of wax. You can't say that you are really serious about the art of acting unless you can test yourself against the classics.

You have to have a point of view about the art of acting and the theater. I'm a humanist and I go to the theater to learn something about human nature, some part of the world we live in. If the theater can't illuminate some aspect of life for me, I don't want to be there.

Phoebe Max

Michael Schulman

Michael Schulman founded his workshop in 1976 after teaching at the Lee Strasberg Theatre Institute for five years, and also at The Actors Studio in New York. The Michael Schulman Theatre Workshop also includes a unit for producing workshop projects since Mr. Schulman believes that "An actor's training must include performing in full productions, night after night, in front of an audience."

He is also a founder and artistic director of the British–American Acting Academy, which grew out of his work at the London Academy of Music and Dramatic Art (LAMDA). At LAMDA he organized and taught in a program that combined British and American acting approaches. The British–American Acting Academy holds courses in London and New York that are designed to help actors learn to integrate the best of British and American training.

In 1985 Mr. Schulman became chairman of the theater department at the Usdan Center for the Performing Arts on Long Island. A *number of his students have become teachers at Usdan, inaugurating yet another generation of acting teachers.*

Mr. Schulman's books and articles on acting are used extensively by actors and students around the country. These include his essays "How to Approach the Scene" in Contemporary Scenes for Student Actors, *"Overcoming Stage Fright," in* The Actor's Scenebook, Vol. I, *and "Creating a Character" in* The Actor's Scenebook, Vol. II. *The primary goal of his work with actors, he says, is "to help them create a unique, authentic, and passionate life with each role."*

Mr. Schulman is also a professional playwright and director. His plays, including his highly popular one-acter Did You Ever Go to P.S. 43?, *have had productions all over the United States, as well as in Canada and England. He studied directing with Lee Strasberg and was a member of The Actors Studio director's unit. He trained as an actor with Tamara Daykarhanova, a Russian actress and teacher, who was a founding member of The Actors Studio, and who had herself trained at the Moscow Art Theater under Konstantin Stanislavsky.*

Mr. Schulman has a Ph.D. in psychology; is a licensed psychologist in New York State; has done research in the areas of creativity, stage fright, child development, aggression, and psychotherapy; and has taught psychology at Fordham and Rutgers universities, Hunter College, and most recently at the Ferkauf Graduate School of Psychology of Yeshiva University and at the New School for Social Research. His writings on the psychology of acting include a Psychology Today *article entitled "Backstage Behaviorism."*

How did you get started teaching acting?

I was studying directing with Lee Strasberg at the Strasberg Institute. He knew I was a psychologist and he seemed to like my work in his directing class. After a while he asked if I would start a class. He was interested in me using whatever was new in psychology to expand and explore the actor's craft. I started teaching a class and then, before too long, had three classes at the Strasberg Institute, where I taught for five years.

I was also asked to teach an acting exercise class at The Actors

Studio, which I did for Studio members. After a while I began to change a number of the exercises. My work began to evolve away from Strasberg's in ways that made me feel that I should be on my own.

How does your approach to the training of actors differ from Strasberg's?

It differs in a lot of ways. One of the first things that I began to realize was that there were better ways to deal with actors' fears than the relaxation techniques that Lee used. Relaxation deals with the central nervous system, what is called the voluntary nervous system, but fear is controlled by the autonomic nervous system, the involuntary nervous system. One of the things I began to do was to develop techniques to get directly at the system controlling the fear. So I developed what I called Confidence Stimulus Exercises.

Could you describe them?

In their scene work actors often use personal stimuli that are objects, people, or events from their own lives to arouse feelings in themselves. It struck me: why not have an actor use a personal stimulus to make him feel strong and confident, just for himself, not for the character.

One of the problems with the relaxation technique was that I found that, frankly, it wasn't working for most people. And it often led to very de-energized acting because people were working so hard at keeping their bodies relaxed. Students had a lot of trouble making the transition from using relaxation as an exercise to using it in their scene work. Also, I found that there was no correlation between those who were the good relaxers in class during these exercises and those who were good actors. Many of the best actors were bad at doing this exercise, and vice versa.

To do the Confidence Stimulus Exercise, I have students sit in a semicircle in the stage area of the classroom and I ask them to think of some object, place, or person in whose presence they feel strong and confident. Students have used all kinds of things: bowling balls, ballet slippers, their grandmother, their dog, lots of different things. One student used a bright light that for her was God. I will tell students to put themselves in the presence of their confidence stimulus and to let it affect them, making them feel strong.

Do you give them any prompts for creating their confidence stimuli?

Yes, I give them reminders to focus on the sensory elements of the stimulus: the smells, the sight of it, particular details; if it's a person, to recall a particular context with that person, a particular look on that person's face.

So it's a kind of Sensory Recall.

Yes. It's basically a sensory exercise. You can generally see visible changes in the students; they seem more comfortable very quickly. Because the stimuli are so powerful for them, their concentration is quite strong. Then I ask them to put whatever they are feeling into a sound—to express the feeling in sound. Now, by having a demand placed on them to do something publicly, a number of them will lose concentration. I expect them to. It's part of what I want them to learn—confidence isn't something you have and keep forever. As an actor, you work with the awareness that there are a number of things that might make you lose confidence. Your job then is to remind yourself to go back to your stimuli, to go back to thinking about the things you've chosen to think about during your rehearsals.

Concentration simply means that you have chosen a target to think about, to place your attention on, and when you check, if you find yourself on target you say, "I'm concentrated"; when you are off target you say, "I've lost my concentration." When you lose your concentration, your job is to tell yourself, "Go back to my stimulus." Actually, I've developed concentration exercises that provide students with effective tools for going back to a stimulus and staying focused on it. The key is to ask a question about the stimulus, such as "What does that look she gave me really mean?" or "Does this taste the way it usually tastes?" Questions are compelling; they bring us back on target.

In the Confidence Stimulus Exercise, when I ask students to express a sound that conveys what their confidence stimulus is making them feel, they often lose their concentration because they start to anticipate the sound they are going to make and worry whether it truly expresses their feelings or whether it sounds silly. Sometimes they start making a sound that is connected to what they are feeling and halfway through, rather than completing the sound, they start to evaluate the first part of it. At that point they have lost their concentration. The rest of the sound is no longer coming as a response to their stimulus, but is instead a response to the initial sound that they made, what they heard coming out of their mouths. When I hear that they've lost their concentration, I remind them to tell themselves to go back to their confidence stimulus, to go back to the sensory elements of the stimulus that make them feel confident—for instance, to feel the weight of the bowling ball, to feel the strength in their arms as they are holding it. I ask them to continue to make a stronger and stronger commitment to making a sound that truly expresses what they are feeling.

One of the other things that I do in this and other sensory exercises is have students close their eyes for a second and picture themselves with that stimulus—with that person or object or environment that makes them feel confident. Then I ask them to hear the sound that this private self that they are picturing wants to make. I tell them to observe passively, as if they were watching a movie of themselves. Usually the private self they are imagining will make a sound that is much more expressive than the sound they have allowed to come out of their own mouth while sitting in their chairs. I'll then ask them to open their eyes and re-create the stimulus and to try to let the sound they have just observed privately come out openly.

This monitoring of the private self is an important part of the sensory exercises that I do. It's another area that is very different from what Lee did. Lee didn't really deal with how to make an actor more expressive. He said, "That's the talent," and left it at that. But the word "talent" doesn't explain anything. What are the talented people doing? That's the important question. We work directly on helping the actor become more expressive, and then people say, "Boy, is he talented." Teaching the actor to become aware of and to express his private self is one way we work on this. Often actors will come off the stage after doing a scene or exercise and say, "There are things I didn't get at. I knew there was more." When you ask them how they knew there was more, they'll usually say, in one form or another, that they heard sounds in their heads they didn't let come through, or that they pictured their bodies doing things they didn't actually put into action; that they held back. They might say, "There were moments when I wanted to scream at the other person on stage with me and I felt myself inhibiting it, not as the character, but as the actor." One of the things actors need to learn is to be aware of those moment-to-moment private impulses in order to express them. As soon as they become aware of them, they have to go back to whatever it was that evoked them, such as the snotty tone of voice their partner just used, and make a commitment to express all the sounds and actions that want to come through.

When an actor uses these images of his private self he needs to be careful not simply to imitate the private behavior. That will feel artificial. First he must re-create the stimulus to which the private self was responding and only then try to express what his private self just expressed. Learning to monitor the private self is a very important exercise for increasing expressiveness. As I've indicated, one of the major problems that one encounters in working with actors is how to get an actor to be more expressive, to use his voice and body more fully and vividly when reacting to the various kinds of stimuli in a scene: the partner, the memories, the plans, the environment.

How do you make sure it's all being expressed? Well, most of us are much more expressive privately than publicly, so one of the things we can do is learn from ourselves, from that private self. For example, in the Confidence Exercises, along with having the students hear the private sounds that want to come out in response to their confidence stimuli, I'll also have them get up out of the chair and begin to move to that stimulus, expressing with their bodies what the stimulus makes them feel. Then I'll have them stop for a second and close their eyes and I'll ask them to see that movie of themselves reacting to the stimulus, to see how their body truly wants to react—not a literal movement like swinging the bowling ball, but some expressive movement or gesture that's a response to the feeling they get from bowling, for instance.

Then, in order to increase the expressiveness of even that private stimulus, I'll often say to them, "Tell that private you to use its torso more fully, or use its arms or voice more fully. Don't tell it how. Just tell it what to use and then observe." Usually the private you will, indeed, use those parts of its body more expressively, and it won't feel forced, it'll feel organic. Then I'll tell the student, "Now open your eyes and re-create the stimulus and try to let those same kinds of motions come through." The goal is not to reproduce exactly what you pictured, but to be guided by what you saw and release an expression that is as strong and forceful and that comes from what you are responding to. This is a very, very useful way to get actors to be more physically and vocally expressive. It is more useful than dance or movement classes, where students learn arbitrary or stylized gestures that have nothing to do with reacting to stimuli or playing a life.

So you may stop actors in the middle of a scene, monologue, or exercise if you feel that they are not expressive enough.

Yes. I'll ask them to observe their private self in the same situation that they are using in their scene or exercise. Let's say somebody is doing an exercise that makes him angry. Often our private selves in life express much more anger than our public selves. For instance, if your boss gets you angry, very little of your feelings may be visible to an outsider. Inside, though, you are screaming at the top of your lungs some very ugly words at him and imagining your body in some kind of violent convulsion, and yet you are keeping it all very contained.

As an actor one wants to be able to let out those screams and convulsions when they are appropriate for a character. Because we inhibit those kinds of impulses so much in life, many actors can't let them out even when they are called for. There are, of course, actors who inhibit strong impulses in life, yet find playing a character a liberating experience when they can let everything out that they normally hide. But for many, the habit of not showing, whether it's anger or love or fear, carries over into their acting work and everything stays very, very small. How to become more expressive has been a problem since the beginning of actors' concerns about their craft. One of the new ways I have to try to solve this problem is through putting an actor very consciously and directly in touch with the expressiveness that already exists in his private behavior.

I'd like to say something else about the Confidence Stimulus Exercise because there is another part to it. Once students begin to express what the confidence stimulus makes them feel, I will have them switch to a stimulus that makes them feel very unconfident— some person or circumstance that brings up feelings of self-doubt, perhaps even self-hatred. I ask them to go through the same process to get them to express that negative experience very fully. Then I will have them switch back to their confidence stimulus. What I want them to do is practice switching from negative, self-doubting feelings to their confidence stimulus so that they get into the habit of going from bad to good feelings. Then, when they feel frightened or inhibited, a little voice that is already well practiced says, "Go to your confidence stimulus." They may need it when they are going to an audition, working in front of someone who makes them nervous, or on an opening night. If they've practiced switching, they already know how to deal with the tugs of doubting feelings that intrude into their thoughts and make them do less than their best work.

In what other ways does your approach to the training of actors differ from your own training?

Many ways. You can think of human behavior as divided into two major dimensions: we take actions in pursuit of objectives and we react to stimuli. Sometimes the same behavior can fall into both categories.

In almost all his work Strasberg focused on the *reactive* side of behavior. All of his sensory exercises and emotional exercises dealt with reacting to stimuli. He hardly focused at all on the other side of life, the side that involves taking actions. One way my teaching differs from his is that I place great emphasis on the actions that characters take in pursuit of objectives. An actor needs to break down his part into what his character wants and what the obstacles are that block his getting what he wants.

When I work with new students I point out that if I move a chair away from one spot it's not a very dramatic event. But if the student sitting next to the chair puts his hand out and grabs it, providing an obstacle for me, suddenly the entire class will rivet its attention on what is going to happen next. That's the essence of dramatic tension: an objective met head-on with an obstacle. Then the audience asks, "What's going to happen next?"

There are theories of the beginning of drama that state that drama derives from religion and ritual. I disagree with those theories. If you want ritual, you don't go to the theater; you go to church. It isn't as if we don't have ritual today. We go to midnight mass, go to Macy's Thanksgiving Day parade, watch the half-time events on football games, go to a carnival. There are lots of rituals. What makes drama special is this interplay of objective and obstacle—a life with desire and something in the way of that life getting what it wants. The earliest plays we know are based on that principle, not on ritual. Plays may take place on religious holidays and have religious themes, but they are still plays. So the theories that state the essence of theater is ritual are not based on any facts we actually know about theater as far back as the ancient Greeks, not based on Sophocles or any other Greek playwright. Audiences then and now seek something special in theater. We seek an understanding of the human experience and not simply a personal religious experience. When we want a personal religious experience, we go to church. When we want to know more about our lives and the human condition, we go to the theater.

I teach students that the obstacle is just as important as the objective. The best way to make sure that your objective is strong is by making the obstacle strong. It is helpful if the obstacle almost prevails two or three times in a scene. That way, as the scene progresses your character has to remind herself just how much she wants whatever it is she is after. There are two kinds of obstacles: external ones, such as another character who won't give you what you want; and internal ones, like the ones felt by a priest who is sexually obsessed with a parishioner.

Whenever possible it is useful to include internal obstacles for your character. A device you can see used by the most expressive actors is alternating between going directly after an objective and going in the opposite direction because of an internal obstacle. A trap for inexperienced actors is that they'll allow their objective and obstacle to cancel each other out so that the audience never sees an action taking place in either direction. The actor thinks the thoughts—"I want her, but I mustn't have her"—but never really starts to do anything, so as far as the audience is concerned nothing is going on. One of the best examples of an actor making his conflict visible is James Stewart in *It's A Wonderful Life*. In the famous scene when he and Donna Reed share a telephone, we see him alternate over and over between his desire for her and his need to break away.

I work with actors on making sure their thoughts and feelings are expressed in behavior. It may be extremely subtle—through a slight gesture or a small shift of posture or change in facial expression; but something must be visible or the audience won't know that thought or feeling exists. In this way my work is similar to Stanislavsky's emphasis on "physical action."

There is an important danger in defining objectives. You don't want to define your actions in advance. Some teachers—Harold Clurman, I believe, was one—teach students to plan out their actions in advance. This destroys any possibility of spontaneity. Until you're actually rehearsing with your acting partners, responding to what you're getting from them and from the environment you've created, you can't know what actions the life you are playing will want to take. Sitting in your room charting out your actions is likely to lead to very conventional-looking stage behavior, and in rehearsal instead of being responsive to what your partners are giving you, you wind up busy trying to fulfill the actions you've planned in advance.

I teach students to come into a rehearsal knowing what has led up to the scene, knowing one's history with the other characters and the place, knowing what one wants, and being prepared with the character's imagery in the sense that if the character talks about an incident with his mother, he needs to have prepared a mother and an incident to talk about. Once you discover actions during rehearsals that you want to keep, you have to make sure when you repeat them that you focus on the same stimuli that led to them in the first place. Otherwise they will feel awkward and look mechanical. And if in a next rehearsal or performance your partner gives you something totally different, you have to be ready to give up actions that no longer are appropriate, even if they felt wonderful before. I've seen actors look awful even though they were repeating virtually identically a performance that had been brilliant the night before, because their partner was now giving them totally different feelings or actions and they weren't responding to any of it. There is nothing more crucial to the acting process than the actor being responsive to what is happening in the moment.

Another way I differ from predecessors is the great importance I place on imagery. For example, I play a little game with new students. I will often say, "What did you have for dinner last night?" Let me ask you that question: what did you have for dinner last night?

Spaghetti and meatballs.

In order to answer me you had to have images. You just had images of spaghetti and meatballs that probably involved more than just visual memories, but recollections of taste, smell, texture. Now if I wrote out your answer and gave an actor that little scene to play, many would not have the imagery that you just had so easily, so spontaneously. Well, if you don't have the imagery that a real person has in life, you don't play a real person. You wind up indicating the attitude toward what you had for dinner last night. So virtually anything that we talk about involves the use of imagery, whether it is about past experiences or plans for the future. If I ask you where you think you are going to have supper tonight, images will start to flash before your eyes. It's crucial that actors have these images. If you are playing Hamlet, you need very concrete images of your father because so much of your motivation in the play is based on the desire to find justice for what was done to your father. Without images of your father—not the actor playing the ghost, but a father who lived for you—you can't experience Hamlet's life in any authentic way.

How is this different from what is often called prior circumstances and given circumstances?

It makes the prior circumstances extremely concrete and brings them into the actual onstage thoughts of the actor. Also, the imagery is a way of making personal everything that an actor needs to know about his character and the other characters with whom he interacts. I find that most teachers and most actors I've worked with don't create their images very specifically. For example, if to successfully create a father for Hamlet you must use imagery, you can do this in two ways: you can use what I call Personal Stimuli—that is, elements from your own life, perhaps recollections of your own father or someone else who was a father figure to you, whom you would have to avenge if you knew he had been harmed. You would think of specific instances from your own past with this person *and* you would have to think of them onstage while playing Hamlet. If Hamlet were actually living through all those events in the play, he would have images of his own father at many moments. The actor playing Hamlet needs those same kinds of images, and needs them onstage as he speaks and behaves. Otherwise he can't create a living being.

The second way to find imagery is to use what I call Character Stimuli, stimuli that are based solely on Hamlet's life, not your own. You can get at these Character Stimuli by a process that I call Private Improvisations. For example, I might have a student playing Hamlet create Hamlet's history for himself through fantasy by saying, "Remember a time when your father taught you a dueling technique that has always served you and without which you know you wouldn't be alive today," and "Remember a time when your father confided some fear of his to you." These will make the father both more personal and more vulnerable for the actor and stimulate the desire in the actor to protect that father. I will put an actor through a number of those kinds of fantasies so that, as Hamlet, he has a history with his father, and I have actors combine these kinds of Character Stimuli with his Personal Stimuli—the face of the person who taught you the dueling technique might resemble that of your own father or someone who was a father surrogate for you.

We do exercises in class to help students develop these kinds of character stimuli.

Would you describe these exercises?

In one version each student creates an imaginary brother or sister. I have a group of students sit in chairs, usually with their eyes closed, and I say, "Remember a time when your brother or sister got blamed for something you did." Then they just sit there and spin out an incident in their thoughts. Other "memories" include "Remember a time when your brother or sister got angry at you and locked you out of his or her room." "Remember a time when you saw one of them kissing someone." "Remember a time when your brother or sister gave you a birthday present." We go through a series of such occasions, perhaps a dozen, creating a full history. I usually bring it to a time when that brother or sister is very sick and you think he or she might die. Then I often see tears streaming down the faces of the students, tears for this imaginary brother or sister who has become so alive simply through this private imagery. Because I take them through incidents at different ages, the physical aspects of their imaginary brother or sister will change, depending on the age. Sometimes it takes a few of these private fantasies before the physical character gets fully defined. Their fantasies may connect to someone they have known. Sometimes incidents they have actually lived through may filter in, and that's fine. But what they are doing is creating a story for themselves and an imaginary relationship.

I use this technique to make sure students, in their scene work, create very full histories. It's one thing to know that you are married and you love your spouse although you have had your ups and downs. It's another to do a fantasy on some of those ups and downs so that when you are sitting on stage with your partner and are in the middle of some discussion, as in life, you suddenly remember a moment that was very exciting for you, or a moment when you felt angry at your spouse. I find these kinds of private fantasies generally more powerful than having the two actors do an actual improvisation on some earlier experience because in the improvisation the actors may not get at things that are going to help them. For instance, an earlier experience may be some torrid lovemaking that the actors may not feel comfortable about improvising. But in your fantasy you can often get to things that are helpful for the specific character that you are playing.

Another exercise I do with new students is called the One-Line Play. I talked before about expressing fully in response to an impulse. Actors feel connected when the lines want to come out, when they *have to* say the next thing that the playwright has given them to say. They feel disconnected when they are thinking "How should I say the next line? How do I get into the next line?" Just as right now I am not thinking about how I am saying what I am saying—I am responding to your questions, I am responding to images. I am responding to this circumstance, I have memories of myself teaching and myself as a student, and all of that is leading to what I am saying and the way I am saying it. When you are playing a life, that's what you want to experience. You don't want to experience pushing your lines out. You want them to come out because they have to.

Well, an actor can only do that if he puts in the right ingredients. So one of the things I do is have a student sit alone facing the class. I then give him a line such as, "Give it back to me." I will say, "Create a circumstance in which that line wants to be said." The student will think of a situation with someone and imagine himself in it and then say the line. If I sense that the line is a bit forced, depending on what I see going on in his face or hear in his voice, I will have him re-create the circumstance and help him find a detail that will spur the line. It might be a particular look on the face of the person he is talking to, or I'll remind him of why the object he wants back is important or under what circumstance that person took the object. And then I will have him try the line again.

Are these circumstances kept private?

Yes. I never ask students to tell me what they are working on. I believe that is an intrusion into students' privacy. I want them to use every element of themselves, but in the service of their art, not for revealing, not for psychotherapy. So I ask them to keep all their stimuli private. I might ask if they are working on a person or an object or I might ask for the general framework of their circumstances so that I can help them pinpoint details, but I don't let them share any private aspects of their lives. This is a principle that Strasberg held to as well, for very much the same reasons.

In doing the One-Line Play Exercise I will put the student through a series of such one-line plays. Another line might be, "I want to go dancing," or "You hurt me," or "I'll get even with you." Through these exercises I put him through a series of different kinds of emotions and the student learns how easy acting is when you put the right ingredients in. You don't have to force anything out. When he goes on to do scene work, I want him to remember the experience he had in this exercise so if he finds that he is trying to figure out how to say something or is forcing, he can recognize it through the contrast between the strain he is having in the scene and the ease he felt in the one-line plays.

Do you do improvisations as well?

Yes. We do a lot of improvisation work. We do it as a way of learning to play objectives without the burden of lines or character-ization. That's its purpose. In this way the students get a sense of how just wanting something impels their action. Here again, when they are doing scene work and perhaps are not feeling so impelled, they can remember how easy it felt in the improvisations and realize that they are now forgetting to focus on what they want.

I use the imagery work in improvisations also. Most improvisa-tions that I set up involve two people. I will give each of them an objective. I will usually tell both some of the circumstances. For example, two people have been having an affair and they meet on a bench in Central Park once a week and spend the rest of the day together. The man is married. Then I will give each character some private information. The purpose of that is to set up a conflict. Each character knows something and wants something that is usually in opposition to what the other knows and wants. Thus, for each character there is an obstacle. In this situation the married man will be coming to tell his girlfriend that his wife is pregnant and that he can't see her any more, and the girlfriend will be coming to tell the man that she is pregnant in the hope that it will finally make him leave his wife.

If I stop with just that much information, the actors will often just "play at" the event; they won't really live through it. So I will give each actor a moment or two to create little private improvisations. For instance, I will tell the woman to imagine a few incidents that led her to believe that the man would leave his wife for her. I will also ask her to create several wonderful times that they had together so that when she walks out on stage it's not just another acting partner who is sitting there but a man with whom she has shared some experiences and who she can realistically believe will leave his wife for her. I will give the man some private improvisations that make him feel a bond to his wife so that now that he has learned she is pregnant, he feels an obligation to stay with her. I will also have him think of a couple of incidents that bond him to his lover. Usually, I will have him think about what he likes about children, what he has observed that makes having a child important to him. This may sound like a lot, but these fantasies don't take very long. Without these private improvisations, the actor is likely to have only the idea of a wife, not the experience of one. And he'll have only the idea of some interest in having a family and the idea of having an affair with this woman, but he'll have no experiences to help him find the reality of the situation. As students progress, I will say less and less to them, letting them know that it is their responsibility to fill in the background. If I see that they haven't, that they are simply skimming the surface, I will ask them if they created all those elements. So I find this private improvisation work extremely important and use it even in improvisations.

This notion of imagery is so crucial. The other day a student who is a very good actor was doing a scene from *The Philadelphia Story*. When he talked about Tracy, his ex-wife, having gone up on the roof naked in the moonlight on a particular occasion, he did it with some gusto, he was playful, but he didn't really have an image of what that moment must have been like—for him to see the woman he loved so exposed, so free. Without that, there is nothing to play. So a lot of my comments to actors have to do with making their imagery concrete and pertinent to the moment their character is living through.

Do you do Affective Memories Exercises?

I handle the whole area of emotional arousal very differently from the way Lee did. For Lee, creating sensory and emotional stimuli was this arduous, frightening, and unclear task of trying to create hallucinations. People used to sit in his class for hours staring at their hands waiting for a cup to materialize. Lee never really described his exercises very well because in his class everybody was working on a different exercise. He had a particular order to his exercises, so that someone who was there for the first time would be doing the first exercise and someone who was there for the twentieth time would be working on another. His classes were two hours long and in that time you cannot describe ten different exercises adequately. So students had somehow to learn what the exercises were about through a kind of osmosis. That was always confusing, and you couldn't really observe what other people were doing because you were doing your own exercise.

I believe that what is at the core of the whole area of sense memory, at least what is of value in it, is nothing more than the creation of imagery. To create a cup or a mug is very easy. As soon as I ask a student, "Is the surface of the side of the mug different from the bottom?" the mug is there for him immediately and in a way that he can actually use if he has to mime drinking or holding or touching a mug. If I ask, "Is the heat on the bottom of the mug the same or different from the heat on the sides?" the student will experience those elements of the mug immediately. All of those sensory exercises that one spent an endless amount of time doing in Lee's class, I find unnecessary and confusing. Also, his students had a great deal of trouble incorporating his exercises into their scene work. What is important in them is simply the imagery work—and you saw how easy that was when I asked you what you had for supper last night. One just needs to be reminded to do it and to create the sensory details.

In the emotional area, I work more directly toward an emotion than Lee did. In his exercises it was taboo ever to define the emotion one was working toward. However, Lee's Affective Memory Exercise doesn't quite follow his own principle because a student really did know what he was working toward. He was trying to re-create an emotional experience from the past so he knew what emotion was involved: a happy one, a sad one, etc.

The whole area of emotion was very touchy and scary with Lee. You could only do an Affective Memory Exercise after a long period of training and you could only work on emotional stimuli that were seven or more years in the past. I found in working with actors that emotions aren't such a big deal for most of them; they like feeling and expressing emotions. It isn't so scary. They don't need long preparations to become emotional. It isn't something they have to be led into so carefully, and the seven-year boundary is not necessary.

Also, contrary to Lee, I found that actors could use fantasy stimuli to arouse emotions; these are events that never really happened to you but that you could imagine happening. If one creates the details of these kinds of stimuli properly they are just as powerful and as reliable as re-creating events from your past—for some actors, more so. For example, we do an exercise in which students see someone they feel protective of being harmed. It's pure fantasy, but when students create their imagery specifically and vividly—seeing their child's or their mother's hair pulled or eye poked, or hearing the person call out to them for help—the reactions are tremendous, and they are very repeatable and reliable.

I found when I worked with actors who were trained in Lee's method that they were having a lot of trouble in the emotional area. Some of the things he said were downright silly, such as his instruction to begin working on an emotional stimulus a minute or two before you need it in the scene. No actor of any quality ever did that. It takes you totally out of the moment and out of the scene. You work on an emotional stimulus at the moment your character is faced with it; otherwise your reactions cannot be organic. If you have trouble creating an emotion in what I call "organic time" it means either that you haven't learned how to provide yourself with the evocative aspects of an emotional stimulus or that you are embarrassed about displaying the emotion and are inhibiting it.

These are problems that you work out in class by doing emotional exercises, not by approaching emotional arousal in an inorganic way.

Because I found so many of Lee's students confused and intimidated by the emotional work, with my students I began to say, "Next week I want you to bring in a stimulus that makes you angry." So they knew they had to find a stimulus to make them angry. I had students sit in a semicircle and begin to create that stimulus and put their feelings into sound, and then into the words of a memorized monologue so that the way the monologue came out would depend on the emotion they were working on. We would go through a whole series of emotions—sorrow, fear, love; and sometimes we'd take the same emotion in different ways. There are many kinds of anger, so it was important for students to learn not to play an idea of anger. Sometimes anger involves bellowing rage, sometimes one cries when angry, and sometimes one is silent. The only danger in labeling the exercise "anger" is that the student will play a conventional idea of the emotion and not be faithful to what the stimulus draws from him. But when students are reminded not to play the label but to play what is true to that stimulus, it's usually not a problem. If I see them play the label, I help them find the stimulus elements that will arouse authentic feelings.

Also, I usually have students work on people to arouse feeling, imagining people they have known. Lee didn't like students to create people in his exercises because he believed that people changed too much as you thought about them, that they might do unexpected things, making the result unreliable. That's why his students were often confused about how to use substitutions, because when he talked about substitution, he seemed to be referring to using a person; but since he never allowed anyone to work on people as stimuli, it was unclear how he wanted you to do a substitution. If I ask students to work on an anger stimulus and that stimulus turns out to be a person, as it usually does, that's what they work on. And, yes, stimuli do change. One of the purposes of the emotional exercises is to learn about those changes and to discover which elements of the person or situation affect you in which ways so that if you want to use a personal stimulus in a scene, you have already practiced it and you know what elements you need to focus on and go back to.

How do you help students learn to use a person to stimulate an emotion—anger, for instance?

I will have them imagine themselves in a circumstance with a person who has angered them, hearing what that person is saying, seeing a particular look on his or her face, re-creating what they wanted or expected from that person, knowing how they wanted that person to treat them. I will have them express their feelings in words or in sound. I will also get their bodies involved so that they are expressing physically. I will have them do that private self exercise, picturing themselves responding to that person in order to help them get their expression out in a fuller way. It's crucial that emotions lead to actions. In life, when you're angry or sad, you want to *do* something, or you try to figure out what to do. Actors who have emotions that don't instigate actions are not being true to life; they look self-indulgent, and the audience tires of their emotion quickly because it isn't going anywhere.

Then the next step in the emotional exercise work teaches students how to use substitution. I will have two people sit in chairs that are quite close, facing each other, and ask them to find in the face of the person sitting before them elements that remind them of their personal anger stimulus. Then I'll ask them to direct their sounds toward each other, and take turns speaking a memorized monologue to each other. That way I get them to practice expressing their anger to another person, which for some isn't easy. Sometimes I will give them a circumstance and have them go into an improvisation. I'll say, "You are two roommates. One of you hasn't paid the rent. The other one is tired of paying your share. Find something in each other's face that reminds you of your personal anger stimulus and incorporate your reactions to that stimulus into the improvisation."

Real anger—on stage or off—is very powerful to witness. Few actors achieve it. For example, you're not likely to see real anger on *Miami Vice* or most other "tough guy" shows or films. Few actors achieve the physiological, the autonomic, components of anger, or any other emotion they work on. Without these bodily reactions the emotion isn't real. Through the emotional exercise work, the actor becomes sensitive to these bodily reactions so he can tell if he is being authentic when he becomes emotional in a scene.

Because I often do strong emotional exercises I also teach students how to get out of an exercise. You get out of a stimulus by going to another one. So I have students learn to switch out of negative emotional states by going to something that makes them feel good. Sometimes I'll have everybody work on a warm bath with wonderful smells of bath oils. Sometimes they will put someone they like in the bath with them, massaging their toes. This is a way to teach students that they are truly in control of their emotional stimuli. If the effects of a stimulus persist longer than wanted, they know they can get out of it.

When students have some concern about using things from their own lives, I remind them that great art can only come out of using one's self. We all have these kinds of strong feelings on one level or another in us, and it's neither a danger nor a betrayal of them to use them carefully in the service of our art.

An emotional stimulus is a complex entity, made up of many elements, so if a stimulus from your own life is going to serve you in playing a character you have to know which particular stimulus elements to go to. Your relationship to a stimulus depends on how you focus on it. For example, there is an exercise I do in which I have students go back to and explore a room that they knew in childhood. When they go back in as an adult and they open a drawer and find some toy they haven't seen in years or an old baseball glove or their ballet slippers, it's a very emotional experience.

After they explore the room as an adult, I have them do the same exercise—go into that same room—but now as the child they once were. To the child these very same objects are just everyday things, often to be tossed aside because they are in the way. As a ten-year-old you don't sentimentalize those objects. So I tell students to use stimuli from any time in their lives. As an actor I have used my dog. I can use my dog for a joyful stimulus or a sad stimulus, because she died. What the actor needs to know is what aspects of the stimulus evoke what reactions in him, and often he will have to re-create the *him* of a particular time to get at particular feelings. If I think of a person that I had a love affair with, am I thinking of the thrilling, early moments in the affair or the sad end of the affair? If I think of it as the me that I am now, I may be very happy that the affair ended, even though I might have been devastated at the time. If I want to get a feeling of devastation, I need to re-create the me of that earlier time by re-creating the needs and fears and hopes I had at that time.

What other exercises do you use in class?

There are many other emotional exercises I do that I have created over the years to help students with different aspects of arousing emotions. For example, we approach the problem of being vulnerable in front of an audience through an exercise called Don't Go. Students work individually: they stand facing the class and imagine somebody in front of them leaving them, or somebody dying—and their line is "Don't go." I help them to create the person they have chosen by asking them to see what that person is wearing, to see a particular look on his or her face, to see whether the person is angry at them or disappointed or sad at going, to think of what is special about him or her that can never be replaced. Then I will say, "Think of something that you have never said to this person before, that you have always wanted to say but have never been able to put into words." They have to ask the person they are visualizing not to leave them. They can use the words "Don't go" or a variation of that if they want.

I find this very helpful because many students have trouble showing that kind of vulnerability. It's a common problem with acting students. When students are working on this I will give them prompts to try to get them focused on their need for the person. They can re-create an incident when someone did leave them or they can imagine someone they love leaving them. I usually won't have the student say out loud what he or she always wanted to say because it's an invasion of privacy. I will have him think it and imagine himself saying it. I will have him put the intention behind what he wants to say to the other person in the words, "Don't go." This exercise ends when I get a sense that the student has gone as far as he or she can go. For one person this may mean that I have seen a feeling aroused to its fullest. It may be a painful feeling or an angry feeling or both.

Sometimes I will end the exercise before anything very strong comes out because I don't want to push the student beyond what he or she is ready to deal with. I don't believe that as a teacher I should pressure students and make them feel that they have to come up with an emotion to satisfy me. My prompts are designed to help them find imagery, but they must remain in control of their emotions. I don't approve of teachers who use the force of their personality and their relationship with students to provoke them into emotions. These students don't know how to repeat the process on their own because it depends on another force demanding an emotion from them.

In another exercise I'll have students imagine someone they know whom they would like to kiss but haven't. This is to remind them of how specific our attractions are. The person they want to kiss may have wonderful lips or great cheekbones or sexy eyes. In life we are drawn to and respond to these details, and it's visible to anyone watching. Actors playing love scenes rarely notice any details; they usually just play the attitude of being attracted to someone. And they rarely have the wonderful bodily reactions that we experience when we are about to kiss someone for the first time. Here again I remind students to become aware of their bodily reactions so that they can tell, when they are playing a love scene, whenever their bodies are reacting fully and honestly.

To this end I'll put students through a series of exercises that I call Autonomics. These include imagining oneself thirty stories up on the ledge of a skyscraper, tasting something disgusting, and encountering something frightening. The focus in each of these is creating vivid and authentic bodily reactions.

What techniques do you use to help students learn to develop a character?

I do a great deal of character work. The great actors—Marlon

Brando, Laurence Olivier—all strive to create a unique life with each character they play—unique physically, vocally, and behaviorally. They rarely simply play themselves. There are, of course, wonderful actors who have had long and successful careers playing themselves. Cary Grant is a good example; so is Jimmy Stewart. They varied somewhat from part to part, but it was often a small variation of themselves. It's not that I dislike actors who do that; they are often extraordinarily appealing and expressive. Jimmy Stewart and Katharine Hepburn are brilliant actors, although they usually don't vary that much from part to part. But those actors who are the most creative, those we go out of our way to see, even if the play or movie they are in isn't particularly good, are the ones who work creatively to bring into being very particular characters for each role. I remember going to see *The Betsy* some years ago, a movie that I heard wasn't very good, because I didn't want to miss what Laurence Olivier was working on. It doesn't matter if he succeeds or fails in each particular role. With him, it is coming into contact with an actor's creative mind that is exciting. With an actor like Jimmy Stewart, the thrill is coming into contact with Jimmy Stewart, who is so intense and appealing.

In class, I'll have actors work on both processes. Sometimes they will simply work on expressing aspects of themselves through a character, but I also encourage and try to teach them how to create unique lives.

How do you do that?

It's based on the way the great actors do it, and that is through the observation of people. Olivier, for example, based his famous Richard III on Jed Harris, the American producer that he worked for and disliked. Brando also uses particular character models. There was a rumor when he worked on *The Formula* that he used the industrialist Armand Hammer as his model. It was an extraordinary performance in an otherwise awful movie. Although Brando doesn't take his career seriously, he does take acting seriously, and those of us who admire him are disappointed because there are so many parts we would like to see what he would do with. There are very few actors you would look forward to seeing as King Lear or Richard III.

You already know what most of them would do with the role—exactly what they did with every other part. Not so with Brando or Olivier or any of the truly great actors. In interviews both Brando and Olivier have talked about the importance to them of creating characters who are unlike any they have played before and unlike those created by other actors in the same or similar roles.

The way we do character work in class is through observation. In the basic character exercise I will ask students a week in advance to prepare five different characters. I want them to think about these people and, if they can, to observe them. To make the five people very different I will usually say, "Pick someone you know who is funny, someone who is very aggressive, someone who is very sexy, someone who is very shy, and someone who is very confident." The idea isn't to play the label—as a matter of fact it is crucial not to—but to set their imaginations going.

At the start of the exercise I ask the students to engage in an activity in a kind of pantomime where they are just themselves either painting, cleaning, or washing, or any other ongoing activity that can last for an extended period of time. And they need a motivation for what they are doing. It shouldn't be an activity for which the sensory elements are overwhelming, like typing a letter, where you have to create the keys, the paper, and so on. But it should be an activity that requires the actor to use his whole body, to walk around, to pick up things. Students will start by engaging in that activity, and I will help them make the sensory elements clear by reminding them to have obstacles, such as the paint dripping or a stain that won't come out. Those kinds of obstacles make the sensory elements of the action very vivid.

Then I will say, "Pick the person you have chosen for the funny character and become 'possessed' by that character." I use the strong term "possessed" and break down what I mean. I say, "Imagine that character moving right inside you, taking over the rhythm in your body, taking over the distribution of your weight, taking over your legs." We will go through the arms, fingers, lips, eyes, and other parts of the body. I'll say, "You are now seeing through that person's eyes and hearing with his ears. Begin to walk around as that person:

feel the person take over your stride, take over your temperament."
I tell the student to find the voice of that person by making sounds
or speaking a monologue or singing a song. He or she needs to find
the rhythms, placement, strength, and style of articulation of the
voice. Then, after a few minutes of just experiencing being possessed
by that person, the student should start the activity over again so that
he can experience how this "new" being sweeps a floor, irons a shirt,
or paints a bookcase.

It's important that the students *not* ask themselves how the person
would do it. It's not an intellectual process. It's letting that being
who "possesses" you play itself out in that activity. Authenticity is
not important. If you act in a play, nobody is going to be comparing
your performance to some model that you have chosen as a
character. You don't need to become an exact replica of that person.
What you are striving for is a sense of the spirit of that person, the
sensitivities and readiness for action of that person, and the kinds of
actions that want to come out of that person, including particular
mannerisms that will help you define that person for the audience
and for yourself.

Once the students have gone through all five characters I'll put
the entire class into a group improvisation. The students are now a
company of actors in a summer theater and are getting the theater
ready for performances. I'll have some students work on their angry
character, others their funny character, somebody else on the
confident character, and so forth, and let them interact with each
other. After a few minutes, I'll have them switch to one of the other
characters and continue the improvisations. We'll switch every few
minutes until each character has participated in the improvisation.

Some students will find certain characters much easier than
others because they are not comfortable expressing certain kinds of
feelings or behaving in certain ways. For instance, some students
may be uncomfortable interacting when they are possessed by their
aggressive character, somebody who is always putting others down.
An actor may back off from fulfilling the character and send off
signals: "It's not me. I'm really a nice guy." If somebody is working
on his sexual character he may have trouble sending out sexual

signals. That's important for him to know because it tells him which areas he is going to have trouble playing. If he gets cast for roles that call for that kind of behavior, he will have to work hard not to undercut what the character needs to express. That's our basic character exercise.

When students work on scenes, I will at times have them use specific character models. Through this kind of character work, students find they can play parts that they never considered themselves right for, that they can truly transform themselves.

An extension of the basic character exercise combines character work with personal emotional stimuli. For example, the actor creates someone from his own past life who makes him angry, just as he would in the emotional exercise work that I described earlier. But now he provides this for himself while he is possessed by a character so that the form that the emotional expression takes is true to the character, not to the actor. Actors, even when playing characters, need to be able to use their own stimuli, but you want your reactions to come out in a form that is appropriate to the character.

We also do improvisations with character work. I will put two students who are doing character exercises into a situation in which they want something from each other. The form their behavior takes should reflect the characters they are working on.

Oddly enough, Lee never let his students use people as character models, only animals. Since so many of the actors he and everybody admires—Brando, Dustin Hoffman, Robert DeNiro, Olivier, Meryl Streep—say they base their characters on people they observe, Lee's objection is an example of a teacher's theory contradicting what the best actors are actually doing.

What techniques do you give students to help them work on comedy?

There are different kinds of comedy and you have to approach them in different ways. For example, in a lot of comedy the character is not trying to be funny. Jackie Gleason in the *Honeymooners* is not trying to be funny. He's funny because of the intensity and extremeness of his reactions. It's the same with Lucille

Ball in *I Love Lucy*. Her character is not trying to be funny. If, for instance, Ricky gives her a vase that she has to protect and she hears it fall off a shelf, the look on her face and the sound she will make when that happens will often be hilarious because of its extremeness. If she had that reaction to seeing her child dead on the ground, it would be appropriate.

I often demonstrate this aspect of comedy to students by saying, "If I see that student in the back row and I love her and I walk around the class to give her a hug, it can be emotional, but basically it will be melodrama. But if I love her so much that I don't notice anything in front of me and I just begin to walk straight to her, up and over the people sitting between us, it's funny (as long as I take it seriously and play the reality, and don't try to pump a laugh from the audience)." A lot of Charlie Chaplin's humor was based on extremeness of reaction.

There is another kind of humor that is very difficult to play and that's wit. In wit the character *is* trying to be funny, as in Noel Coward or some of Neil Simon. The character is going for the laugh. One often hears acting teachers say, "You never go for the laugh." Well, in certain kinds of humor that's true, but if you are witty in life, you know you go for the laugh. You look for the laugh and you set up laughs. If you are playing a witty character, looking for the laugh is something you have to play in order to be true to that character. If a student is having trouble playing wit, it can often be solved through a character exercise, by "getting possessed" by somebody he knows who is funny.

Some years ago I directed an actress who was playing a character who was witty and she was having trouble getting it. She tried character work and used W. C. Fields and it worked. Every line was hilarious. Fields gave her a funny perspective on everything. But she couldn't use Fields in the production because it was too obvious. When she switched to someone witty she knew from her own life, she got the same effect, but the audience could not be aware who her role model was. So that's one way to get at playing wit, especially if you can't find the rhythms and timing that you need to be funny.

How do you approach working on Shakespeare?

There are a number of aspects of playing Shakespeare that have to be solved. One is the language. A lot of good American actors have trouble with Shakespeare's language because they try to make it sound natural, they try to bring it down to ordinary speech. They wind up sounding unnatural because they leave out all emphasis. They are so afraid of doing a mock British-style performance that they wind up emphasizing nothing and the intention behind what they are saying is never very clear.

When we speak in life words are actions. We make points with them and in so doing we emphasize certain words and isolate others. Words are also reactions. For instance, we may have an image of something; say, someone we love. The image leads us to say something—to describe her to a friend. In life the way those words come out would reflect what we saw in the image. When you cut out all emphasis from Shakespeare or any other playwright, you wind up sounding very unnatural. The American actor is often afraid of emphasizing in an external way and rightly so. But you can solve that problem by making sure you know why your character is using those particular words and phrases, what intention is behind those words, and what stimuli those words are a response to.

There is another important element in owning Shakespeare's language. Most of Shakespeare's characters make brilliant arguments and describe their feelings in brilliant ways. If you are going to create a character who is going to own those words, there has to be a sense that the character has that kind of brilliance. It isn't just the emotional passion that is important in Shakespeare. The characters, for the most part, are highly intelligent. You need to create human beings who could say those kinds of things. If you speak Shakespeare's lines with a typical New York accent, the problem for the audience will be that it doesn't ordinarily hear that kind of brilliance and eloquence spoken with a New York street accent.

I also tell students to ignore iambic pentameter totally. The reason is that the only way you know that Shakespeare wrote in iambic pentameter is by speaking the lines intelligently. There is no footnote on the bottom of a poem by Robert Frost or any other poet to tell you what meter to speak it in. You know it by speaking it. The meter does *you*. Shakespeare is the only one who comes with a footnote by the authorities telling us how to speak it. So many of Shakespeare's lines are not written in strict iambic pentameter—he breaks it for effect. How can you tell when he breaks it? Because you speak it intelligently and it naturally comes out broken. Shakespeare didn't leave notes saying where to break it. If you speak it intelligently, the iambic pentameter is there or it breaks at appropriate places, with no special effort needed.

It's clear that Shakespeare wanted real and organic emotions from his actors, so we handle the emotional work in his plays the same way we do in contemporary plays, finding personal and character stimuli to arouse real feelings. In *Hamlet* the player, described as a great actor, who comes to visit the castle starts to weep real tears in the middle of a monologue he is giving. Hamlet is very impressed by this and puzzles on how the actor accomplishes it. Polonius, who is mocked by Hamlet, gets upset when he sees real tears and wants the player to stop. Hamlet makes fun of Polonius, saying, "He's for a jig or a tale of bawdry, or he sleeps." Also, in Hamlet's speech to the players, Shakespeare makes it quite clear that he wants realistic acting, wants actors to "imitate humanity" honestly and dislikes bombastic, artificial acting.

How does one learn to play the classics—Molière, for example? The basic way actors usually learn it is by learning the tradition of how it has been played in the past, by observing and working with actors and companies who are doing it in a way that we consider acceptable. But what is acceptable now may not, in fact, be at all the way Molière wanted his actors to play his plays. As a matter of fact, if you read Molière on acting, he wanted naturalistic acting, yet Molière is played in very stylized ways today. We don't know what naturalism looked like in Molière's day, but he made clear that he detested the unnatural acting of the established companies of his day. Over the centuries the way Molière is "supposed to be" played has evolved in ways that Molière would probably find artificial and offensive.

You can see a better example of that kind of evolution of performing styles if you look at some of the wonderful old films of

Shaw's plays that were made when he was still alive and compare them with current productions of Shaw. In his essay to directors Shaw said he just wanted actors to behave like real people. And these actors—Wendy Hiller and Leslie Howard, among others—did. They were surprisingly simple. But if you go to a Shaw production in the 1980s, the actors are trying so, so hard to be funny, eccentric English people that all reality disappears. Even in English productions, the actors are working so hard at some image of how Shaw is supposed to be played that all reality is lost. It's a bit like my whispering something in your ear that you then whisper to someone else, and so on, until the phrase no longer resembles what I originally said. Another good example is Noel Coward. When you see some of his films with him in them, they don't look anything like the way Noel Coward is played today. Today everyone is trying to be so arch and eccentric. In the old films, everyone is so comfortable; it's all so effortless. They have a sense of those lives as people, not as theatrical types.

One of the biggest problems in doing Shakespeare is figuring out how his people are supposed to behave. Unlike a lot of other period playwrights, Shakespeare didn't write about his time. None of his plays is set in Elizabethan England. Half of them are set in Italy. Do we play them as Elizabethan characters? Well, we don't exactly know what that is, and what sense would that make anyway, since the plays are not about Elizabethan manners? We don't go to Shakespeare to see his comments on Elizabethan manners. We may go to other playwrights for the fun of seeing their period mocked, but not Shakespeare. So it's often a problem for the actor playing Shakespeare to find an authentic life that will accommodate his characters and their language and behavior.

Another point about period character: it is crucial that students learn the intention behind the mannerisms of a period. In Restoration, for example, male characters carried their arms in a certain way, often with arms raised. Students who have had character courses in universities or have studied in England will mention that they learned that the reason Restoration characters carried their arms that way was because they wore big billowing sleeves that would have dragged on the floor otherwise. That is totally useless for an actor and nonsensical information. No one would wear sleeves that could drag on the floor unless there was a psychological purpose behind it. No one would allow a fashion designer to put clothes on him unless the clothes reflected things he wanted those clothes to say. People certainly wear odd and uncomfortable clothes, then and now, but only because the clothes reflect something they want to express. The Restoration male character carried his body and arms a certain way because he was peacock, because he was saying, "I'm powerful. I'm elegant." If I ask a student to learn a Restoration walk, and he just walks with his arms up in order to keep his sleeves from dragging on the ground, he will feel and look awkward. On the other hand, if I say, "Do an urban street swagger, the kind we see in New York," most of my students can do it fairly convincingly without any special training. That's because they understand what is behind that walk. It says, "I'm cool. I'm tough." Without that understanding, the walk looks silly. Actually, one of the things that both contemporary and period playwrights often do is write in a comic character who tries to affect the externals, the walk, trying to look cool and tough, or elegant and powerful, but who really isn't any of those things on the inside. His effort becomes something to laugh at. It's very important when learning period mannerisms for both men and women to understand what they are expressing about the character's personality and desires, what that walk is supposed to sell.

One way to find the reality in certain periods is to study them: go to museums to observe paintings and sculpture; read about the period, particularly books written by people from the period, but also what historians say about it. Keep searching for the realities of those lives. Don't simply imitate the theatrical style of another actor, who probably learned it from an actor he saw, and so on back a couple of hundred years until it no longer reflects any reality at all. Also, in period plays make sure you have created your environment and your character's relationship to it very fully. Contemporary plays take place in kitchens or living rooms or other environments with which we are familiar, and even without a lot of very careful work our characters are likely to be affected by aspects of these environments.

But too often, when playing in period plays, actors don't pay attention to the environments of their characters and wind up missing out on a lot of stimuli that would help them feel the lives of their characters and establish the characters' realities for the audience.

Another common problem for actors when working on Shakespeare is that they have to talk to the audience. The solution is to create a relationship to the members of the audience, just as you would with anyone onstage. You have to want something from them, to get them on your side, perhaps, or to win their understanding or their sympathy; or perhaps you want to frighten them. You need to talk *to* them not just toward them. I've had students who were told to talk to the exit sign rather than directly to the audience. All that says is, "Because I am afraid of the people out there, I will avoid them." Well, your character is not necessarily afraid of the audience. He has something he needs to say to it, and that's what you have to play, that need and that relationship—not some mechanical way of avoiding contact with the audience, because that will take your character out of the scene and you will always feel awkward.

The same issues keep coming up in acting that have been coming up for centuries. The Roman critic Horace said to actors, "If you want to move me, you had first better move yourself." He was essentially saying that he wanted to see reality on stage, real emotions and thoughts. Even when playing in openly antinaturalistic plays, as in Goethe's work, you still need to find your character's realities—what he wants and what he is reacting to.

Goethe didn't want his theater to be naturalistic; he wasn't interested in writing about everyday events. But if you read his writing on acting, he still insisted that his actors create all the realities in the sense of people reacting to things, wanting things, and pursuing goals. But the form of expression was not to be naturalistic—just as you can have great, realistic, but nonnaturalistic acting in opera; and just as you can have great nonnaturalistic acting in *The Honeymooners*. Theater has seen many such cycles of periods of naturalism followed by periods of antinaturalism, and back again. After a period of naturalism, theater people begin exploring larger, more universal issues and seek more abstract forms. But the forms often wind up being more important than the reality being expressed. And after a while people start reacting against that and say, "We need to get back to life," and suddenly a period of more naturalistic theater comes about. Then, after a while, the portrayal of life becomes more and more mundane, more about illustrating life than illuminating it. Then others say, "That's not why we go to the theater. I want theater to get at some basic human truths, and I want to see it in forms that are richer than everyday life." Then we move back into an era of more expressive nonrepresentational theater. Those cycles have repeated themselves for generations. But students need to realize that within *any* form an actor can be real in the sense of reacting to stimuli and taking actions in pursuit of objectives. Those two elements create reality in any form, whether it's naturalism or expressionism.

Lonny Black

Terry Schreiber

*Terry Schreiber is highly acclaimed for his direction of the Broadway
productions of* K-2, The Trip Back Down, *and* Devour the Snow.
*Off Broadway he has directed at The Circle Repertory Company and
The Roundabout Theatre Company. He has also directed productions
at many leading regional theaters, including the Tyrone Guthrie, the
Syracuse Stage, and the Pittsburgh Public Theatre.*

*The Terry Schreiber Studio in New York City was established in
1969. Along with basic acting classes, it offers workshops in body
dynamics, auditioning, Shakespeare scene study, Victorian scene
study, and vocal production; a playwright's lab; and a director's
unit. His technique is based on "a Stanislavsky/Method approach" to
acting and he states that the work is "designed to ultimately free the
subconscious to behave spontaneously," thus enabling the actor to
fulfill "a very real and richly developed stage life."*

* * *

How did you get started in teaching?

I came to New York in 1960 bound and determined to be an actor and thinking that I could never do anything else in my life. In the mid-1960s I began to get a lot of acting work. One of the jobs I had was with the Portable Phoenix Company, an APA adjunct, and we went touring on Title 3 (government) money. That's when I started to teach. We would present our program of one-act excerpts from plays in schools and then we would stay on and play theater games with the students. I really enjoyed it. In 1969 I decided I wanted to stay in New York. I was married and I didn't want to keep going out of town. I thought, what could I do to earn a living without doing office work? So I applied to a couple of places to teach and I was accepted. These places worked out very well and I began to attract students.

After a while I decided to rent a space and start teaching on my own. I started out very small on Third Avenue. We added productions to the classes and I took the first two out to New Jersey. The following year (1971) I moved in and shared a space with Milton Katselas and Michael Shurtliff. I not only had classes there, but I also continued with productions, this time in New York, so it wasn't only a theater school, but a place where people who studied could perform as well. I cast totally from people who were studying with me.

For the next four years of what became an off-off-Broadway theater, I continued to cast strictly from people who were studying at the studio. It just grew from that. Then I added a movement and vocal production teacher. So I've been teaching since 1969. That's how it started. There was never any conscious decision on my part to stop acting. It just happened that I suddenly got very busy teaching, directing, and producing, and found it much more involving than acting. I just gradually dropped away from acting and became solely a teacher/director.

How has your own training as an actor influenced what you do as a teacher?

The main influence in my training has been Michael Howard. I studied at another place when I first came to New York, but that shall remain nameless. It was just a disaster. Later, after I worked with Michael, I totally rejected the work that I had been exposed to at this other place.

What was it you felt was not helpful?

Let's just say that I felt that the particular classes were more geared to performance and result work. There was an attitude of "Let's entertain the teacher." I felt that it was not a class that was conducive to doing the actor's basic work and learning a process. The exercises were external and didn't help me learn to get concentrated in my acting. It seemed all very external and result-oriented rather than process-oriented and I feel that acting class, no matter how advanced, has to be dedicated to the work process. You see, actors are subjected to result work from the time they step out of a classroom—whether they go on an audition or are in performance. And let's face it, even most rehearsal work for a play is result-oriented. There has to be some place that the actor can go without people auditing (and I hate auditing), without people observing him in any capacity other than that of an actor taking a class. An actor should be protected in that area.

Why are you against auditing?

The first place I studied in New York had ten new people sitting there every time I walked into class. As I said, the class became all result-oriented. I feel it is unfair to the actor's work process because a class should create a nonjudgmental atmosphere and encourage the actor to take the risk of falling on his face—taking some chances. That's the only way he can expand and grow. If people just come to sit and audit, to make value judgments about the actor and teacher, it's very unfair to everybody. I always admired Lee Strasberg on that point. When the studio got really big in the 1960s and people called to come in to observe, he said, "If you want to observe the actors, you can see them in the lobby between 10:30 and 11:00. At 11:00 the doors shut and it's about us." That's the right attitude.

In terms of your own approach, what techniques do you use to help your actors cope with stage fright?

The way I go about it is to help the actor get in touch with what he is feeling at the very moment that he is tense. I think that acting is an unnatural act, a presumptive act. You're working on a stage and you are asking people to laugh and to cry and to feel with you. It's a big presumption that you can move an audience to that. I think there is a lot of tension that comes with the work whether it's on stage or on camera. I do go back to the basics of an actor knowing as much about his body and his instrument as possible and knowing how to do relaxation exercises to combat the tensions that come up and result in stage fright.

Another thing I do to help an actor get in touch with what he is feeling is ask him to stand onstage and talk about how he feels about being there. I think it starts with that. Anything that comes up is valid. It shouldn't be suppressed, but used. For instance, if it's a tremendous shyness or a fear, that energy shouldn't be stifled. The actor shouldn't say to himself, "I shouldn't feel this." Instead, he should allow it to flow, to use it, because it is an energy source. So I do one exercise that I've put together from a bunch of other exercises I've worked on to deal with this problem. I use phrases with the exercise such as "I'm scared, I'm frightened, I'm really terrified."

You were saying before that you talk someone through the fear. Could you describe that in more detail?

When tension comes up, let's say in the middle of a scene or sometimes before a scene, I attempt to get the student to say out loud what he or she is feeling or thinking. I ask the student what he or she feels in the body. Someone might say, "A tight fist right in my stomach." Then I'll work with that. I'll tell that person to breathe into the fist and allow whatever comes up from that, whatever feeling comes up, to be expressed. I'm not going to analyze where the feeling came from. I just feel that once actors can start to face some of their blocks, they can start to open up their instruments much more and be available to much more. Also, if they are free enough to express the emotional life of that particular feeling, they've opened up another area of themselves that they are free to call on more readily and to use.

After this exercise, does the actor go back into the scene he or she was working on?

Many times in a scene I'll have the actors go in and out of the dialogue, sometimes using their own words as a substitute, or using their inner monologue. But I only let them do that when I feel they really know what a scene is about, when they really know what's going on.

Sometimes I'll do a Place or Space Exercise to help someone overcome tension. If an actor is supposed to be standing and looking out a window in a scene, I will ask him what he sees or smells. I'll want him to verbalize that because that will pull him in deeper. We are all verbal beings and it makes us concentrate when we have to put thoughts into words.

Do you use the Song Exercise?

Yes. The process one goes through as a teacher is interesting. When I first started teaching it was around the time that Esalin and that kind of work was popular. So I started to use a lot of those kinds of exercises in my teaching. And now I see that in the seventeen years that I have been teaching I've come full circle, come back to the original exercises—the Place Exercise, the Song Exercise—that I started with. The exercise for fear that I just described is a lot like a song in the sense that it's spontaneous and one just verbalizes things aloud. I'll run the gamut with an actor in what I'll ask him to verbalize, all the way from "I'm a little boy" to "I'm silly." In other words I will give an actor phrases as we are moving along that will be the equivalent of the actor making loaded choices for himself and playing a scene.

I have also come back to a strong belief in the Affective Memory Exercise. I do that in three steps, starting with the basic exercise and then adding elements.

The first step is to have somebody bring in a personal event that was traumatic. It doesn't have to be unhappy. It may have triggered great joy, great surprise, but it is something that ended in a great emotional response or intense feeling. Then I want that person to work through it sensorially in front of us. I don't want actors to give me a descriptive narrative. They can start with five minutes before the event happened. I want them to recreate it as if it were happening right now, so they will put it all in the present, and when they talk about it, it will be something like, "I'm in my backyard . . . St. Paul . . . summer . . . not summer, June . . . late afternoon . . . blue sky . . . some clouds . . . green . . . green shingles." That's an example.

I want somebody to pick an event that has been 98% emotionally resolved. I don't know if we ever totally resolve an emotional event. That's debatable. But I want an event that is at least seven years in the past of the actor's life. That makes us work harder and call on our imagination more. I don't want something current and I don't want something that the actor has not emotionally resolved. I don't want an actor to act out of neurosis. It's not healthy. Incidents from childhood are usually good. A woman recently did a wonderful affective memory about getting a horse as a present when she was a child, and seeing it out in the backyard. Another student recalled when she saw the Beatles live for the first time, and another student did one about being elected a cheerleader.

There have been some very serious Affective Memory Exercises— a drowning incident, for example. But if actors use something from childhood, I want it to be something from childhood that they are really resolved about. I ask them to stay away from things that are very conflicting with parents that are still troubling. You know, there are certain areas that I just don't think an actor can use every night in order to get an emotional response and still remain healthy. Good acting is not about personal neurosis.

The second step in an Affective Memory Exercise starts by asking a student to select an overall activity, such as preparing for house guests who are arriving in fifteen minutes. I ask him or her to choose five tasks that must be done to get ready, such as making a salad, putting out liquor, putting out canapés, putting out wine glasses, prettying oneself up, whatever. I then ask the actor to do the emotional recall or Affective Memory as an inner monologue while doing the five tasks. So you can start to see that as the recall works, it's going to affect the way the actor does the tasks. And as he or she is doing the tasks, the tasks are going to affect the recall. Also, of course, the time limit affects both. The goal is to put the actor's emotional life and behavior together and have them affect each other.

The third step is to take a monologue from a play that has a similar moment to the one the actor is working on—for example, Catherine's big monologue about Sebastian in *Suddenly Last Summer*. Then I ask actors to choose where they want to be in their own emotional recall prior to starting Tennessee's words. Step three includes the five activities of step two. These three steps tie it all together—the life, the behavior, and the words.

One of the frustrations I had when I was studying was that I didn't understand how to unite the exercises and scene work. I didn't know how to put them together. I want actors to come out of my classes with tools that they can use in rehearsal and in homework to solve problems in scenes.

I've used Affective Memories with actors in plays that I have directed. I directed *Suddenly Last Summer* and I remember the Affective Memory the actress playing Catherine used for her big monologue. Once the Affective Memory really works, the actor can just flash images of it and be affected. It's amazing how the mind works, what it can be trained to do, and how you can trigger the subconscious. There is an actor, Denis Lipsky, who worked with me a lot and now is a successful film actor. We worked on the character of Danny in *Night Must Fall* and we used an Affective Memory in a few places where Danny flips out. Well, Denis still uses that particular recall in his work when he needs to play crazy. He said that he terrifies cameramen in Hollywood because he can flip out in thirty seconds. "All I have to do is sit down and use my Affective Memory. I've told cameramen many times during a shot that all I was going to do was to sit down in a chair and I asked them to stand by because I would be ready to go in thirty seconds." So it really can work. I believe in the exercise.

Do you think it's better to use an Affective Memory from one's personal life to stimulate an emotional response or should actors try to use the circumstances of the play?

Great question. I think that if an actor can respond to the material, that's great. Why do all this work? I disagree with teachers who feel that everything has to be internalized and personalized. Many times an actor will pick up a piece of material and just respond to the event. I mean, if he can be free enough to give himself to it, why make all that extra work? Why make it that difficult? I think an exercise like an Affective Memory is helpful when you have to create an experience that is heightened, extraordinary, like the one in *Suddenly Last Summer*. What actress has had that kind of heightened experience in her own life? Most actresses don't have experiences like those of Blanche Dubois, so what will they use if not something else, something that's personal? I saw a woman do a beautiful job with one of Blanche's speeches by using a drowning incident that she witnessed at a pool when she was eleven years old. Every time that gunshot was supposed to be heard in that speech, her Affective Memory was there for her and all she had to do was to use a sense memory of the pool incident. So when you can't get the heightened response just from the material, you use something from your own life instead.

I'm the first one to say that if an actor can respond to the events of the script and to the writer's words, I'm pleased. That's what I want.

The other exercise that I still use from my own training that I fought doing myself when I was a student is a Private Moment. I resisted it for a long time. You know, these exercises take tremendous courage—especially a Private Moment. I think it's the most difficult. It is an exercise that I have come back to and have used very heavily over the past three years. I think it is one of the best examples for teaching someone to be private in public and it also really deals with staying in the moment and allowing feelings to come up. Plays are filled with private moments and sometimes they are very difficult for an actor to execute. It's very helpful to me when I'm directing and an actor comes to me in rehearsal and says, "Terry, I will try what you are suggesting (to do a Private Moment), but I gotta tell you, it's very difficult for me. Would you clear the room so I can try it alone?" And I'm more than happy to do it so that the actor can try it. I don't know how shy or vulnerable an actor might be and I want to give that person the privacy he or she needs.

Could you describe the Private Moment Exercise and what it's purpose is?

I do it in three steps. First, I ask the student to bring in something that he does at home that would be private and hard for him to do in front of others, something that he might do with someone he lives with, but would be hard to share with the class. I ask the student to pick something that would be hard, harder, hardest for him to do. When you do those three, you end up putting a whole storyboard together.

Do you do them all together?

No, at separate times, in separate classes. One month someone will be working on Private Moment No. 1, the next month on No. 2, and so on. I always want the exercise discussed ahead of time with me, so I know what it will be. I don't want actors ever to pick something that would really violate them or something that they would not do on stage or in a "legitimate movie."

Plays and films are filled with private moments. That's the purpose of the exercise. Someone is left alone on stage and has business or carries on an activity during that time. But that person is also living through a whole life. And it's hard to do. I mean, anybody can just go and do by rote the business that's given by the writer, but frequently an actor has to come up with some business of his own. Especially in films. I always think of *An Unmarried Woman* as an ideal example of a private moment. When Jill Clayburgh got out of bed in the morning and announced that she was dancing at the New York State Theater that night, she was doing a Private Moment, a wonderful fantasy moment. Frequently in Private Moments people get into fantasy.

I think it's also a wonderful way to do homework on a character. After you do your own Private Moment, do the character's. For example, I had a student do a Private Moment of Hedda Gabler's when she has the pistol and contemplates shooting herself. It was a wonderful exercise. I'm going to direct *Hedda Gabler* this year and

I'm thinking about using that moment because it was just marvelous.

Does that mean that after a student has done a series of Private Moments of increasing difficulty you then ask them to find Private Moments for the character they happen to be working on?

Yes. What I want them to do is feel what it's like to do their own Private Moment first, before they can hide behind a character. There's a nakedness that I want to get at, a figurative nakedness that I want to help the actors achieve with this exercise and I want students to leave themselves open to express whatever occurs to them. For instance, if suddenly, during the exercise, you get fire-engine red with embarrassment, it's wonderful. Allow that. It's a piece of human behavior. I feel that frequently we grit our teeth to do something and we don't really get as much out of it as we would if we were open.

I'll give you a good example of how it's helpful. I directed *Ashes* a few years ago in Pittsburgh. First of all, the producer was terrified of doing the play in Pittsburgh because it's very graphic. Also, the theater was awkward because the audience is on all four sides and it's tiered so that the audience is right on top of the play. The actors worked with me very privately in rehearsal and they developed a wonderful trust and freedom and intimacy with each other. There's no nudity in the play, but there is everything else. These two actors were so comfortable with each other that by the time we opened there was not one audience member who was offended at any time. There were no letters from anyone in that community condemning the frankness of the work.

So a Private Moment Exercise helps the actor learn how to be totally alone onstage. The actor will then either use the circumstances of the play or, if that is not possible, re-create his own Private Moment to achieve that sense of authentic privacy in the play.

Yes, and Private Moments are important because writers like Odets, Miller, and Williams put them in their plays. So did Ibsen. In the *Hedda Gabler* that I am going to direct I've already spoken to Jean Ruskin about a Private Moment that I want to do at the opening of the play.

Ideally, good acting is like watching somebody through a keyhole.

To me the definitive thing about a Private Moment is being able to be private in public.

What kinds of things do people choose to do as their Private Moments?

A good example is a student whose first choice was getting ready for bed and looking at herself in the mirror and, without commenting on it, really being very private with herself and her body in front of the mirror. Her second choice was kneeling down and saying her prayers out loud rather than to herself. Her third choice was not being able to get to sleep and fantasizing that she'd won an Oscar. But instead of just lying there and having a fantasy, she got out of bed and came down stage center and did her acceptance speech to us and thanked her grandparents, her parents, me, etc. That was a wonderful one. It was beautifully constructed.

Another student who lives alone and sometimes feels the walls moving in on her when she feels lonely will pretend that she has a man over for dinner. She cooks the meal for him, serves it to him, and talks to him throughout the dinner. She brought that in as a Private Moment, and it was terrific.

Do you have any specific exercises to help actors become more expressive?

I think that a Song Exercise and the Phrase Exercise are good for that.

The Phrase Exercise?

That's where an actor will just stand on stage and the first thing that I see on his face I will put into words for him. If I see that he's scared, I will give him phrases like "I'm scared," "I'm a little boy," "I'm shy," or "I don't want to be here." And I'll ask him to repeat them. What that winds up doing is helping the actor to find many sides of his personality. When using phrases like "I'm a little boy, I'm a little baby," I might ask him for his nickname as a kid, at which point an actor might start to giggle. Sometimes you wind up with a two-year-old standing in front of you. It's really what the words suggest. From there I will go on to phrases that are harder, like "I don't know," "I give up," "I can't," "I quit," "Hold me, daddy," or "Love me, mommy." That usually stimulates vulnerability in the actor. The actor will repeat each phrase five or six times and then I'll move on to some other phrase. Usually each phrase will cover a different aspect of one's life. I usually stay with those emotional areas that are more difficult to express than others.

What are you looking for when you ask the student to repeat these phrases?

I'm looking for the phrase to affect the student. What is it like for the student to say, "I don't know how" and for him to stay with all the conflict and the struggle that that phrase brings up? It's an exercise designed to help actors open up in front of others and share themselves. It helps actors find the freedom to do that in an arena where no one is going to judge them as being weak or cowardly or a bad person because they express these things. In a way, it's giving the actors courage. We work through all kinds of feelings with that exercise. I do the Song Exercise in the same way.

Would you describe the Song Exercise to me as if I were a new student?

Choose a ballad, a slow, romantic ballad with simple lyrics, something that you might sing in the shower. Then I want you to sing the song through once in front of the class. After that I may try to relax you in various ways, having you drop over, shake out, use neck manipulation, loosen your jaw, and so forth. Then you'll sing the song again, and I might have you do it in a falsetto, or hold your arms up, or do various things to try to get your body to open up. Then I might have you do the song as if it were a march, or just move as you sing it. I want you to allow the song, the music, the rhythm to affect your body. From there I will ask you to do it as a waltz or a tango, as if you were a go-go dancer, a punk rocker, a stripper, whatever. The object of the first part of the exercise is to exhaust you so much that you are wide open for the second part.

In the second part I tell you to sing the song to your mother. Put her there and sing it to her. I may ask you to switch to your father. I may put an empty chair on stage and tell you to sit on your mother's lap. I may ask you to sing your song to the first little boy or girl you fell head over heels in love with and I might ask you to verbalize his or her name. (Doing this usually brings out a wonderful childlike quality.) I may ask you to sing the song to the first person you ever made love to, or to your child. I may even ask you to sing the song to someone as if you were making love then and there—vacillating between being aggressive and being passive.

I encourage body dynamics awareness. Both myself and Gloria Maddox (one of my teachers) are very bioenergetically based people. So is Carol Reynolds, the body dynamics teacher. She uses Feldenkrais and Pilates technique as well.

Could you describe how bioenergetics might be helpful to actors?

For me the work helps someone to get down into the body. I feel that the main energy source for all of us is connected to the ground. I find that most actors come to me and they are only acting between their shoulders and their nose. That's all that's happening in their bodies. For me, bioenergetic work really gets somebody grounded down into the body. It focuses on breaking open the chest, getting down into the thighs, calves, and pelvic areas, allowing the lower half of the body to breathe. A lot of the time people work with tremendous tension in the lower half of the body. Many times when I'm working with actors, they start to pull their energy from the sky, from the shoulders up. They get into a high area, and the next thing you know, the emotional life is hysterical and you can't understand a word they are saying. What is the good of an emotional life if it's locked up, not free to express itself?

Carol Reynolds (my movement teacher) helps each person with body alignment as well. She brought me a picture of a male student, a before and after. My God, the changes in his body were incredible—even his complexion. He suddenly got his blood flowing and began breathing into his body. I also start to see certain mannerisms disappear. One actor here has a lot of talent, but was very effeminate in his movement. He broke the barrier through just this kind of work. His personal life is his own, but it's going to limit him getting cast as an actor if he can't control or get rid of his mannerisms.

We have a yearly evaluation, and at our last one there were several people who did scenes who I felt needed to work only with movement and voice. I felt it was wasting time for them to continue in scene study class. I asked them to take a year off and just study with Carol and Chuck Jones, our vocal production teacher. Their physical problems were so severe that I couldn't make progress with scene study. Their instrument was locked and needed the kind of freeing, unlocking, that Carol and Chuck are so wonderful at.

This movement and vocal emphasis has really become major for me over the last few years. Most of the work for actors these days is out in regional theaters. I don't think any actor can limit himself or herself to just realistic, naturalistic work in class. Too many don't put enough emphasis on their bodies and their voices, as well as working on the classics.

Do you have teachers who work on period movement and dialects?

I want to expand in that area. Carol Reynolds does a very special advanced class with a movement group. I'm encouraging Bob Smith, who teaches Shakespeare here, to take on the Jacobean and Restoration periods and Molière as well. We just have to get people trained in this area. I was amazed when I saw Shaw's *Arms and The Man* at Circle in the Square. The problem with American actors was just laid out in front of me. Whereas Raul Julia, for instance, took on that material and was absolutely wonderful, John Malkovich and his wife, Glenne Headly, were much too small for these roles. Their work was honest and real and it was good acting, but it belonged in somebody's garage. It never rose to the size of the material. I was especially upset because I thought Glenne Headly had everything you would want for the character of Raina, but she was doing a performance in somebody's clothes closet. It was a good example of what's missing in our training.

How do you advise actors to approach a script?

First, I want them to read the full script carefully. Then, I want them to sit in a chair with their partner and just read their scene without any obligations to do anything or to express the emotional life they might think is there. I want them to read it almost like idiots, as if they had never seen these words before. That gets into the area that you asked me about before, about getting actors to relate to and get comfortable with each other. In the second rehearsal they can begin to make choices about the scene and they can discuss the kind of set that should be used, whose house it is, etc. We don't get into interpretation in class. I leave it up to them to make a choice, to find the character's spine in a scene, and to choose their objective—that is, what they came on stage to do (although I feel that at most there should be two objectives in a scene).

I like students to start making choices by answering the "I must" question about a scene they are working on; for example, "I must seduce" this person. "I must persuade" this person.

By the third rehearsal they should have a clear idea of what the scene is about. Then I like actors to start breaking down the scene into beats (a beat being the beginning of one action to the beginning of another—and you have to be very clear about what that action is). These actions should be sustained in one way or another throughout the whole beat. Then each actor has to decide what adjustments he is going to use to fulfill that action. For example, if a scene is a seduction scene, how will he do it? Will he charm? Will he cajole? He may also want to cross out all stage directions in that scene and find new activities for himself.

By the fourth rehearsal, I think the students should be committed to the organic life of the scene, meaning the feelings and emotional responses of their characters.

By the fifth rehearsal they should be editing and cleaning up and discarding things that they no longer find useful in the scene.

Usually I see a scene when it's at its second or third try and I stay with it five or six times—especially if it's a good scene for a particular actor and we are really hitting on his acting problems and are beginning to solve them. I don't see any sense in doing scene after scene and repeating the same problems. Frequently I will put the scene on hold for a while and assign an exercise that I think will be valuable for that actor and ask him to do the exercise prior to doing that scene again. Many times I will assign a scene because I know that it taps an area of difficulty for that actor so that we can find a solution.

Can you give me an example?

Let's say it's very difficult for an actress to work on being aggressive or assertive. It would be good for us to find a series of ladies who are assertive for her to work on.

When I was studying practically all we did was Tennessee Williams. Every time actors tried something like *The Importance of Being Earnest*, they got their head handed to them. So nobody brought it in again. I really want a wide variety of material here, especially in my advanced class. Of course, the tendency is for actors to want to work on contemporary plays. I had two people working on *The Seagull* and they went through the tortures of the damned. But if you don't take on that work here, where *will* you take it on? Every regional theater has a season that includes Chekhov, Shaw, and Ibsen, and American actors have got to get acquainted with that material.

In a way we have come so far from that theater of the 1960s. Sam Shepard cannot be played with stereotypical Actors Studio intro-spection. It would die. I see actors get up and do *Fool for Love* and try to make the scenes naturalistic and it just dies. We have to hear the music of the play and the stakes and meet the challenge. It's what the English are so good at. I think we could do it more deeply, but we are missing the step of hearing the music in the language. So many times the actor has no sense of the rhythm or has simply not been exposed to enough theater.

That's another problem that goes on in New York. True, theater prices are prohibitive, but just to see other actors is to have some guideposts. I think actors should see everything from Charles Ludlam to summer stock musicals.

Could you describe the different classes in your school?

We have a twofold approach. Advanced students can just take our special classes, like my professional scene study, or Bob Smith's advanced Shakespeare, or Carmella Ross's classical class, which includes working on Wilde, Shaw, Molière, and Restoration com-edies. Or they can take the audition image class, which is a real marketing yourself class, everything from monologues to photos to clothes. It's an overall commercial class. We also have a basic exercise class beginners can take. But not the advanced Shakespeare or my advanced scene study. So, advanced students can select what they want, including body or vocal work, any class that might help them with a specific acting problem. All beginners go into a basic exercise class for three months that covers relaxation work, concentration, and the imagination. They learn how to relax and find their center. They also learn sensory work.

The classical notion of sensory work?

Yes. I do them in groups because I think that it's a wonderful way to start. People sometimes feel freer at first in the anonymity of a group rather than being thrown up there all alone. I don't understand classes where somebody walks in for the first time and is asked to do a Private Moment. That's the most difficult exercise I can imagine, and I think it's terribly unfair to ask a student to do that right off. You have to build up the courage for these exercises and understand how to do them, and that takes time.

What is the basic sensory work like?

It's a way to get out of your head, into your senses, all five of them. After you relax, you start to re-create your basic morning drink, whether it's a cup of water, a glass of juice, a cup of tea, whatever, just working sensorially, creating what's in it, the cup, the liquid, not just miming the cup but, even with just one finger, finding what kind of material the cup is made of, if it has a chip, the weight of it. You're never actually going to feel that, but just a flicker of a sense memory will come alive just as it might in daily life. The mistake is to think that you are ever actually going to feel it. If you do, it's time for Bellevue, not acting class. But you are just looking for the cup because in the looking for it you are taking your consciousness and involving it, immersing it in something that you are doing as a task. By doing that, you are kicking off the subconscious. And that's what we're after with the work—a way of getting the subconscious to behave spontaneously.

From there we'll work to getting the cup up to your mouth, to smelling the liquid, to see what you can find with your nose, to tasting it, to see what you find with your lips, your tongue, your palate. Does it make a sound? All the senses are explored any way the student wants. We go from the basic coffee cup to other morning activities like washing your face, brushing your teeth, or shaving.

I've really come back to Strasberg's basic exercises. They're wonderful.

We also work on a lot of the sensory conditions that a playwright may require of an actor—like getting drunk or feeling heat, pain, or cold. We work on these sensorily by first relaxing and exploring the conditions with the whole body, what it's like to be drunk, where that affects you. We'll work through all the parts of the body right up to the top of your head. I may take a condition like getting drunk into an improvisation and tell the students they're now at a party. It's amazing to see students discover what their own body feels like when it's hot or cold or drunk. If they trust their senses, they'll find much more interesting behavior than if they just slap their arms to denote cold. That's not very interesting and you and 9,000 other people are going to do that. I think that oftentimes working on a physical condition in a scene can help you get to the feeling and emotions of a character. If you're working on a blinding headache, that's certainly going to dictate a character's temperament or psychological condition.

In my more advanced class I work on more advanced sensory exercises like a Place Exercise. I ask students to pick a place from the past that is filled with a lot of memories. Let's say an actor's working on the bedroom he grew up in and let's say he brought in three objects that still have wonderful memories for him. I ask him just to work on walking into the room, just to work on creating the space sensorially—touching it, feeling, smelling, looking out the windows—and just to discover the objects as if he hadn't seen them in twenty years. At times I will ask the actor for his or her inner monologue.

What do you mean by inner monologue?

To verbalize what he's seeing, what he's smelling. It just deepens the event. I may say that someone just walked into the room and is looking at him. That usually calls up all kinds of connections.

Again, plays are filled with moments like that and it helps the actor to be alone on stage and to become concentrated enough so that we are really watching him just exist in that space. It's also an amazing exercise because I've seen people in their fifties become eight years old in their bodies. And it's an organic way to find out how to move like a child. Actors frequently need to appear many years younger for a role in a flash. It's a wonderful way to help them. For example, I worked on *Foxfire* last year and there is a flashback for Hecter and Annie (who are both very old) where they are kids again when they first met and kissed behind the corncrib.

Are there any techniques you give your students to help them create a character who is very different from themselves?

I find animal work just wonderful for anything from Noel Coward to a period piece. Once a group of women were working on Giraudoux's *Madwoman of Chaillot* and they all went up to the Bronx Zoo aviary to study birds. When they came back they did an improvisation as birds. I didn't ask them to imitate the birds, but to find in their bodies what would be similar to what the birds do, then to allow themselves at home to cook a dinner or make a bed or do something as that bird. It can be wonderful for finding the carriage of the person from another period, for finding a way to hold the body.

Animal exercises can also help when actors have difficulties with particular emotions. I was once working with someone who had a very hard time displaying his feelings and we made a whole breakthrough with animals. He was doing *Otherwise Engaged*, playing the character who commits suicide. When he did him as a lizard, he was able to express the feeling through the animal that had otherwise been so hard for him to get to.

Do you advise students to observe people?

Yes. If students work on a scene that requires a specific kind of person, a dockworker, as in *View From the Bridge*, or a streetwalker, I ask them to observe those kinds of people. A scene from *Family Business* was done the other day and a student brought in a stereotypical gay man. I took that all away and told him to observe some more and he found something more interesting and much more his own for the character. I don't think actors can observe enough.

Do you use improvisations? Could you describe how and to what end?

One of my teachers, Gloria Maddox, teaches a class in improvisation. I use them if I want to get actors closer to the event of the scene. I might say, "Play the scene as if you were his mother or as if you were his sister. Let's improvise." Scenes break down into role relationships a lot, as they do in life. For instance, in *Family Business* there is a scene in which one of the characters has to confront an authority figure. Well, we may just do an improvisation where I will ask the actor to re-create a time when he had a run-in with an authority figure. I might ask him to set up those circumstances in the scene and to improvise around them. Many times I'll go back and forth between the words of the scene and an improvisation on the scene in which the actors use their own words. I think it's a wonderful way to get closer to the material.

I don't go to improvisation automatically. I've worked with directors who say, "Let's improvise" in the first week of rehearsal. Improvise what? I don't even know what the material is about yet. And I think that's where we get into trouble in the theater. It's a valuable tool once you are really steeped in the material, and I do use it in rehearsal, but usually in about the third week. By that time the actors are deeper into the material than I am. They better be or I'm in trouble.

Are there any acting techniques that you feel an actor should avoid?

I have enormous objections to what is going on in some acting classes. I don't think the current "isms" belong in acting classes—EST, Scientology, and Primal Therapy, for example. What we are doing in an acting class is walking a tightrope. We are not therapists. We are teachers. Of course, some actors should be in therapy, but I don't think that teachers should start to play the role of the therapist.

I think a lot of actors spend too much time in acting classes just working on their own psychological aspects. To spend year after year coming in talking about how I am feeling today is overkill. Eventually we have to get to the acting work and get off "I." That's the kind of thing I don't feel is good for actors. Many times I think students are using acting class as a substitute for therapy and that their teachers are encouraging it. You can't learn how to do Chekhov by studying EST.

I remember years ago a teacher was doing theater games with actors and an actor wanted to use the game in a rehearsal for *Uncle Vanya*. Chekhov did not write from Theater Games. I don't like going way off on tangents like that—what the hell does it have to do with the work at hand? I don't think it's useful for actors to run all over the theater, shouting and doing cartwheels, when they are going to do a scene that is confined to ten feet of playing space, period costume, and, most of all, *words*. I mean, what's the point?

Are there specific techniques that you teach your students to use for TV or film?

I'm in the process of getting somebody to teach on-camera technique because I think it's really needed. It's a different style of work, a much smaller way of working. People who have watched Robert DeNiro work in front of the camera say you'd have to be standing on his shoes looking up at his face to see what he's doing. It's all in his eyes. It's the subtlest kind of work. I think frequently people who do stage work have a hard time adjusting to film. Good film work seems to be composed of very rich subtext. So is good stage work; however, the camera is much closer than the audience.

What do you feel has been your main contribution as a teacher?

I guess being supportive and giving people confidence. And I would say with a lot of people I've worked with, well, I guess I've helped them grow. They may not choose acting in the end, but I think we've hit on some areas together that will be helpful to them in their lives.

What advice would you give someone just starting out on a career?

I have very strong feelings about training. Just an acting class is not enough. Actors should put much more time into their bodies and their vocal instruments. We need to pay more attention to these. We can't just rely on scene study. We need to pay more attention to the technical side of acting.

We have to look at the market. We have a wild influx of all these English actors coming over here. I will go to my grave believing we can do that work and do it more fully than they. But we have to prove it to the powers that be. And we haven't because we lack a classical background. Actors don't put enough time into the technical areas and they don't go out there and take risks with material. We need to overcome the materialism of wanting to get into the movies or TV because it's big bucks. We need to come back to this business to really work on the craft of acting. There is nothing more exciting and rewarding than stage acting.

Isn't one of our problems that our most skilled actors leave the stage for film and often don't come back?

Yes. God bless Al Pacino and Dustin Hoffman for returning to the stage. We have lost so many good actors to Hollywood, but a few have come back to visit now and then and to remind us that some of our best film actors know how to work on the stage.

John Strasberg

John Strasberg is the director of The Real Stage in New York, where he teaches acting, and is a founder and associate artistic director of the Mirror Repertory Theatre, where he has directed productions of Paradise Lost, Inheritors, Rain, *and* Ghosts. *He is an international teacher and director as well and has conducted seminars and workshops on acting and directing in France, Germany, Canada, Spain, and Italy. In 1983 he founded a branch of The Real Stage in Paris. He is also a professional actor and has appeared on the Broadway stage and in film.*

Mr. Strasberg is a member of The Actors Studio, where he studied with his father, Lee Strasberg, for many years and later taught at the Lee Strasberg Theatre Institute. Well grounded in the Method approach to the teaching of acting, Mr. Strasberg believes that it is important for the actor to "understand the sensory exercises, and certainly to understand the principles behind them." However, the "actual practice of them can be limiting for some actors." He feels that he is at his best as a teacher when he can "help an actor come into contact with an emotion through the circumstances of the play," rather than using incidents from one's own life as his father taught at The Actors Studio.

In what way is your approach to the teaching of acting different from or similar to your father's?

You probably ask that question not only of me but of anyone who is teaching acting today. Most everybody does a slight variation of the Method. I think that what I do is a little different from what my father did. What he did very well, aside from inspiring people, was work out a system of well-thought-out exercises so that if an actor studied he could learn a very simple, clear way in which to come into contact with his feelings. And that served an awful lot of people in a variety of ways. I think it's an important part of the actor's work to understand those exercises, and certainly to understand the principles behind them, because the principles are beautiful. The actual practice can be limiting for some actors. I find that a lot of actors, especially those who are very sensitive and have a great deal of imagination, have a great deal of trouble using my father's Sense Memory Exercises. Many shouldn't do those exercises because it can inhibit them rather than help them express feelings.

What defines a great actor? I think the most important thing is his imagination; everything else comes after that. I think that my father's work, to a great extent, centered on teaching an actor to stimulate and manipulate his emotions. And I use his work carefully because I do think that acting can be just a manipulation most of the time. On the other hand, when you watch wonderful actors on a good night, you'll see purely spontaneous moments—within a very structured form—but it's totally spontaneous. My father's work really didn't permit that to take place. Not that some of his students couldn't do it. An actor will take anything and basically adjust it to himself anyway.

Are you saying that your father's work focused actors on creating substitutions rather than living the life of the character?

Yes. He believed that actors should make up a parallel line or life to the one they were playing, a life that came from their own personal experience. It was almost like asking them to write another play. And maybe that's not necessary. You know, sometimes an actor doesn't have to do that. As a matter of fact, I think that the best work comes when actors are lucky enough to be cast in parts that they are well suited for. Some reach a point in their careers when they can choose those parts. It's hard to make a mistake when you get that kind of role because there is something in your instinct, in your own organic understanding of the material, that's right. Then your problem is to try not to think about it too much because if you do, you're going to ruin it. Which is what often happens. I'm critical of certain "methods" if I think they are too intellectual. There is a danger in that and I think it also leads to a lack of pleasure in acting. And pleasure is very basic to the profession. It's a lousy profession to begin with, so you might as well enjoy what you are doing. And that enjoyment comes when a piece of material or a role strikes your imagination. You begin to think about it and dream about it. That's 50% of an actor's work. And yet very few people nowadays, especially in this country, approach acting from that point of view.

Everybody is trying to work out a "method" and it tends to be a little too mechanical. I was trained that way myself and it took me years to break that habit. In several conversations with my father— sometimes in front of a lot of people—I raised questions about his method. He was not the easiest person in the world to talk to about his work because he would get very threatened when questioned. Whenever someone asked him about spontaneity or imagination, he would always say, "Well, listen, you use the exercise if you need it." Like, if you're sick, you take an aspirin. And that was how he defined what he did when he felt a little cornered. He was all for spontaneity, it's just that he didn't incorporate it in his own work. I think he had ideas about what plays were about that I'm not sure I would agree with.

An actor is at his best when he is working spontaneously. You can't will it, you can't control it, you can't say, "I'm going to be inspired." It is impossible even though a lot of acting methods hold out the promise that actors can be spontaneously inspired on cue.

You can learn a craft—which means that you can go on stage and tell a good story in a realistic fashion—and realism is the primary cultural choice that we made in America. We want it to be real, which is what people like about our acting, especially in our movies. Our movies are as good as anybody's in the world. But in theater, since we don't do much classical material, we don't learn the craft as well as the English. You have to work on the classics to be able to do those successfully; you can't just do movies.

What do you do to help an actor break free of the constraints of Method technique and stimulate his imagination?

First of all, if you are talking about acting as an art form you have to ask yourself if you can teach someone an art. *Can* you teach people an art? I don't think so. I do think that you can give them the principles of the art form and you can expose them to a variety of ways to think about creating life in a play form. The main question is how do you make acting real? That's what everybody wants to do. You want to be able to take something that never happened to you, that happened in a different time, a different place, in a different language, a different culture, and you want to create life within that form. How do you do that?

I believe you begin with the play. You can have people in New York City come into an acting class without having read the play because they don't think it's important. That's a very bad attitude, and it's dangerous because they think they know what they are doing even though they haven't even read the play they are doing a scene from. They have nothing that stimulates their imagination. They think, "I'll just read the scene and make some sensory choices and then make a substitution for a character and do this for that." And if they think they'll create a life this way they're kidding themselves. What they are doing is approximating life on a mechanical basis. It won't really be spontaneous and it won't really be alive because alive is alive. When you are real on stage, it's not *almost* life, it's real. Now that scares people a lot.

The whole principle of The Actors Studio was absolutely beautiful. It was one of the great movements in the history of the art of acting. I don't think anyone can dispute that. People may not like what it's led to and where it ended up, but you can't question what it was. But sometimes people believe that the system of exercises or the system of training that my father developed is the same thing as the group of artists that got together because they wanted to create life in the theater. There's a tremendous difference. People should be aware that Marlon Brando and James Dean and everybody else whose name is bandied about didn't do what they did because of a series of exercises.

There is no art form that will tell you that in this situation or in that situation this is what you should do. You won't find a karate master, you won't find a singing teacher or anybody who will tell you that. But you will find acting teachers—too many—who will and you can imagine the effect on you if you are a young talented person and vulnerable and somebody is telling you that there is a very specific way, an exact way, to do it. You could become terrified that you aren't good enough because you couldn't do an exercise in class—which is criminal. So you have to be very careful about choosing a teacher.

Most of what I do that I think is different is based on the concept that the art of acting is the ability to create life within the form. But it's spontaneous. Therefore, your whole craft is based on the analysis of a play, which includes sense memory, which includes a tremendous knowledge of yourself. You can separate a lot of actors by their ability to perceive themselves. A lot of people can't perceive themselves and if they can't do that, they won't know what they are doing wrong and they won't know how to fix it. Nobody wants to be a bad actor. But some people just can't perceive when they are off or feel it and you have to be very respectful of that in people. If you start to tell them that you've got this method that will start to make them feel, that will summon their emotions, you've got a potentially dangerous situation.

Any time you work with an actor you are dealing with his habits, and his habits depend on where he studied. If you're familiar with the acting scene in this country, you can tell who studied with whom. There is something wrong if you can do that. You shouldn't know. You should just see a person and you shouldn't even think about that.

Can you give me an example?

I can tell when someone's doing an exercise because I see him or her focusing on the back of the head. He or she focuses the energy on the back of the head and the eyes are off. And you can see it in the movies and on TV. It's a little harder to see it on stage. But it has a premeditated, pensive quality to it. At times it can be very effective, very powerful. But it can also be destructive. If you've ever been in a room with ten people doing Sense Memory Exercises, after half an hour of sitting in a chair you are going to see those people react out of sheer frustration if nothing else or because someone else is feeling something and they don't want to be outdone. I don't do those exercises, although I do have people in my school who teach them because I think that an actor should know the basic system of Sensory Exercises, which may include, depending on the individual teacher, certain kinds of exercises that deal with self-awareness.

When you say "a system of Sensory Exercises," what do you mean?

Like my father had a system. He had it all worked out. You go from drinking an imaginary cup of coffee up to doing a series of five to eight exercises at the same time. That might include a Private Moment, a Personal Object, an Affective Memory, smell, taste, and then a combination of those. That's what my father's work evolved into, which is fascinating if you like puzzles and things like that. But if you start to believe that you are actually creating life by doing things like that, you are mistaken. And if you do have spontaneous moments, it's not because you've learned how to do it through the Method, but because you've had the ability beforehand. And I could prove it if I took someone and worked with them long enough. I could get the same moment out of somebody just by stimulating his imagination through the piece of material—if the actor's capable.

As specifically as you can, would you describe the exercises or the work that you do to stimulate the actor's imagination?

It's hard to explain, but basically what I will do with a student is have him read a play and then ask him to tell me what the play is about. I know what most of the actors that I deal with professionally are going to do before they open their mouths at the first reading. I know what the performance is going to be. Now people may find that very arrogant to say, but I really don't mean it that way at all. When I direct actors professionally I spend most of my time trying to get them not to plan what they are going to do so that they will just try to live in the moment. Because life is life, and if you talk to me about creating life, it should feel exactly like life. In life what you have is your past and your circumstances, but you don't know what's going to happen. And in a good play, for instance, you don't need to know, because the play is going to lead you where you have to go. It can be a lot of fun to act like that because you are not planning what's going to happen on the next page.

But most of the time the actor is planning so that when he gets to the next moment he's going to be ready for it. And I think that's a big mistake. It takes a lot of fun out of acting. It may look real, there may be tears and anger, but it's not coming out of the life of the moment. It's coming out of a story that the actor is telling himself or herself. And I think that's the playwright's job and that the main mistake that most actors make is that they think an acting technique is playwriting. That's the biggest mistake. They make up a parallel story for themselves and they play that story out with a series of exercises and substitutions. I don't do that. I don't like it. It's not fun to me. I know that some people, depending on their limitations, need to do certain things like use substitutions in different parts or manipulate themselves if they don't understand something and have to get at a moment. It's good to know how to do that. But when an actor's craft is working properly he doesn't have to make up a parallel life. That's not how it happens. Therefore, I work from the life principle so that anything that I'm teaching involves talking about the life of the play.

I remember that at The Actors Studio there was a whole period when the idea that you were telling a story was considered to be "indicative," which was a really dirty word there. Well, telling a story is probably at the heart of the art of acting because back when theater began it was the first thing that an actor had to be able to do. This is something that I think is critical and also fun. The audience likes it because it knows what's going on if you tell a good story. A lot of people think that it's somehow beneath them to tell a story (and by that I don't mean commenting on the play or doing representational acting because I come out of the realistic school). What I want is for an actor to tell a story so that everything he does looks and sounds real—whether he feels anything or not. Feeling is for pleasure. You don't have to feel to be a good actor. I know an awful lot of good actors who are cold as ice, but they can fake it. They can cry and get angry.

Let's get back to your notion of telling a story. Let's say you have a new student. How would you start with that?

First, I'd find out if he ever read a play, because lots of students don't read plays these days. They come to study acting and they've read two plays in their whole lives. This is the first time in my life that I feel there are too many actors. I never felt that before.

You feel there are more than there used to be?

There are just more people who think it's a nice life and a good way to make a living. Little do they know. But the very basic thing I do is try to find out if a new student knows what he wants to do, because most don't. They usually have absolutely no idea. There are a few, and you can see a drive in those people when they come in. There is something else going on.

I may watch a scene and afterward say, "I can't tell what is happening in this scene. I couldn't tell if you were happy or sad. Were you in love with the other person?" Just ask fundamental questions about what they think the play is about. After I ask those questions and discuss it and decide what is going on in the scene, I say, "Now do it." I'm not so arrogant to assume that everybody has to learn how to act from me. An actor may know a lot more than I think he does, you know. I have to find out what he needs to learn rather than selling him a "method." I don't do that. Some people like that. They feel comfortable: it's safe for them to feel that they can go to someone and learn A, B, C, D. But that's not what it is to me. The art form is not about that to me, and I would never say that doing A, B, C, and D was creating life. That's just connecting the dots. It can be done very well, it can be done beautifully and professionally, but it's still *almost* like life, it's not life itself. And I'm looking for that totally spontaneous moment. That's what my work is all about. That's when it feels best and it's the only reason to do it.

How do you help an actor overcome stage fright?

It depends on the person because, for instance, you can literally divide amateurs from professionals by their willingness to overcome their fear.

Let's say an actor is willing to overcome his fear but he doesn't know how.

But that's not true, that people don't know how. That's the lie that people tell themselves. In other words, nobody puts feeling into you. The one advantage that an actor has over any other artist is that he has intimate knowledge of the material he works with because he is working right from himself and he has been living with himself. If an actor is having a problem entering into contact with whatever is going on in the play, first of all you have to know the person well enough to know if it's a problem that he has with the scene or if it's a problem in all his work. It may be a particular problem he has coming into contact with that particular emotion. I would say, "Well, pick a scene where you have to get angry." Then they might come in and not do it because they are afraid, for one reason or another. So then I'll say, "Let's do the scene again." What I will say will depend on the person. Sometimes I'll say, "I don't care what you have to do. I don't care if it's bad. Just get angry." It's very easy to get angry on stage. You can pick up a chair and scream.

Finding out how to stimulate the person depends on the person. Sometimes I'll be very direct with them and say, "You don't have to feel angry. Just pretend. You don't have to feel anything. As a matter of fact, if you don't feel anything, it's better. Just pretend. Fool me. Make it look real. If you are such a good actor that you can fool me into believing that it's totally spontaneous and totally real, go ahead." People are shocked because they think that it requires some secret or manipulation. It's not true. Sometimes you can just do it.

That's where acting training can really get carried away, and I wish we would all read a few more plays and talk less about technique. We'd learn more if we read a little more Shakespeare. Read Shakespeare and it will teach you more about acting than a lot of acting teachers. Read Shakespeare and you'll learn a lot more about human nature than most psychiatrists know.

I'm not one to break people down. I won't do it and I don't think that's what this business is about. I know a lot of teachers who enjoy that. They like being a guru and feeling important. They approach it from almost a therapeutic point of view. I don't. I approach it more from a love of acting. If you like to act, then find out what you like to do. Maybe you don't like to do scenes where you have to get angry? I don't care if all you want to do is comedy and make a million dollars and be on TV or whatever. That's your business. If I don't want to teach you, I won't. But if I do want to teach you, I'm not going to try to teach you to conform to what my idea of an actor is. I have too much respect for people. Which is not to say that I'm irresponsible, but I also don't make the kind of judgment that says one thing is better than another. You live once and you might as well try to do what you want to do. I'm serious about my work so I want to be able to do everything.

One of the sad things about the realistic school of acting is that everybody thinks it's only about crying and negative emotions. Nobody thinks that doing comedy is worth anything, you know. If you want to look at a great actor, look at Charlie Chaplin. How many people have you ever seen on the stage or screen who can do what he did? Where is that coming from? How did he get to do that?

The thing that people forget about Stanislavsky is that he had a tremendous problem expressing himself and he writes about it. So a lot of his method came out of trying to solve his own problems. Now, he was very lucky to be working in the Moscow Art Theater, where he had two or three great actors in the same company at the same time. And he could watch them every day. Any actor who is worth anything will tell you that he learns more about the art of acting by watching people than anything else. I meet students who say they believe they can only learn by doing it, and I say, "You've got a lot of problems. If you haven't got the eye, you can't do it. You have to see it in order to do it."

Let's go back to this hypothetical student who has trouble with anger. You might say, "Pretend. Make believe. I don't care if you really feel it, just convince me." What happens if the student gets up there and is really phony? What do you do then? Do you ask him or her to use substitutions at that point?

I will sometimes say this is like an "as if" situation. First of all, a student can get a lot of help from the play, much more than he thinks. Rather than say, "Why don't you use a substitution and think about someone else?" I'll say, "What has this person done to you in the play?" And they will say, for instance, "This person has raped me and murdered my child." I'll say then, "Did you ever have a child?" They might say no. I'll reply, "Well, do you want one?" "Yeah." "Well, how would you feel if that happened to you?" Sometimes when you talk about the circumstances of the character you will literally begin to see the energy change in an actor. You can begin to see him think about it as if he hadn't taken it seriously before. It's a big difference. Actors say they want to be real. Everybody says it, but very few people do it because they don't want to enter into that state. They don't want to come into contact with that part of themselves.

My work is at its best when I can help an actor come into contact with an emotion through the circumstances of the play. I'll try that before I'll try something else, and if none of that works, I will tell him to go study with someone else in my school and learn more about acting before he comes back to me. That's what I say. I say, "You need a grounding because you have difficulty making contact with your feelings and when I tell you certain things you don't yet have enough self-perception. You need to work with someone who can do certain kinds of basic work with you so that you will find out more about yourself and what you have to do when you're in a play." In my school I do have people who teach a variety of basic exercises.

What kind of exercises?

Like Sense Memory, which includes everything from Affective

Memory to Private Moment. It's all from my father's work but most teachers have watered it down into their own personal versions, which, in my honest opinion, is usually less useful than what he did because most teachers nowadays are not active enough in the profession. I think it's very important to be active in the profession and not just to teach. It's an old-fashioned idea, but I think you know more about it if you've been through it. When I direct I know how to talk to actors because I've been an actor.

How do you help a student create a character who is very different from himself?

I'll tell him to read the play. I also ask people if there are parts that they have ever dreamed about working on or if there are characters in Shakespeare that they find really interesting but that they don't think they are like. In other words, I try to find out what their personal interest is in wanting to play a character rather than just give them something to do because it's a challenge. I try to work from the pleasure principle. I think you should like acting. So if you are going to try to do something that is really hard for you, get all the help you can. And make it as easy as possible because it's hard enough anyway.

Do you advise students to observe people or work on animals?

If you have to tell students to observe people, they shouldn't be in this business.

I ask that because some teachers tell their students not to observe people when they work on character because it will lead to imitation. How do you feel about that?

Those are people who have never acted and have never been on a stage. If they had they would know that you have to have a very clear ability to observe nature, which in practical terms does lead to imitation.

I try to find out what interests an actor. There is a difference between being interested in Macbeth or Richard III or King Lear. They are very different characters who come from different cultures and different countries. Once an actor chooses I'll tell him to pick either a monologue or a scene from that play. Sometimes I'll have the actor do a reading first, because if a student is inspired he may do brilliant work. You know often when you don't do a lot of thinking you do your best work. That's very important in terms of how you teach people because if you teach them that in order to act they have to be thinking about what they are doing all the time, they're in trouble. Sometimes they have to think about it until they master it to understand what the process is, but in the end if they are doing their work properly, they're not thinking at all. They're just living. Just as in life. There is no difference.

For instance, French actors will start by doing a whole characterization immediately and it's totally superficial. American actors do the opposite; they hardly ever start with any physical behavior because it's all coming from the inside out. So when I work with actors I tell them what I see. If an actor starts with a character, that's what I'll begin with, and I always try to point out where in the play I differ with the actor's interpretation—where I get my analysis—so that it's not just a personal opinion. That's a very important thing. I try to teach people structure and script analysis on a practical basis, not in an intellectual way. Most people don't know how to read a play. It's one of the hardest things to do.

Do you give the students questions to ask themselves about the play before they start to work on a scene or monologue?

No. I don't like to do that beforehand because that would absolve them of responsibility for it and I think that if they want to create something they must take responsibility for whatever they are going to do. The acting profession tries to teach the actor to do what he is told. That's less true in the United States than in Europe, but still the actor is at the bottom of the rung and isn't encouraged to take responsibility—except in the movies, where stars control everything.

What happens after students have read the play? Are there specific questions you want them to ask themselves or that you ask?

I ask them to tell me the story and tell me what they think about it. Do you like the character? That's fundamental, too. I'm very basic. I think there is a lot more common sense in good acting than people would like to believe. It's not so secretive and mystical. You don't have to kneel down and pray and light incense all the time, if you know what I mean. It gets a little tiring. I don't mind if people do that if that's what they want to do. But to start telling actors that they cannot create life if they don't do those things, I don't like that. Anybody I've ever known who was any good had their own way of doing it. If you've ever been in a dressing room with Geraldine Page, it's chaotic. She's just sitting there listening to the radio during the performance. That's how she works. That doesn't mean that I'm going to teach everyone to do the same thing. But it works for her, and I'm not going to criticize her and say there is a better way. And you have to allow that to function, you must allow that to take place. When you teach you must be very careful not to turn principle into something that's rigid. It's very dangerous.

Do you teach relaxation?

I don't teach a lot of warm-up work. I tell people that they have to be ready to come on stage.

What does that mean to you?

For me as an actor what I do to get ready to go on stage depends on the material. If it's a modern comedy, which is not that difficult for me to do, the main thing I have to do is relax. Being relaxed does not mean going into some numb state or meditating. It just means being the most human that I can be. I think that rather than trying to be perfect in your art form, what you have to try to learn to strive for is to be the most human you are capable of—which is very hard to do. What parts of yourself you bring to what you are doing depends completely on the material.

Being ready means being concentrated, so that when you are working you are dealing with the plan and the circumstances of the play. But some days you can be more concentrated than others. I think that if you do your work properly your work will be relatively consistent. You don't ever have to be bad. You should always be able to tell the story. You may not be inspired or feel a feeling, but you should always be able to go out there and tell a simple, clear story.

I think it's the same thing in rehearsal. Even though I have a book in my hand, I'm still talking to my partner, trying to make contact with him or her, trying to discover what kind of relationship we may have. I'm trying to see not only how I should act this material, but also what life is taking place. If we were the Macbeths and we were sitting here getting ready to kill someone and nothing was happening to me it would bother me. I would feel that I'm doing something wrong.

Do you use the term "prior circumstances?"

Oh, yes. I think that's more important than anything. Ideally, all my acting work should be about what happens before I come on to the stage. I should literally know the play like a piece of music. It should be like Beethoven. It should be read like music. I don't think that any artist will tell you that if you know material well, it will prevent you from being inspired or being real. Only actors will tell you that. And that's ignorance. That comes from The Actors Studio and we are paying the price for it. But that's being corrected because everybody is aware of the problem. If I have a problem as an actor, it's because I haven't done enough at the beginning. I will eventually get there, but I think about it a little too much, before I make choices or take risks with them.

There was a period, though, in my work when I would just do something and all of a sudden I would believe it and it was real. Sometimes I would just do it, cry because I was supposed to, and surprise myself and really feel something.

Don't you think that's because crying and laughing are physiological events as well as emotional ones and can be triggered?

That's right. A lot of the people who are doing body work are aware of the fact that memory is in the muscle, even sense memory. Therefore, you can trigger it from the outside in as well as from the inside out. Ideally, the actor should feel free enough to get it any way he can. It doesn't matter how you get it. It only matters that it works. That's what's wrong with teaching "methods" of work rather than principles of life, of reality. Other people think that it's not what you do but how you do it that's important. That's only important to the teacher who is taking your money. It's not true for the actor or the play or the audience. And I don't like it. I've seen too much of that happen and I've seen work become distorted. That's sad and I guard against it. I'm in the unique position of having seen that kind of work rather intimately so that I understand it very well. I also understand it from my personal experience as an actor having to solve my own problems, some of which came not just from my own personality, but from some of the things I was taught at The Actors Studio.

I remember my family going to the Berliner Ensemble in 1961 right after they put up the wall. They were replacing a lot of actors because many had stayed in West Berlin. They said their biggest problem with the new actors was that it took two years to untrain them. My father said, after seeing their work, that they had the courage to be simpler than anybody. They just talk, and it's interesting and theatrical.

When students are afraid to do something simply I will say to them, "Do you know that you are overdoing it?" They often say, "Well, I guess I think that I have to do more." I tell them, "Look. You're paying me money. Trust me. I'll tell you when you are not doing enough. Do it so that *you* believe it." That's something I say a lot. Make yourself believe it. Fool yourself. Remember, if you're really a fine actor, you can fool the audience. If you're a great actor, you'll fool yourself. That's true. And that's just common sense. I think that it's valuable for people to hear that because it takes some of the mystique out of acting.

Do you use improvisations?

I do, more than I used to. I didn't like improvisation at first, the kind where two actors paraphrase the words of a scene and play it in their own words. I felt that if an actor needed to improvise to get to the reality of the event, nine times out of ten even if he got it in the improvisation he couldn't put it into the scene. Actors who could put it into the scene didn't need the improvisation. However, I'm a little easier about that now. Sometimes it does work because it gives people a certain freedom to make mistakes during rehearsals.

One of the basic premises of my method of work is that actors should risk making mistakes. When they are not sure about what to do, I tell them to make a big mistake, because if you make all the mistakes possible, you'll get it right. There is nothing like trial and error. There is no better method in the world. How you apply trial and error depends on what you think acting is about. To me acting is spontaneously creating life within the circumstances of the play. It has to be real—which also means real within the style of the play. People think that the style of the play will change the basic life in it and it doesn't.

The problem in this country is that people don't have enough training in style. When we do the classics all our wonderful American acting, which is simple and real, goes out the window and we look like slightly watered-down versions of the English. I can criticize and say that in some of their tragedies their moments are forced and not as real as they could be. But I would rather not complain about the English until I think that we are better. For us to be better we need to do more Shakespeare filled with the kind of life and energy that American actors are capable of. It would just knock people's socks off.

Do you agree that the British do Shakespeare better than Americans?

The comedies. They do the comedies well. They have a sense of ease and feel at home with them. When it comes to the emotional moments, which you notice more in the serious plays, it depends on the actor and on the night. A lot of English actors are talented, but their training ignores the principles of reality. They just don't deal with it. They say you either have talent or you don't. And then they leave it alone. In some ways that's fine, and in other ways one of the strengths of our work is that we accept the reality principle as fundamental in training the actor. I like that.

We don't do Shakespeare in New York, not because we lack the talent, but because Shakespeare is not commercial. And you have to do it in New York to make it viable throughout the whole country. I know that there are people outside of New York who do Shakespeare and the classics, but most of it is not first-rate. I know that some people will say, "Who the hell does he think he is, saying that?" but I've been there and I know the difference. In London the Royal Shakespeare Company and the National Theatre always have a production of Shakespeare, even if it's a bad year. It's a tradition of theater. That's not true in this country. Not yet. And I think that it needs to become true. I've no objection to the commercialism of

Broadway. It doesn't bother me at all. But I think there has to be a place for wonderful theater. We could do the equivalent of *Nicholas Nickleby*. But what producer could you go to in the United States and say, "I've got an idea. I want to convert a novel into a play, and I'm going to use forty-five actors." Maybe Joe Papp would say, "Okay, go into a corner somewhere," although even he would be more interested if it were musical.

As associate artistic director of the Mirror Repertory Company I'm concerned with doing classical theater. Take Geraldine Page, for instance. An actress of her stature in most other countries of the world by this time in her career would have played more than 200 great roles. And Geraldine has done about twelve, of which about six have been in the last three years with us in the Mirror Rep. There is no respect for the classics in this country. We respect power and we respect success, but there is no respect for the craft itself.

Warren Robertson

Warren Robertson is the founder and artistic director of Actor's Repertory Theatre in New York City, where he currently teaches acting. He also travels to Holland each year to work with professional actors, and a grant from the Canadian Film Board takes him to Montreal, where he conducts classes on a regular basis. A prominent drama teacher for more than twenty years, he has also performed on Broadway, on TV, and in the movies.

Mr. Robertson is the author of Free to Act, *a book about acting that "presents a revolutionary new method of using body, mind, and emotion to break out of habitual behavior and self-defeating attitudes."*

In what ways have you been influenced by your own training?

My first training was in the arts. I didn't become an actor until I was twenty-three. I studied fine arts in three different universities before I became an actor. Then I worked in the movie *Sayonara* with Marlon Brando and became friends with him. When I heard from him about the work that was so new and stimulating that was coming out of Russia and The Actors Studio in New York, I decided that I would go to New York City. I was interested in the relationship between the human interior and exterior. I observed classes at The Actors Studio and that's when I became a serious actor. I got into a couple of Broadway shows and started doing some TV. I also did a one-man show of Will Rogers that was quite successful for a while. I started teaching inadvertently. The things that were being done at the Studio and the things that I saw being done in the theater plus what I brought from my own life and education and my own natural talent made me feel that there were other ways to approach acting.

I started with a group of actors in a living room. We were all working and doing scenes. Little by little I found myself more and more in the position of moderator and teacher. Then, what started out to be a collection of actors in a living room turned out to be thirty people and I realized that I was working a couple of times a week and giving all this information out and putting all my energy into it—so I might as well look at it from the point of view of officially being a teacher.

This was in the 1960s and there were a lot of dynamic things happening. I was discovering many new ways of stimulating and releasing energy and ways to integrate that back into movement, back into the voice, into the gesture, into the surface of the body. Suddenly there was a demand for what I was doing, and when the demand got greater than I could handle, I taught other teachers my methods, and that was the beginning of my school. It was not a school by design. It was a school by necessity.

I discovered that there was a very clear division between schools of acting. There was at this time (in the 1960s) a distinct gathering of schools on one side that seemed to be very concerned with the externals, the traditional—movement, voice, diction, mannerisms, props, and physical stances. And another school that seemed to be very concerned with the interior, the psychological, the internal. These schools seemed to be very much at odds with each other. It struck me that neither of them was complete. It wasn't a question of one school or approach being right or wrong. It's just that a human being has both an interior and an exterior, a content and a form, and when the content and the form balance—whether it is in writing, in dance, or in acting—it then becomes whole and complete.

I found a lot of the schools putting an emphasis on the externals at the expense of the interior and vice versa. The interior approach sought psychological truthfulness, but had not been integrated into movement, speech, dialect or a character's behavior, given circumstances, and so forth. While the external schools taught actors how to speak, how to move, how to design a character, they had no inner reality, no inner justification. I thought it was not a question of one being right and the other being wrong, but an understanding of the degree to which each was correct. I thought training should be about the self-education of the body, of the feelings, of the voice. In the end, it is a totality. You can work with the parts, but the merging in the end is a wholeness. The exercises I saw being done at The Actors Studio were emotional, physical, and vocal, but I also saw some very good things being done at schools that put more emphasis on motion, styles of movement, and freeing the voice.

Which schools?

Let me narrow it down to individuals; for instance, the difference between Lee Strasberg and Stella Adler: to me Stella was this marvelously theatrical person who had been born into and was fully involved in the art of acting. She had a tremendous capacity to diagnose a scene and analyze a character and to describe the externals of characterization for an actor. On the other hand, Lee had this incredible perseverance and insight into each individual. He could stimulate and uncover emotions in actors and could free them up from a lot of external pretensions and indicating.

At the time I came into theater there was great controversy over which approach was right, and coming in as an outsider without having been schooled in either, I just thought it was a question of understanding the essentials of both. Instead of resistance there should be a flow.

But I see this in everything. In creation there is both an interior and exterior. One is dark, unknown, and turbulent, and the other is knowable and willful. It's the rational and irrational and how they merge. It's what gives something its creative wholeness.

My first work was trying to reconnect all the parts in a continuity of exercises. Instead of having an actor work only on a sense memory or affective memory, or just having him move or use his voice, I wanted to get back to the origin of the whole process: how a person originally has an impulse or a feeling and how it is released through sound.

Would you describe how you combine an Affective Memory Exercise and movement?

I often have an actor do an Affective Memory Exercise on his feet instead of sitting in a chair. And at moments I'll have him try to integrate feelings into his body. I'll have him lift his hand and wave goodbye, and he will remember, without even trying, who he is waving goodbye to. The body is a means of finding a specific feeling. This waving will connect with something. There are key terms that were our first spoken language and there are key movements that were our first physical language as well.

Also, rather than have actors sit in a chair and, moment by moment, do a sensory exercise, I found that when I asked them to raise their eyes, something in the raising of the eyes connected with something inside. Then I would ask them to remember who they used to look up to with certain needs, and as soon as they extended their hands outward, it brought that feeling up. Once the feeling was aroused, I would do something different with each person. If, for instance, while one was feeling something, I thought her fingers had no dexterity, no vocabulary, no gesture, I would have her play an imaginary piano, try to create movements in her hands and arms to express what she couldn't verbalize yet. I would have the students do anything as a means of getting those feelings to move out of the body and convey what they felt.

I had seen that it was not enough for an actor to feel. What is important is the motivation for the feeling. The feeling itself is not acting.

Are there any specific techniques you give your students to cope with stage fright?

The first thing I do is to get them to accept fear because it is also energy. I've worked with about 36,000 people over twenty years and I've observed that energy is neither good nor bad. It is all life. And if you interfere with one kind of energy, you somehow interfere with all of it. There is just life, and energy transforms it. The energy behind fear is the same energy we laugh with and cry with. I'm not interested in how to make a person go against his fear. It may be energy that at the moment is inappropriate for a character, it may be energy that is not yet in the actor's command, but he or she has to get familiar with the energy we call fear.

How do you do that?

In any craft or training, it's how you apply something. The same rules, the same exercises, applied by two different people will get two different results. Exercises themselves are so creative. There is something that happens between the teacher and a particular student during an exercise that's a dynamic in itself. So knowing how to use an exercise at a given moment is like electricity. Giving people the right amount of knowledge so that they can experience the unknown is also a dynamic.

Many of the people I've worked with were already schooled in all the areas of psychology, but they couldn't feel anything. The first task is to get just enough knowledge to the person so that he can taste something of the unknown in himself—the unknown being feelings, not just knowledge. The teacher has to try to clarify for that person the relevance of feeling and its relationship to the whole art of acting. We don't want him to become enamored of the fact that he can now laugh and cry once again and push that into everything he does, believing that that's all acting is about. That just qualifies him to be a human being. That's just reclaiming the roots of our birthright.

To me you cannot teach a class, but you can give a class knowledge. In the arts only individuals learn. I can teach a class of fifty people and only one may get something out of it. What I mean is that it will become a process for him or her. That person will be able to put the knowledge to use. Forty-nine other people may be stimulated by what you're saying and understand you, but it may not move anything inside them.

I work with the group overall, but my work is always geared toward the individual. It cannot be any other way. That's why I have always resisted institutions or academies; they tend to formulate a way of doing something that is supposed to hold true for the whole group, sometimes at the expense of the individual. The human dynamic is such an original and individual thing, you just can't apply all of these rules and laws and expect to get one result with everybody. It's a very delicate and personal thing.

Teaching is a great commitment. Once I started teaching I gave most of my energy to it. I'm devoted to teaching, but I still perform once a year. When I work with a person, that's a big commitment on my part and I ask for a big commitment on his or her part. I resist teachers who tend to use these formula exercises, of which there are so many now. That wasn't true when I started. Then it was like a new frontier because The Actors Studio was just beginning to use what was called the Method, which was a compilation of certain exercises to get a result. But the whole field itself, the human potential movement, hadn't begun. Today even housewives are familiar with these things. When I started it was considered revolutionary.

Can you give me an example of what you mean?

Just moving the emotions back into the voice and the body. It went along with the whole movement in the 1960s of going back to the individual and the potential of that individual.

For instance, after a student is fully relaxed I'll ask her to say the word "child" or "fear" or "alone" or "hurt" out loud and tell her not to do anything else, just allow whatever feeling comes up to happen. I don't want the emotion stopped. I'm looking for an emotional response and I want the actor's sensitized body to react to the imagery and emotion that these words arouse.

Is there a specific movement in psychology that you feel has influenced you the most?

No. I've never gone with the movements in psychology.

You mentioned the human potential movement.

I don't incorporate. I was a few years ahead of my time when I started doing these things. That's why I got so much attention when I first started teaching. Today the exercises that I came up with have moved into the human potential movement. But I don't use the movements of psychology as a guide to where I am going. I use the state of the individual in the class. He or she represents to me the overall state of the whole establishment.

I would like you to describe some specific techniques that represent your work.

The first one that I remember was a kind of improvisation. At the time, an improvisation was where you would let go of the text— you'd assume you were the character and then improvise around what you thought the character would do. When I was teaching I saw that if you let actors choose something from themselves instead of trying to act the character with their own words, that if you asked them to try to find something analogous in themselves and base their improvisation on that, it was more authentic. I call that personalization. It's what makes acting different from ordinary conversation. Once you give a person a situation that he has been alive to in his own life and you define it by a need to complete an action—such as to confront someone or to make an appeal to someone or to accost someone or to charm someone, or one of those 2,000 verbs— suddenly things start happening, big things start happening. As far as I know, when I started doing improvisations that way, it was a discovery for me. I said that this is not only a problem in particular exercises, but this is also the general problem in acting itself. People are learning how to feel, how to move, how to speak, but they do not understand the through line of the action of the play. When actors don't understand how to score a text by its actions, they wind up playing ideas of actions; they don't try to complete actions.

You mentioned personalization. In what way would you say that is different from a substitution?

It's not different from a substitution. When I started teaching, substitutions were done as sense memories. We weren't using substitutions; we were doing sensory recall.

When I do personalizations in class, I'll ask a student to recall, for instance, someone he loved very much who hurt him and then to choose actions to demand, to criticize, to challenge that person out loud. I want him to include his whole body and let the emotion affect him.

Do you believe it's always better for actors to use personalizations or should they use them only when they can't use the circumstances of the character?

Ideally, someone is sensitive enough or talented enough to respond enough to the text so that it prompts a belief in him. But, of course, the ideal is not usually the case, so actors need technique. Understanding the application of an exercise is as important as being able to do it. I've seen people go rampant in scenes or monologues in which they display all the marvelous things they have learned, but it's total chaos, it's madness. They didn't understand the relationship of the parts. Often it just becomes an indulgence. So again, how to keep the student constantly aware of the relationship of the parts to the whole is the point. Sometimes the exercise becomes the actual work in a scene and sometimes it can be a stimulus for something else.

I realized that my work with actors shouldn't start with getting them to be active, but with releasing the stress, the tensions, the blocks, the resistances to reception that they have. When one is receptive, one finds an action. In acting jargon that means that an actor takes the given circumstances and ambience of a play. In that moment he doesn't intrude upon something with an action. His action comes out of his reception. How he takes the action is based on his character. In other words, the action and how it's attempted will reveal his character; therefore, one doesn't *play* character. That's revealed moment by moment in how he attempts something, in how he either conceals or reveals something.

What gives an actor force is what he's concealing. That interests the audience. A well-written play gives a character something to contain, an obstacle that keeps him from revealing something. A person engages in a physical task in order to conceal something. He's angry, and the anger, rather than being revealed instantly, is contained by putting away some papers or fixing his hair. All of these become part and parcel of a whole way in which we go along with an audience wondering when this person will reveal what he's holding in. In a great play a character will reveal something that will transform him for the rest of his life, something he didn't know about himself.

Do you feel that your contribution as a teacher has been more in terms of how you work with people, the force of your own personality, rather than the specific exercises you use?

No. I feel that my gift is my ability to amalgamate the rational and the irrational, the feeling and the expression of that feeling. You see, to me creation is just that. When you say acting, you're using a very advanced term. Some of the things that I see called acting, that people get paid for—I don't know what you should call it, entertainment or acrobatics or whatever. But if you're talking about it as an art, it's a very rare coming together of things to which the word "creation" is applied. And creation means that even I haven't been there before. So no matter what I know, no matter what anyone ever knew before, this has never been. Knowledge has got to drop you somewhere into the unknown if you are really going to create. Some people stay safely in the known. Some people drop into the unknown.

I feel that my skill has been the ability to convey information and let people experience the unknown. I have that ability, somehow or other. I don't have a school that operates by semesters—you know, first, second, third. I work as a specialist, and my skill has been in finding why a person's acting doesn't consummate, why it doesn't evolve into a totality. And sometimes it's just like taking a grain of sand out of a carburetor. Then the car goes terrifically well. But if you don't know it's the sand in the carburetor, you take off the tires and overhaul the engine and spend years working on it and the car never runs any better.

So your special contribution is being able to diagnose a particular problem that blocks an actor's potential?

My contribution has been the ability to take the essentials out of vast amounts of words and information and to bring them down to actable tools for the actor and then make those tools personally effective for that actor.

What about character work? What techniques do you teach your actors to help them create a character who is very different from themselves?

The principle holds true for any style of theater. Take Blanche Dubois, for instance. I've seen so many attempts at her that it's painful; the southern accent, abstract motions and gestures, and intonations and outpouring of emotion—all of it. But first of all, the actress needs a very free body. If it's a New York actress, she needs to be free of any local mannerism or fixed gestures, any speech or behavior that is recognizably from the Bronx or Brooklyn. With regard to the southern accent, I tell her that an accent is only the symbol for the whole person. For Blanche, her accent is only a representation of a whole complex human being. Don't start learning the dialect until you understand the origin of the whole personality. Her particular southern dialect is different in its quality and intonation from that of a woman who is not brutalized and seriously disturbed.

To me Blanche is a symbol of a whole genre of women. When she is hallucinating and working from memory she tends to disembody, she goes into her head, her tone goes up and her hands actually lift. That's why they have so many frills and so much lace on the head and hands in the South—so they can keep their hands above the center of the body, where the reality is, where the heart is. That's why the voice is high. You could say the same thing about anybody who is haughty or aloof. Blanche has become unhinged, but there are moments when she is very lucid. When she says, "God can appear so suddenly," at that moment she is lucid and her voice and gestures are more centered. When she is really into the deep disturbances that go down into the primitive, sexual, pelvic areas, the female areas where she has been brutalized and misused (as well as into the horrors of the tubercular family and the dying), then things get very deep, the tone, the gestures, the whole body are going in and down.

When you talk about an actress playing Blanche Dubois you are talking about an actress understanding the relationship between the voice and its intonation—not just the accent, but the register of speech from the high pitch, the middle, or bass. It's just like playing a piano. Also, the gestures—where in the body they come from or if they are elaborate or covert—plus the feeling. How Blanche avoids terror or pain is to revert into a high, joyful, pleasant hallucination of the old plantation where she was Scarlett O'Hara. These things become demonstrable in a class. I never give an actor or actress a piece of information without letting him or her experience something of it, so that what I say doesn't have to be accepted at face value.

The kinds of divisions you were talking about—the head area as opposed to the pelvic area—do you use those often to help students find a character?

You can't find a character without that; you would be doing a caricature. You may do it intuitively, but working knowledgeably you have to start with body gestures, voice, and their relationship. You have to know where the centers are in the body.

Do you advise students to observe people as a way to develop a character?

I advise students to observe all the time and not to dream or to live in dreams. I advise them to be aware right now, not to miss anything. That's their God-given right, to live instantly in this moment. Be aware, wake up. Don't keep living internally in reflections.

If I were going to play Gittel in Two for the Seesaw, *for instance, would you advise me to observe a New York "broad" type?*

I would first get you to observe that which is Gittel-like in yourself. The actress might have Gittel qualities she is not aware of. They may be there all along but she doesn't realize it. That's when we often go out of bounds on a character; we're already some of that character but we don't see it.

If the actress is from the Bronx in New York and she is very capricious and independent, sort of her own big brother, and very enticing, you would start from there. If she's from New York but has a far more subdued life and is accustomed to being acted upon and having regular personal relationships, a lot of work will be needed.

Let's say two actors are working on a scene in class and you feel they are not relating to each other on a moment-to-moment basis. How would you deal with that?

That is the very essence of acting—action and response. In other words, I attempt something and in that moment I have to be very receptive to your response, which will, in turn, become a reaction in me. All training leads to this. First of all, I know what I need to get from you. I define that as my intention, my motivation, my action, whatever you want to call it. It's a verb. But in order to get feedback on how I'm doing with that verb, that action, you must be in my field of play all the time. It's like fishing. The fisherman and the fish go together. I believe there is an invisible connection between people that is called communing. Communing means transmitting to and receiving from each other without using words. Then I use the words in order to complete what I want to get. And when an actor doesn't understand that, he tries to make the words that action. But the words only aid me in completing an action.

Can you think of an incident from the past when an exercise led to a very dramatic change in a student?

Yes. There was an actress who became quite famous. She had never acted before, but she had a childlike ability to commit totally to something. She didn't have many blocks or an attitude of "Show me," or "I already know this." So when I gave her the exercises I mentioned before—the ones where you find the dynamic of feeling in the body—she was able to respond almost immediately to them. What she achieved was a kind of ferocity and, at the same time, a great vulnerability. Doing exercises gave her a big visible and emotional life, which made a great difference in her career.

Are there any exercises that you feel work the most reliably?

My observations have been that every human being has a secret person inside. You do, I do. It starts to collect in us very early in our lives. It sometimes advises us not to do this, or go ahead and do that, or it reminds us of a punishment we got, or it reminds us of a time when we got angry. The first thing you know, by the time you are an adult you have a whole secret person inside. This kind of makes you into two people: the one that has the impulse to do something and the one that monitors.

The most dynamic exercise that I have is my first exchange with a human being. Somehow or other I seem to be able to talk to that inner person. When that inner person is allowed to manifest, it's thrilling, because that's where people put away their most important feelings, thoughts, and memories.

When do you suggest that your students work on technical skills like dialects or period movement?

At a certain stage of training, if they have already had some experience or training. Otherwise, technical training is premature. Most of my work seeks to get behind all that technical training in someone's head to find the human being, that which is individual and creative, before it becomes laminated by too much early external training, too much knowledge about behavior that wasn't integrated properly into the whole actor.

Do you have new students start with certain exercises first?

Sometimes I'll try to get them to be more receptive through a Color Exercise, for instance. It's one to help a student sensitize her awareness of her surroundings. An actress can do it anywhere, at home, in the street, on a bus. I tell my students to pick one color a day and then spend just ten minutes noticing all the different objects and things in their environment that are that color. It makes them very sensitive to their surroundings.

Another exercise, Habit Breaking, can help stimulate a student's imagination. I tell him to think of different ways to get out of bed each morning. He can crawl, stand up on the bed and walk off, whatever. It's a good way to break ingrained habits and it sensitizes the student to other possibilities.

Some people come in who are already in very good shape for acting. They may be very ready to do something in a film playing someone very close to their own personality. That doesn't mean they are going to be able to do Ophelia or Mother Courage. That may still be beyond them. Some actors come to an acting school to get on a soap opera or to be in the movies. Others come only because they want to be on the stage. Any of those can be correct or incorrect. But it's still a very personal statement. It should always be a personal statement. The seed that will flower in a human being is such a personal thing that training can be the worst thing that can happen to him.

That may sound funny coming from a teacher, but I do think that wrong or premature training can keep the individual from fulfilling himself or herself. And it's got to be individual. A person must be acknowledged and addressed as exactly who he is right then and there. I'm very against blanket judgments like Class I needs this or Class II needs that. It's antithetical to my whole school. That's why my school is not designed academically.

Are there any techniques or approaches to acting that you feel actors should avoid?

I've always had an aversion to acting teachers criticizing each other. It's a question of who is practicing it, who is applying it. I've seen some very good techniques and exercises that are totally misapplied. I've also seen very good results coming from people who really don't quite understand what they are doing. Teaching is immediate, just as acting is immediate. You can find certain laws and you can define certain exercises, but it's in the moment with each individual that a particular exercise is realized.

Some teachers encourage students to reveal their personal lives in the belief that it is in the service of their craft. Other teachers shy away from that. How do you feel?

I don't think that the person should ever be violated. I don't subscribe to the school of acting that calls for people to reveal personal things. But the actor does need to experience the feeling that he can publicly reveal how he feels about something. He should be able to experience himself deeply, richly, privately. He shouldn't have to reveal personal information about himself. Acting shouldn't be analytical. It should allow the individual to explore his inner world and the experiences that have collected there. It shouldn't be like a group therapy session in which a person reveals all of his private life. There may be teachers who do that and somehow it's right for them, but it doesn't seem right for me.

Are there steps you take students through to help them to be private onstage?

Again, to me private means to be total. If a person is really involved in a total way, he *is* private. My way is to get a person to become so involved sensorially that he becomes private. It's a selective privacy. But as far as a person getting on the stage and performing a private act or acting out certain kinds of private moments, I don't find that necessary. Being able to be private in public is a very important part of the creative process in acting because when you are private you do things for yourself or for the other person on the stage. When you're not private, you do things for the audience and you limit what you do out of concern for what it will think.

How do you advise students to begin working on a script or a scene? Are there steps that you feel are the most helpful way to begin?

I like to let students start from wherever they are, however they instinctively want to start on something. I see the results of whatever they do and then I can determine from that where I need to start with them. One actor may need to start with clarifying for himself what the character needs or what his motivation is. For another it might be how to get more at ease on the stage, how to get more of the reality of the situation. For someone who can't remember lines, the first thing may be how to get his mind off the fact that he can't remember lines. When actors don't try to remember lines, they remember them. It's a question of attention, primary and secondary attention. I don't think you should tell students that one thing is their primary consideration. Even if I see five different students doing the same part in the same scene, there will be a different definition of what each of them should do first for their own personal growth.

I would say that, in general, it's a good idea for students to break down a scene and decide what their objective is, what their intentions are, and what actions they will use to carry out their intentions.

Do you teach audition techniques?

There are different degrees of auditions. Sometimes you get a script and some time to work on it. Other times it's a cold reading. I think intelligence is so important here. Students will go up to do a cold reading and try to do in-depth sensory work. That's just not intelligent. But if you're working with a director who says, "Take the script home," and you bring back the most obvious kind of result playing, that's not intelligent either.

There are such things as cold reading or audition classes, which I think have a value, but I don't concern myself too much with them. If an actor seems to be having trouble in an audition, I try to find out what he may be projecting or what insecurities are keeping him from working as fully as he could. If it goes beyond that, I usually suggest that he go to an audition class or that he take the script-reading class that we have in our school. That's different from learning how to act because reading and acting are really two different things. Some actors come in and do the best acting they ever do in their first reading. Maybe they're nervous, or maybe something happens to them because of fear, but they can't repeat their performance. On the other hand, some very good actors and actresses are miserable readers.

Do you feel that today's actors approach their craft differently from their predecessors?

I think that in the last twenty years actors have had access to so much. They have insights into themselves and to humanity that were prohibited by religion or by the establishment for centuries. The movements of the 1960s, '70s, and '80s have given us a chance to look at things in a new way. Actors have such vast accessibility to ways of working on themselves. Each new generation has the advantage of all the accomplishments and knowledge that the past generation has provided. I feel very fortunate. I stand on the shoulders of people like Lee Strasberg, Stella Adler, Stanislavsky. I learned from them and I had a chance to say, "Hey, what's next?"

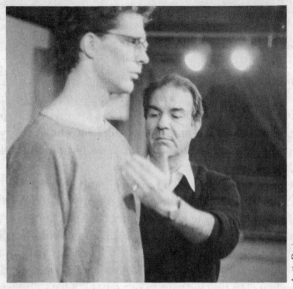

Justin Davis

Ed Kovens

Ed Kovens is director of The Professional Workshop in New York City. He studied acting with Lee Strasberg for twenty-five years and was a founding staff member of the Lee Strasberg Theatre Institute. He has been a member of The Actors Studio since 1968, and is a member of the Society of Stage Directors and Choreographers.

Mr. Kovens is also a professional actor who has appeared on Broadway, on TV, and in feature films. He feels that acting is vital for a teacher because it keeps him in touch with why and how certain techniques are helpful and important to the development of the craft. His approach to actor training is Method-oriented. But these techniques "weren't written in stone; they were a way of looking at acting problems. . . . I try to stay as close as possible to Strasberg's techniques as he did to those of his teachers. The changes that I have made have been more evolutionary than revolutionary."

How did you get started teaching acting?

126

Originally I went to art school and was a commercial artist, but at nineteen, after acting in high school, college, and stock, I quit college and became an actor. I went to NYU at night and studied acting and directing, and after six months I actually thought I was trained and went out and got work in radio. For the next four years I worked as a stand-up comic, had small parts in film and on TV, and directed some plays and revues. At twenty-three I stopped working because I looked like five hundred other guys who thought they were John Garfield. I was no longer a juvenile, and I was dissatisfied with my craft. This was 1957.

This led me to start studying again. By the way, originally I was very opposed to Method acting. I thought it was a lot of mumbling and scratching, that kind of stuff. But when I made a list of the actors that I liked, the ones that touched me, I found that they had either studied privately with members of the Group Theatre like Strasberg, Stella Adler, or Sandy Meisner, or had come out of the Second Avenue Yiddish Theatre. Later I found that the actors who started the Yiddish Theatre were the nucleus of the Habima and had originally been trained by Stanislavsky's protégé, Vakhtangov. No matter where I looked, the actors who moved me, like Paul Muni, turned out to be Method actors. I admired Olivier, but he never made me cry. However, I remembered seeing Brando in *The Men* when I was sixteen, and he was so good that I was convinced that he was really a mean, nasty person. Previously I always knew that someone was acting. With Brando I wasn't sure. Up until then I had basically been an intuitive actor, if inspiration came—wonderful— if it didn't, I was in a lot of trouble. I knew when I was good, but I couldn't repeat it, and I knew when I was bad, and I didn't know why or what to do about it. From studying art and playing sports I knew there had to be certain principles involved. I knew I needed a craft.

The Group Theatre influenced acting in America. It had been influenced by the Moscow Art Theater, which came to the United States and left some of its people behind. Strasberg trained with those people at the Actor's Lab. The Actors Studio, though, has influenced world acting. There is no acting community that doesn't know something about Method training. When I saw The Moscow Art Theater production of *The Three Sisters* here in New York in the 1960s, I saw that it was stuck where Stanislavsky left off; that it was very old-fashioned.

In 1957 I started studying privately with Strasberg in a small studio above the Capitol movie theater. That was the time of the biggies: Monroe, Fonda, Hoffman, even Streisand. A lot of people studied with him who never talked about it. Subsequently, I also studied with him at The Actors Studio, where I became a member in 1968. I kept on studying that way basically until his death in 1981. In 1965 a bunch of Strasberg students came to me and asked me if I would form a basic exercise class, since his private classes were so crowded. They wanted to study with me and Lee at the same time. So I charged one dollar a person and we did exercises. And I've been teaching ever since. I still act, because I think that's revitalizing to a teacher. If you just teach, you lose touch with the "why" of what you are doing, and how you should be doing certain things.

When Lee started the Lee Strasberg Institute in 1969 he asked me to teach for him. I was one of the founding staff members along with John Strasberg and Walter Lott. After five years there, I left the Institute—more over business differences than artistic ones—and I started my own classes, called The Professional Workshop.

What have you retained and what have you rejected from your training with Lee?

I don't think that artistically there are any differences. I truly feel that what Lee taught, at least what I learned from him, was fine.

Let me clarify something first. Stanislavsky didn't invent a new acting technique. He simply was the first to formulate what good actors had always been doing. At the same time, the theories of Pavlov and Freud were being formulated and he was aware of them. Strasberg was taught Stanislavsky technique at the Actor's Lab by Maria Ouspenskaya and Richard Boleslavski. He then, rightly, adapted and adopted those theories. I try to stay as close to Strasberg's techniques as he did to those of his teachers. The changes that I have made have been more evolutionary than revolutionary.

His techniques have worked for thousands of actors throughout the world, so why fool with them? The changes that I've made have come about through more than twenty years of teaching, using the Method as an actor, and also through the discoveries in psychology that we have all been exposed to: Lorenz, Reich, etc. By the way, Lee introduced me to those people and told me to read them. Lee's work evolved also. At first he adhered to Stanislavsky and the principle of "What would you do if you were in this institution?" Slowly he adopted Vakhtangov's principle of "What adjustments do I need in order to do what the character does?"

Could you explain the Sensory Exercises you learned from Strasberg?

Everyone thinks that Lee's major contribution has been with Sensory Exercises and emotional expression. That's a misconception. Lee told me that when Stella Adler came back from Russia after her meeting with Stanislavsky she stepped off the boat yelling, "You're all wrong. I got *the* word from Stanislavsky." Stanislavsky's emphasis at that time was on action and so she told Lee that everything he was doing was wrong. She also talked about beats. The story goes that the translator she used kept saying "bits," but with his accent it sounded like "beats."

Sandy Meisner disagreed with Lee also. What's important, he said, is the interpersonal relationship between the actors on the stage, which is really a Vakhtangov principle.

Lee felt that later in his life Stanislavsky was searching for and making up for what he hadn't done in the beginning. Stanislavsky realized that he had left out the carrying out of tasks. People came out on stage and were static, so he added actions, physical actions or mental actions. At the Group Theatre, Strasberg never ignored actions. There are three component elements to acting: the carrying out of tasks, the interpersonal relationship between the particular actors onstage, plus the creation of sensory objects to ground an actor in a reality. Lee always focused equally on those components. People erroneously said his work was all sensory and all emotional. I never got that message from him. When we worked on a Sensory

Exercise, if an emotional element arose, fine, but sometimes it was physical. We were not out to have emotional breakthroughs and psychic breaks.

In my estimation some of the most important work that Lee did was in the area of relaxation. Lee claimed that the inability to relax and anticipation were the two biggest problems of the actor. The first area in which there has been a major change in both Lee's work and my own has been in relaxation. In the beginning we would sit in a chair and literally try to fall asleep. Then later at the Strasberg Institute when Lee was exploring kinesis, he started using movement during relaxation. That would open up the body physically and allow emotions to come pouring out. Lee started using this technique after reading Lowen's *The Betrayal of the Body*. It's gotten to the point now where some teachers use movement for the sake of movement.

My understanding of Strasberg's work was that nothing in the training should be done to form new habits in the actor. You are trying to break down habits and mannerisms so that each character that the actor plays has a whole new set of mannerisms. So what I have now incorporated in my work is having my students sit in chairs trying to fall asleep and moving their bodies easily and subtly (as they would on stage) in an effort to locate the areas of tension and break down the habit of how they relax, because even that can become habitual.

Ideally, what you want is to be able to get into any position on stage and be in a relaxed state. I am not talking about lethargy or somnambulism. I am talking about the excessive use of energies. If I were a dancer and was extremely tense, I couldn't do more than two or three combinations. I want the student to use only the amount of energy that he needs to move. Stanislavsky saw that actors in a relaxed state seemed easy and that emotion and logic flowed easily from them.

As students begin to relax, the emotions are often elicited. The first sign is that the eyelids will begin to flutter. I then tell the students, "Make a sound from the chest." When they do that I will often hear an emotion connected with it; they may sound angry or sad. I ask them if something happened today, if something upset them before they came to class. Is there something coming up that they are anticipating? Is it that they are onstage and feel themselves being judged? Often that alone can be the cause. They ask themselves these questions and often people start crying or get very angry as they make the connection with what's affecting them. As the students start expressing what they are feeling, they relax; they clean the slate, going to a zero state. That ensures that when they start the sensory exercises, whatever response comes up in them will be purely from the exercises and not some extraneous matter they brought in with them. This, by the way, is not only a training device. Relaxation is done every time they get up to do an exercise and during the preparation of a scene or a monologue. It is then continually checked upon throughout the piece.

The students in my class also learn to relax without a lot of visible movement. At times I don't want to see them actively working on an exercise. This comes in very handy on a film set when an actor is between takes and wants to go off into a corner and do his work but doesn't want to look like some idiot doing that Method exercise and have the crew make fun of him. So actors learn to do it surreptitiously. They should be able to do it publicly without anyone knowing that they are doing it. If they need more than a minute, they should go into the dressing room or, if need be, the bathroom. Unfortunately, most directors don't understand what an actor needs to be able to create.

I once went up for a part and the director said, "Oh, you're one of those Method actors. You're not going to do any of that crap here, are you?" I said, "Don't worry. You won't be able to tell that I am working. If you know that I am working, then I am not working correctly." And that's what I try to teach my students.

My classes are broken down into two two-hour sessions. Two hours are devoted to exercise work. I have expanded what I do in the class to include the Song and Dance Exercise, which is one of Strasberg's most important exercises. I also do commercials, cold readings, character study, and improvisation. After the relaxation period, students start on sensory exercises. We all respond to sensory stimuli without realizing it. If I play some music and it reminds you of an old boyfriend, it's the music that is triggering your feelings.

This kind of triggering was studied by Pavlov. Most people don't realize that Strasberg was a Behaviorist, a Pavlovian, and not a Freudian.

Absolutely. Lee's emphasis was in the doing. People have all these strange ideas about what he taught. The students are put through a series of sensory exercises to discover how they respond to certain stimuli, what makes them angry, sad, etc., which is highly personal. Different students may respond to the same stimuli differently. We then use these exercises while doing scenes to create realities for ourselves that coincide with the responses of the character. While a good deal of class time is spent in the creation of these exercises, it is still only a part of the work that goes into a scene.

The sensory exercises that I saw in class and as they evolved were very simple but very meaningful, so I try to stick as closely as I can to them. Lee had students work on creating a cup of coffee. Why a cup of coffee? You need all five senses to create that simple thing. So what a teacher is looking for in that first exercise is how many of the actor's senses are working.

The second exercise is generally looking into a sensory mirror and trying to see yourself putting on makeup or shaving. Here the teacher is discerning if the student is merely following a sequence, or really exploring the objects sensorially and if the person can see himself in the mirror or not. This reveals whether he is a subjective or a nonsubjective person. Subjectivity in this sense refers to a person whose feelings do not get expressed; the more deeply he feels something, the more inward it goes. He is the kind of person who goes into the corner and broods and then explodes over nothing. When a student says he can't see himself in the mirror, that's a sign to me that I must help him to get the emotion out rather than sit on it, as is his habit.

If a person doesn't have a problem in life expressing certain emotions, it stands to reason that he shouldn't have trouble expressing them on stage. The difference is that the audience can become a barrier. It's my job to get the student to respond and act as fully on stage as he does in life. If he has a problem in life expressing certain emotions, he goes to therapy to work it out, which is not what I am there to do, but I can help him get over self-consciousness, especially through the use of private moments. Laurie Hull describes this well in her book *Strasberg's Method*.

After shaving, the next sensory exercise is putting on your shoes and socks. So the order is (1) coffee, (2) mirror and shaving or makeup, and (3) shoes and socks. Next is looking in a full-length mirror and putting on undergarments. Often people do not really look at their bodies. I look for whether they are self-conscious or even inhibited. Then next is sensorially creating three different pieces of fabrics. These are all externals in the sense that the actor is visibly manipulating the objects as he creates them. After that students create sunshine and actually try to feel a sense of the sun on themselves.

You and I know about psychosomatic illnesses, about false pregnancies, and so on. These are all sensory responses. You know that you can put a piece of ice on someone's skin and say you are burning him with a poker and the skin will respond as if it were burned. If the mind can do something like that, it can also create a feeling of sunshine. As a student you might say, "Why do I have to do all this?" Why? Because on stage you are not really going to be in love with the leading man, you are not really going to be poisoned. You have to believe it. If *you* believe it, the audience will believe it. If *you* believe it, you will act within that environment in a truthful enough way to convince the audience, which has also suspended its belief for this period of time.

The funny thing is that as you create an object sensorially, everything else falls into place. From this stimulus that you know isn't real, suddenly all the other false things become real and you start behaving truthfully. Stanislavsky saw that the difference between the good actor and the great actor was the ability to be relaxed, to stimulate oneself, and to be private in public. This is nothing new. There are stories of the Kabuki master who sent his protégé to walk in the snow in his bare feet so that he could then come onstage and create it properly. For years actors have always tried to find things that would help them create reality.

But it must be noted that it is not the successful completion of these exercises that's important. It's *trying* to use them. Even if you get 50%, it's better than 0%. The exercises also put you into a state in which inspiration can take place. By the way, Strasberg once said that the use of drugs and alcohol that is so prevalent in our profession often comes out of a search for excellence, because the actor knows that when he is relaxed and easy, things happen. So the actor says, "If I take a drink, I will relax." Unfortunately, there is no control over that, and before you know it the very thing you were trying to achieve has been eaten away. It's such an epidemic in our business today. It's shameful the amount of talent that is being blown away—sometimes not from a negative search, but from a lack of craft.

When the actor works on creating sunshine he is really getting to the first internal exercise, because the teacher cannot see what is going on. Then we work on pain, and then exercises involving single senses: taste, smell, seeing, and hearing. Hearing is the first exercise in which I begin to work on verbal patterns. Then we do sensory work that involves the external body and overall sensations, like showers, rain, sunburn, being drunk or ill. After that we go on to personal objects, anything that might have some sentimental value for a student.

How do you instruct students to work on a personal object?

The student examines it, trying to create its weight, the feel and color of it. I don't want a student to work on the real thing, but the sensory object. Often the student already knows what emotion is going to be elicited by that object. It's so important to train the sensory response, because it's so easy for actors to work just for the result, just for the emotion. Then they wind up saying that the object doesn't work for them anymore. If they work with just the senses, the senses will keep feeding them over and over again.

At sunshine it gets complicated because we add a monologue. When I studied with Lee I was with him for three years before I was allowed to use any actual material with the sensory exercises. When he said, "Now do the exercise and put a monologue to it," it became a problem. This brings us back to the second problem of the actor: anticipation. If, as an actor, I know what I am going to say, how can I make it sound as if I am saying it for the first time? If the character is responding to a given situation with a certain emotion, the emotion will color the words. Change the emotion and the meaning of the words changes. Punctuation is a writer's device. No one talks with punctuation. There has never been a writer who could write something so that two people would say it in the same way. The only thing a writer can do is create a character in a situation. It's the same thing for the actor. The character is in the situation. If that situation makes him angry, the words come out angry. The language a writer employs is his style.

Everyone in my class learns a monologue and he or she learns it without meaning or punctuation. It's generally a non-Shakespeare and nonverse monologue. The students start to work on a sensory exercise and it brings up an emotion. I ask them to make a sound so I know how it's affecting them. I believe sound is the purest form of emotional expression. Then I will tell them to give their monologue in gibberish. Then I tell them to go back to the words. I observe to see if they allow the emotion to color the words in the pattern the gibberish elicited or if they revert to the way they learned it originally. What I am trying to do is break down the verbal patterns that people unconsciously learn and allow them to speak extemporaneously, *with* the lines that they have memorized, to allow their emotions, not their intellect, to take over and color the lines.

In the next exercise the students begin to work on creating an overall sensation while they are working on a personal object. This leads to two different reactions. Now I will take them over the same lines with each of these different sensory exercises individually. Ideally, the way they say the lines will be altered because the exercise will be changed and affect them differently. Then I'll tell them to put both stimuli together. That way I get people laughing and crying at the same time because they are combining exercises. The words are now coming out in a third way. Then I get students doing four exercises at the same time and also doing an everyday task, like making the bed or having a cup of coffee—or we may impose an animal on it or a character study. You may ask, "Why are you doing all this? They will never have to do all this in a play." Well, if you want to train to run a mile competitively, you run twenty miles every day. Lee never went to that many exercises at one time; he never used gibberish that early in the work. That's another area in which I feel I took the work a little further.

Working on four sensory exercises at the same time, such as an overall sensation, a smell, seeing somebody, and a personal object, is preparing students for doing an Affective Memory, where they have to use all five senses. Many teachers give new students an Affective Memory and talk them through it, and they have big emotional breakthroughs. But then the students can't do it by themselves on stage. The teacher has to be there. If students are trained sensorially, they can do an Affective Memory whenever they want. I also do the same work with singers. Instead of monologues, they use songs and arias.

How do you use this sensory work in scene work?

In *Alice Doesn't Live Here Anymore*, Ellen Burstyn is having a good time with a friend when the phone rings. She has to pick it up, hear that her husband has been killed, and break apart. You think that's easy, going from one emotion to another like that? She could have done it by creating an Affective Memory that gave her the emotion that was applicable to the character at that time. Strasberg stressed that it wasn't important for the Affective Memory or any object or substitution to be similar to the event in the play. Anything that will give an actor the same emotional response as the character is valid.

If I had to play a scene in which I had to cry over my father's coffin, and I used my real father's funeral, I would get angry (as I actually did in life), not cry. So I would use something that made me cry even though it wasn't a similar event.

Why, then, the effort to be yourself on the stage? So you can more easily recognize the difference between you and the character. Where you and the character are the same, you leave yourself alone.

Where you and the character are different, you need an adjustment or an exercise to give you what the character has or do what he does. Most of the material that you are confronted with as an actor is easy to do. But what if I had to play Caligula? I've never killed anybody, and Caligua not only kills, but he enjoys it. However, I know I do enjoy swatting mosquitoes and smashing them before they bite me. I get off on it. How do you apply that same emotion to killing a person? Well, it's not a person anymore. When I hear the buzzing of a mosquito, I start to get excited and annoyed and the actor becomes a giant mosquito to me. I can take that emotion that is mine and expand it into a character trait. So I'm still being myself, but using that emotion in a different area.

So the sensory work and the Affective Memory work are only to be used when the actor can't use the circumstances of the character.

It's a circle. First you read a piece of material and it affects you and you respond. Then you start working on the material and you find you're not responding anymore. Then you have to get back to your initial reactions. Actors should always have an exercise ready so they can re-create the initial response, not imitate it. And by the way, the more training you get the less you need to get turned on to the stimuli of the script. Often it's a simple thing like tasting the coffee that will do it. After a while you need less, not more.

You use Lee's Song and Dance Exercise. Could you describe it?

It's a very simple exercise. Lee originally devised it for singers and then he found that the same problem affected all performers, actors as well as singers.

In the first part of the exercise, the actor is asked to stand aligned, so that he can breathe properly, in front of the class and make eye contact with the people in the audience and without moving sing a simple song. He is then asked to intone the song note by note and syllable by syllable, taking a couple of breaths in between, and holding each note for relatively the same length of time. The sound is to be strong and from the chest. At the same time, he is asked to allow himself to express whatever emotion he is feeling at that given time. Sounds simple enough. It's very hard to do.

Now what does the actor have to do in a play? He generally is asked to sit or stand onstage (although in a lot of films today he is asked to lie down), and he is asked to say words fully from the chest that he has memorized while making contact with his partner or the audience, and to control his movements and allow whatever he is feeling at the time to express itself in the words. Therefore, this exercise is the acting problem in a nutshell. But there is nothing to hide behind, no scene or character. Anything an actor cannot do in this exercise he will not be able to do onstage. If he can't go moment to moment in the exercise, chances are he couldn't do it onstage; if he can't control his body, chances are he couldn't do it onstage either. But since the actor is being judged, suddenly you can see all the things affecting him from his present and past. You show me a girl who was the tallest in her class, and I'll show you a girl who unconsciously stands in a way so as to minimize her height. That's what happens at the beginning of this exercise.

As an actor begins to make sound, I sense the person and what he is feeling. I ask him questions, but I don't want him to answer me, just to think about them and to make a sound. As he makes a sound, often an emotion comes up, because he is thinking about what is upsetting him. What I have done with this that's different from what Strasberg did is that when the person starts to have a feeling and, for instance, cries, I then teach him how to rechannel the emotion. I say, "Take these tears and rechannel them into anger or laughter." He goes right into it because the organism is open, you see; the veil is lifted. I teach the person how to take his emotional temperature before he walks into a scene. After all, the actor is his own instrument. If he is aware that he is feeling angry and he has to go out and be happy, he can rechannel that emotion and go on and play what he needs to.

In the second part of the exercise the actor sings the song again, note by note and syllable by syllable, but this time it's done in a short explosive sound. He also starts any movement and repeats it. If he repeats it seven, eight times, he's created a rhythm. He then has to sing the song independently of the physical rhythm that he has established—when his will says sound, and not when the rhythm in his body demands it. One time the sound may come out on the third movement, the next time on the second, and so on. Then I say, "Change the movement," and the actor has to create another rhythm, and the song will come out of that. We are trying to separate the voice from the body, training actors to use them individually. This Song and Dance Exercise, more than any other, calls on the intuition and the perception of the teacher.

So the song and dance is a way for students to get in touch with their moment-to-moment feelings and impulses and react to them.

Yes. It puts them in touch with what they are feeling and trains them to control and use those feelings.

I also do the Mirror Exercise, where actors stand facing each other and "mirror" each other's movements and facial expressions. There is a lot of psychological information I can get from watching that exercise. For instance, which actor likes to lead and which likes to mirror a behavior? Does one actor monopolize the exercise because he never gives the other person a chance to lead? Does he see what he is getting from his partner? Is he or she simply a reactor? Is he always depending on his partner? The Mirror Exercise helps you when you have to fit into a cast in a play that's already been performing, when you have to replace someone. It enables you to fit into other people's rhythms, to do scenes that have already been set because they've already been directed. So this is a seemingly simple theater game, but it has many manifestations and repercussions for actors. In Viola Spolin's book, she used this to find out how well an actor could mirror another person's movement. But there are other skills to be learned from it. This is how we integrate psychology, theater games, etc., into a craft to help the actor. Only artists, by the way, have the audacity to think that they create wholly from themselves. A scientist would never deny his debt to his forerunners, would never claim that he discovered something on his own. Well, actors are not any different.

What I do is based on the principles that Strasberg handed down. They weren't written in stone; they were a way of looking at acting problems. A lot of teachers use these kinds of exercises, use the sequence, and that's all. They don't really understand what problem is being solved, what to look for in the student when they are doing it. Teaching is asking yourself, "What am I giving a student at this specific time that will answer his need?" A lot of teachers don't know what is behind the exercises, as I tried to explain with the Mirror Exercise. I spent a lot of time talking theory to Lee, asking him what specific exercises were designed for, and that's what I've kept till today. Most teachers in colleges and even professional workshops talk about sensory work, but don't actually do it. They believe in it, they say, but they don't teach their students how to do the exercises.

How do you help your students learn to work on comedy?

I started out as a stand-up comic and always had a feel for it, but could never break it down for myself. The best theory of comedy I've come across is that comedy is real people in a real situation behaving in an unreal way. For instance, in *The Odd Couple*, one guy can't be a "little" messy and the other guy a "little" neat. That wouldn't work. So the behavior has to be unreal, but done in a real way. You take it to the extreme. There is a fine line between comedy, farce, and burlesque. Farce is real people in an unreal situation behaving in a real way (as in the movie *Kind Hearts and Coronets*) while burlesque, I believe, is unreal people in a real situation behaving in an unreal way. I once played a very neat character, and I had to clean everything in my environment. So if I was in a restaurant, I decided to clean my silverware, the table, the chairs, etc. That's comedy. Now take it a step further. The waiter comes over and my character starts cleaning off the waiter—that's taking it to the next step, and that's burlesque. That's what Sid Caesar as a tramp would have done. All comedy is logic taken to an extreme, while tragedy is illogical behavior.

How do you use improvisations?

There are three basic improvisations that I use for scene work with students. In the first I ask the student to do the scene with the dialogue, but putting himself in the situation and reacting to the circumstances as he would himself. Then he will know where he and the character differ. Wherever he differs, he will have to make an adjustment. In the second improvisation I tell him to act out the whole scene without the dialogue. He can grunt, whistle, anything he wants. What does this do? It tells him what actions he should be taking during the scene.

He didn't come into the environment to play a scene, but to do something, and the scene interrupts that action. Sometimes I will have actors do the lines in gibberish. Gibberish will force communication between them. They know what the lines are, but it will also solidify for them what the emotion is.

There is something else I use that Strasberg innovated. Instead of the lines, I will have students talk out the inner monologue of their characters, and sometimes, when an actor comes up against a block at a particular moment, I will ask him to go through the scene saying the lines, but adding his own feelings and thoughts—not the character's, but his own. That's very interesting because often the actor is blocking something he or she is afraid of and if he talks it out, he can get to what it is.

Improvisation is an interesting tool. I remember reading that the first actress who worked on Hedda Gabler acted out scenes that were not in the script because doing just the scenes in the play didn't give her enough knowledge about Hedda. I also ask students to do that.

The other improvisations I do are really from theater games: exits and entrances—where you are coming from, where you are, and where you are going. You know, an actor never makes an entrance. He is never coming from the wings. He is always coming from another place. I used about two dozen different ones, like character studies and animal exercises, but time doesn't permit going into all of them.

Are there any approaches to acting that you disapprove of?

One of my pet peeves is that the acting student today is being taken advantage of by many so-called teachers who are not accredited, have not had accredited training, and have never studied to be actors or ever acted or directed. What they teach, then, is opinion—theirs. Students do a scene and they tell them how they think it should be done. They don't teach a craft. A lot of these teachers are casting directors or agents and claim they teach soap opera acting, film acting, or commercial acting. That has nothing to do with technique. And the hidden promise is that if students study with them, they can get them a job. You might ask, "So what's the damage?" The damage is, apart from it being dishonest, that these teachers take money away from young actors who would otherwise use it to study with legitimate teachers who could teach them a craft and a technique they could use to make a living. They are robbing young actors of a livelihood. There is an old saying: "If you give a man a fish, you feed him; if you teach him how to fish, you teach him how to feed himself." These people are hurting potential artists and destroying our business. They should be ashamed of themselves.

What advice would you give someone just starting out in acting?

When you look for a teacher, see if you can audit the class for free or for a single fee. Ask about the teacher's background. Who has he or she developed? Get training and keep training. You train for the future, not today. And decide what you expect from a teacher. Realize that a teacher cannot make you talented. He can only help you develop what talent you already possess. A teacher cannot make you an artist. He can only give you a technique. How you use that technique makes you an artist. A teacher's task is to recognize what is individual about a student and quickly and fully develop it. A teacher should give you roots and wings.

Gerry Goodstein

Elinor Renfield

Elinor Renfield is a New York–based acting teacher and director. In addition to her private classes, she teaches at the Circle in the Square Theatre School and has conducted classes at New York University, Brooklyn College, and Hunter College. As a director, Ms. Renfield has had productions at Circle Repertory Theatre, Theatre for the New City, New York Shakespeare Festival, and Ensemble Studio Theatre, as well as in major regional theaters across the country.

Ms. Renfield was trained at Hunter College, Emerson, and The Central School in London. She uses her own training as a departure point and focuses on action in her teaching. She believes that when an actor builds a part he has to locate what she calls "the unspoken truth of the character, the unrevealed truth that every character comes on stage with—something he or she cannot say. . . . I think a great deal of what action is consists of resisting that unspoken truth."

How did you get started teaching acting?

My training was essentially organizing the chaos of my needs to express myself. I was a child actress and worked with Muriel Sharon at the 92nd Street Y. She was a great legend. This was in the 1950s. She was an ancient Bohemian with a gift for bringing natural dramatic talent out of children if it was there. If it wasn't, she gave them the ability to articulate their feelings to the degree that they could work with each other on the stage. The material she used was often very European. She had a real love for the commedia del l'arte and French farce. We would do improvisations, of course. We did improvisations around stories, and literature, and poetry. The material was often biblical or mythological, so our imaginations were stretched and honed. Those early days were very vital to me. She had a production group in addition to her classes and you got to perform at the Kaufman Auditorium at the 92nd Street Y. Then she had an even more professional group called the Pocket Players, a group of young adults, actor/artists. They had a kind of gestalt approach in that they painted, they costumed, they invented, they did everything. I worked with them as a child and we toured the city and suddenly I was in children's theater.

I was also a dancer and studying with the company that was known as the Merry Go Rounders. They were the great modern dancers at the 92nd Street Y who did programs for children. They were offshoots of Doris Humphrey, who was a disciple of Martha Graham. At the Y at that time Dylan Thomas was writing *Under Milk Wood* in the basement, so it was a gold mine of theatrical energy. In my dance classes we were learning to contract and expand in our bare feet while my other little friends were doing ballet at Park Avenue schools. That is a very clear image in my mind. I was trained in the mold of progressive liberal thought. I never had classic ballet or acting lessons or elocution lessons. From an early age I was given a freedom, an improvisational feeling, a feeling of releasing one's most subjective self into the material.

Did you study with any of the popular New York acting teachers at that time?

No. I never did the rounds of any of them. What I did was go to the High School of Performing Arts. That's where I got my first taste of the Stanislavsky method—and I hated it. It felt derivative. I hated the idea that I had to follow the formula of having to write my objective and subtext down on my script. This is comparable to the interpreters of Freud. There are great original thinkers and by the time their ideas get to you—a thirteen-year-old at the High School of Performing Arts being taught by a frustrated out-of-work director—it's not really the Stanislavsky system anymore. It's somebody else's system and it's a way of subduing all the wonderful chaos of adolescence into some kind of form.

I went on to Emerson College, which was a continuation of Performing Arts. We would rehearse in somebody's living room in order to present a scene in class, not knowing what to rehearse for, then come to class, where somebody would criticize our execution of our objective or the way we handled the objects. It seemed to me that there should be areas of real specialty where one class would simply be about creating a character from the way you work with objects, or another class would be about nonverbal work, or another about improvisational work or sensory and emotional memory exercises, and another about text and action. It's very difficult as a teacher now to get in all the things that have to be gotten in when, in fact, with a three-hour class, you never really get more than twenty-five minutes per scene anyway. What I can give as direction depends on what my focus is, and it can't be everything. I felt that in my training through Performing Arts and Emerson, both of which had good theater training programs with big productions, the emphasis was too scattered and too imitative to be inspirational. I have never been in a classroom situation in which the teacher was a great master and something in me as an artist was really released.

I took my junior year at Emerson abroad at The Central School of Speech and Drama in London and immediately got turned on to Creative Dramatics, which was a program used in the school system to release the imaginations of children by improvising situations around lyrics and stories. I would read children a story and then they would act it out. You would essentially be teaching them about conflict and obstacles without calling it that.

In my senior year I began to read Viola Spolin seriously and that was to me the essence of what I was trying to say. It was wonderful to work with children using her material. I loved the theater games. I loved teaching children to act and making theater with them through improvisation, through a psychological approach, through short stories, with no script, no technique.

After Emerson I immediately started teaching in the humanities program at Hunter High School and then made my classrooms a continuation of this. I came out of a mishmash of training and rejected it all.

Story Theatre and Peter Brook's *Midsummer Night's Dream* were happening at this time and that's what I was drawn to. Every time I saw an Actors Studio production I felt as if I were being sewn into a very boring environment. It felt very archaic and I must say I preferred bare feet and gymnastics.

Then I ended up taking over the children's acting program at the 92nd Street Y while I was taking my master's degree in theater at Hunter College. I did that for about three years. During that time I restructured all the classes, but essentially continued Muriel's thinking and used improvisational storytelling as a way of teaching acting. This was in 1971 and I was also getting very interested in the Open Theatre and Andre Gregory's group, The Manhattan Project. I felt he was doing the same thing I was doing, but with adults.

I began to bring in more experimental material for my students to work with—Harold Pinter, for example. I would take the names of the characters off the script, referring to the parts as X and Y, and let the students define the who, what, why, where, and when of the circumstances. From scene to scene a new event would emerge. I was helping them see that everything lay in how they interpreted the text, and if they changed the circumstances, the interpretation would change, and that, to me, was wonderful.

When I was working with these kids, instead of using a Sense Memory Exercise to create a physical environment, I would say, "Now we are going to create a cold day. We start by working on the 'where.' I want you two students to say the alphabet back and forth while I give you an environment to find for yourself." I might say, "Create a subway environment in which you've been waiting for a train for two hours, with water dripping on the platform." They would find that cold. I didn't have to stop and say, "Now feel the cold."

How do you begin working with a new student?

I believe that what happens when an actor builds a part is that he locates what I call "the unspoken truth of the character," the unrevealed truth that every character comes on stage with— something he or she cannot say. The actor has to understand what the threat to himself would be if he revealed it. Even if I told you I hated you or loved you, there would still be something in my heart that I cannot reveal. I'm always interested in finding out what that is because I think a great deal of what action is consists of resisting that unspoken truth. Again, it's not that you play the unspoken truth. What makes good acting is how many different channels of information an actor is pumping into his performance, his interpretation.

Harold Clurman once said that really good acting and directing are all connected to the degree of interrogation; the more you ask of the script, the more it will yield. You might say, "Yes, but then the actor needs technique to make that possible." That may be true, but I look at some actors—Judd Hirsch, for instance. I don't know where he was trained, but I do know that in certain parts with certain tasks to be done, he's tops. Then I look at some of the people who went to Yale or studied for years with someone who taught a "method," and they may be very good at sweating or screaming but that's all.

What practical instruction do you give students to help them develop a character?

A student brings in a piece of material and we talk. The first thing I ask is what I think any good acting teacher will ask: literally, what does the piece say? I hate you, I love you, whatever. Is it a love scene, an appeal, a tragic moment, what? That grounds the text in an objective reality. From there the given circumstances are defined. For instance, it is May, it is hot, we are in the living room, I am forty-six, and I am sick. That is indisputable information.

The next step is to move into the subjective realm. That's where action and objective come in. There is no answer in the back of the book when it comes to developing a character. It is drawn totally from the actor's subjective interpretation of the action of the scene. It is the accumulation of the action in a scene that constitutes character.

When actors first start studying with me they are a bit confused because I ask them to use their minds. I welcome them to a class where no impulses are required, no sense memory work or emotional memory work. I trust that they've done that. I'm a director and they are actors. I work with them in the same way I work in a rehearsal. When actors pick up a scene and start working on it, I have to go in there as a director with an idea about where the scene comes from and what it wants to achieve. That's what I do with them. I make it clear on the first day. If they need work or want work on the organic development of emotional impulses or sensory impulses, on the expression or rage, freeing themselves to find the realities, I can recommend about five superlative teachers who do that. What I do is help them pick up a script and get ready to act— meaning plucking an action out of the script—and trust that all their subconscious homework will come back to them. We start by deciding what their character is pursuing in a scene.

If I am going to direct *The Seagull*, for example, I'm not interested in when the last time was that an actor went to the bathroom. Something is wrong if an actor needs that in order to play the fact that the scene is about not letting yourself lose control. If I work with an actress playing Nina, we have to find out what Nina is resisting. What she cannot do in the last act is go out of control because there is a threat to her objective, her need to break away. It doesn't matter if she asks about the objective first or the unspoken truth first or if she asks what she needs. I don't call it an objective, by the way. I call it "a desired response." It's more specific than an objective. When an actress says, "I need him to free me, to say go," it's a different way of saying, "I need to get out of here." It makes it more specific and dependent on the other characters in the play.

You mean it always involves a relationship?

That's right. There have been times when I have actually called the action of the scene the "stragegy." That's how conscious I think it is. As the character you know what you want, you know that there is a threat to revealing something, and you know that you have to find a way to prevent something from getting out, and to get something else. That's how manipulative acting is on a certain level.

I often use a subtext exercise if a student can't get it. Somebody was doing a monologue today from *Loose Ends*. This character thinks his wife is sleeping with somebody else. He calls up a mutual female friend of his and his wife's and says. "This is the problem. I think my wife is out with another guy." The piece eventually comes around to him propositioning this friend on the phone. The first thing this actor did was go for the proposition as the thematic line of the piece. I said, "Look. He loves his wife and he's really deeply hurt. What he is not really saying to this friend is 'Ouch, I'm hurting.' Let's try this. Get down on your knees and just for one minute feel what it's like to beg for love. Now try this piece again and explore it from the subtext, which is pain and hurt and needing love. Find where in this piece your character is begging to be held, for affection, for comfort. This is an exercise to help you understand what the character cannot reveal—that he wants some comfort but is afraid of revealing the vulnerability of pain." If this actor says the scene is about getting a woman to go to bed with him, he has to ask himself, "What is not being revealed?" This approach may come from my early romance with the Andre Gregorys and the Joe Chaikins, but I never saw them understand a piece of text to mean anything other than a point of departure. I am trying to get actors to challenge the actions of a scene, to see it as something more than just their moment-to-moment impulses. If they don't, they have nothing to rehearse.

Suppose a rehearsal is about finding out how to keep myself from punching you in the face and I have to do that in a nineteenth-century drawing room comedy. Now, the unspoken truth of a Gwendolen or Cecily in *The Importance of Being Earnest* is something really ugly, vengeful and competitive, something really uncivilized in an era when that was not allowed. To me the real comedic value in all those plays is the dichotomy between the unspoken truth and the action. Something extremely uncivil is being resisted. It's like watching an actor have a bad stomach cramp but having to play the scene. It's that profound when you really know that the scene is about not letting others know how angry you are. If an actor looks at it from that point of view, he has something to focus on, and other things fall into place.

Is this a technique that you use when you work on comedy?

It's not a question of comedy and drama, but of style and the writer. Directing a Noel Coward comedy is very different from directing a Neil Simon comedy because this is where your basic homework comes in, in the biographical data. Noel Coward comedies are written as a kind of joust, and the action is in scoring points. A certain exercise that I've done with Noel Coward is to find the action in the dialogue that is related to the competition for winning points, and not worry about anything else until I've seen what's in there. There was a time when conversation was about not telling the truth. Noel Coward is almost a perfect paradigm for my exercises in that it's such a far stretch from what's really happening to what's being revealed. It's stretched so far that the emotional interaction is related to who has been able to outscore whom. The characters stay in the scene in order to score another point as opposed to achieving some other objective.

I might work with people on material with more external obstacles; say, you are having a furious fight with your husband at a public function and people are looking at you sitting at a little table amidst seventy-four other tables. This way students can get a feeling for how to keep a charming exterior while they have a fuming interior. I'll always find an applicable improvisation to help liberate students from the text if I feel that they are having a hard time making a leap into the subjective text.

Do students use the text or their own words in these exercises?

It depends on the actor and how instinctively he picks up the direction. If an actor has access to self, I can ask him to improvise, to get into what begging feels like, for instance. If he has problems with that, I'll have him use the script or I'll give him a situation. I might ask him to beg the president to stop nuclear testing. I mean, anyone can get on the ground and beg for that. In other words, there is a way into everyone's sense of what the scene means. There is an "as if" for every student. It's a question of feeling out what each one needs and helping him to get in touch with it. These exercises are about touching the truth of a scene before you find the mask for it, finding the pain and then sitting down and playing a seduction scene with a beautiful woman when what you really need is for her to tell you you're great and your wife is crazy. A good actor intuitively understands how to put a mask over something.

A lot of events that actors play—"I am coming from a fight with my mother," for example—provide them with a launching place that is not subjective. It's given in the script. But why should actors play the obvious? If they ask themselves, "What *action* am I coming from?" that's not so obvious.

By the way, I do believe that a good playwright instinctively knows this—that the merging of the unspoken truths is the event of the play.

Think of Arkadina in *The Seagull*. Her unspoken truth throughout the whole play is how she despises her son, who is always pulling at her. How guilty and despicable he makes her feel. So she spends most of the play resisting that unspoken truth and being the perfect mother.

Let's say I'm working on a scene that requires me to fall in love— the balcony scene from Romeo and Juliet, *for example. If you don't see that happening, how would you help me work on it?*

The first thing I would do is interpret. I would say, "What does falling in love mean to you? Is love surrender, is it safety, what does it mean? Let's talk this through a little bit before you have to get up there and fall in love." Then I would ask, "What do you, as the character, feel has been keeping you from falling in love all along? If you have defined falling in love as a surrender, then in the course of the scene you have to yield. As someone trained in dance, I know that if you are going to release, you have to understand what a contraction is. If the scene is about falling in love, you want to know what is pulling you in the opposite direction. The way to act a scene like that is to uncover the source of the opposition, release yourself from it, and go toward something else. That's how I would work it.

I would say, "Take the given here: fear of being hurt. Let's start with that as your unspoken truth. You have felt strong passionate feelings toward this man for a long time, and in this scene you surrender to him—which means that you have to give up your mask against fear. Your unspoken truth is the fear of being hurt; the action of the scene is the way you resist being hurt. Now, how would your character cover up her fear? she might be evasive, or chatty. How would she show somebody that she was not vulnerable? Let's explore that." Then I would do exercises around that. For instance, "With this character, I want you to improvise making dinner for him, or taking a walk in the rain with him. Take the same situation as the one in the script, one in which you protect yourself from the surrender, and find that as an action, as an activity. It's not just an emotional event. Emotion is the by-product of action. Exhaustion, fatigue, depression, and joy all come as by-products of playing actions."

Do you have a procedure for helping students become more expressive? What if I need to play fear, for instance, and I can't?

Of course, I will encourage students to use their own experience, to get in touch with it and remember it. But I don't believe you can play an emotion. What I would say is that the tension in the scene is the result of one thing resisting another. I would try to define for the actor what is happening in terms of an action, not a feeling. Somebody is pulling a gun on you, you are in a dark alley, it's late at night, and you are terrified that you are going to lose your life. What is the action, the resistance, the opposition? What you would like to do is kill this other guy, so maybe what the scene is really about is resisting your desire to kill this guy. Perhaps that's where the fear comes in: it's the part of you that would be released as a killer. This kind of analysis produces an interesting tension. Play someone getting mugged who wants to kill the mugger and knows that if she shows aggression she'll be killed. The scene may evolve into one about resisting your own aggression in that moment. Now, that's interesting.

How do you help students cope with stage fright?

I yell. I say, "What the hell are you doing in this class if you have stage fright?" What can I do? Sometimes I get very tyrannical with certain students. They need it and ask for it. That's their unspoken truth. They are provoking me into doing that and I do it for them. Others are genuinely needy of a certain kind of help. I can't help them on that level, but I can send them somewhere else.

Do you teach relaxation techniques?

I think all of that is wonderful. But when was the last time a director said in a rehearsal, "Now we are going to spend a half-hour relaxing." We have eight hours a day to rehearse and twenty-one days to mount *The Cherry Orchard.* We don't have the time for you guys to relax. If you want to use your relaxation technique, come to rehearsal a half-hour early. What I do with students is essentially what I do in a rehearsal. I urge them to come in with some degree of preparation, ready to roll. They don't have time to warm up. The fact of the matter is that there is a certain point at which the student has to learn to change gear, jump in, and act.

Are there any approaches to acting that you disapprove of?

By the way, I don't disapprove of Stanislavsky. I'm sure he was a genius and I'm sure Lee Strasberg was. That's not what I objected to before. I read *My Life in Art* and I think that Stanislavsky's understanding of action, by the way, has been grossly misinterpreted by many teachers who don't see the genius of what he was saying. He was a contemporary of Freud, Einstein, and Marx. He was part of the twentieth-century movement that wanted to strip down the facade of reality. He was a great philosopher and his particular method of finding the truth of behavior was extremely applicable to the kind of actor who came from an artificial mode. So you got the slice of life with his approach. But since then we have TV and that has destroyed the slice-of-life approach for everybody. If the world moves in action–reaction cycles, we've come full circle. We need another way of finding the truth of a scene than making it more lifelike.

The true nature of man's aggression was only beginning to be revealed at the turn of the century. First it took Freud to uncover the true nature of the animal in all of us, then the industrial revolution to take us into this century with an understanding of our genocidal lust. How, in the late 1980s, can you not bring that information into the subtext, knowing that in every scene there has to be some degree of aggression, of violence? Even in a play like *The Philadelphia Story* an understanding of aggression has to exist and has to be so subdued that it creates an eccentricity of behavior in its attempt to conceal it.

As a director, do you give your students advice on how to work with directors?

Yes. I always say a good actor is a director. The problem with most actors, as I perceive it, is that they never look at the whole body of the play and how they function integrally with the other people. They immediately put yellow ink over their parts and follow that path right through the play as if that were all the play is about. How often, as an actor, do you step back and look at the obligation of your character to the whole play? The idea of the play has shaped your character, and you have to understand the idea of the scene and how you and this character together are bringing an idea forward—not just a series of emotional moments.

How do you help students create a character?

One exercise that helps starts with the class sitting around in a circle. I ask each person to describe himself in five verbs, to put himself in the third person to objectify it all. Who are you based on what you do? Give me five actions that sum you up. This forces a student to decode a simple description. If someone tells a student, "I've got a wonderful part for you. It's a female who is five feet five inches, dark haired, smart, and tempestuous," that doesn't do anything to the muscles of the imagination. But if I say, "This is a wonderful part. The character procrastinates, she perseveres, she relinquishes, etc.," that will whet your imagination. Character is what character *does*. Hedda Gabler is what Hedda Gabler *does*.

I give students practice in thinking this way by asking them also to pick five verbs to describe themselves or a character they are working on, and to do the same for people close to them, like a parent.

I don't have a lot of exercises. What I do have is a way of stretching the actor's ability to make choices in the playing of the scene. It may not be applicable to another scene, but as a frame of reference it helps. Once an actor knows that there is a high stake in every scene, once he knows that there is something that cannot be revealed, once he finds out what he is resisting in the scene, he can up the stakes; therefore, his objective or desired response becomes very immediate. Once he knows what the obstacle is, what has to be transcended, what cannot happen, everything becomes a question of life or death. My feeling is that a lot of actors keep themselves very insulated with too much sensory exercise work and emotional memory work and scene study work and don't really get up there and chew up the scenery.

I will do exercises that are organic to the scene. Someone in class was doing a scene from *Private Lives*, the "Don't quibble, Sybil" scene. The husband's objective in that scene is to get Sybil out of the hotel immediately. The desired response ultimately is to get her to cooperate in leaving. The unspoken truth is the urgency; therefore, what Eliot has to do in that scene is to avoid alarming Sybil or scaring her or giving her any reason to believe that something horrible is going to happen so he can enlist her cooperation. The text is filled with warnings. The unspoken truth is escalated in that scene because Sybil is not moving. Now, here's an example of just what happens if you learn how to play those two in opposition to each other.

I give an exercise or improvisation in which I tell a student that he is in a room where a bomb will go off in three minutes, but he can't alarm his wife because, if he does, he won't get her cooperation in leaving and they will both die in the explosion. So he has to get both of them out of there without playing it like an hysterical person. The man is suddenly forced to make every choice but directly dragging his wife out of the room. I had an actor practically dressing his wife in this improvisation, moving furniture around, giving her every signal except the one that something horrible was going to happen. At one point this actor was so up against the wall, in such a fit of sweat in his inability to reveal his desperation, that he started putting pieces of the hotel room in a suitcase. There were some fresh tulips that were part of the set and he packed them too. I thought that as a director I couldn't have given this actor those choices to act. It wouldn't have dawned on me to pack the tulips. His action was to resist telling her of the urgency. His unspoken truth was the urgency. He was stuck and it created a physical life in which there was nothing else he could do but pack the tulips. It was a wonderful coming together of task, action, and objective.

At a certain point, after actors have worked with me for a couple of weeks, they know essentially the way I am going to direct them and they start to think that way. I ask the same questions over and over again: what do you want, what do you think you want, what is threatening that, what is your character's unspoken truth, and how are you concealing that unspoken truth?

What advice would you give an actor just starting out in acting?

Don't depend on your ego to get you anywhere. The best artists in the world are aware of how they fit into the world. Acting is not a solo act. Focus out. Read, observe people, keep your ear cleaned. Conversations are taking place all around you that are loaded with subtext, loaded with unspoken truths. Learn how to be a better detective.

Ernie Martin

Ernie Martin is director of the Ernie Martin Studio Theatre, a drama school in Manhattan. He is also artistic director of the Actors Creative Theatre, an ensemble company that is housed with his school. His school offers classes in scene study, technique, and improvisation. The Ensemble Company has an in-house Playwright/ Directors Unit to develop new material for production. A member of The Actors Studio, Mr. Martin was a teacher/director for both the New York and California branches of the Lee Strasberg Theatre Institute before opening his own school in 1977.

A director as well as a teacher, Mr. Martin has directed In the Boom Boom Room, *which won the Los Angeles Drama Logue and Drama Critics awards,* All My Sons, Awake and Sing, Mamma's Little Angels, Diary of a Madman *(in Barcelona, Spain), as well as numerous other productions both in New York and California.*

Mr. Martin's vision is to have a modern-day Moscow Art Theater in which he will teach actors the Method established by Stanislavsky,

157

Vakhtangov, and Strasberg. But he is careful to add that "sensory exercises are just the catalyst." It's important that the sensory work be applied correctly. "It's a way to open the actor up and help him learn how to personalize his work. It's not an end in itself."

How did you get started teaching acting?

After I came out of the army in 1953 I wanted to be a singer so I auditioned for the American Theatre Wing. I started with musical comedy classes and the students had to take classes in acting to help them present a song. My teacher was Jim Welch, and when he talked about Stanislavsky and acting I had a feel for what was going on. I remember him asking me what I thought acting was. I said I guess if I were to act, I would have to be truthful in life in order to be truthful on the stage. He thought I would be a good actor because I was already concerned with being truthful in the craft. I worked on some scenes and he encouraged me and told me never to lose my sense of truth. I never forgot him. During that time I also studied at Berghof Studios, started to do TV work, and went to California.

I dropped out of acting for a while, and then in 1970 I took scene study classes with Lee Strasberg. I sat in on Lee's class and just tuned in. I felt that he was brilliant. When I did my first scene for him, all I did was simply listen and react. I did no more than I had worked for (a preparation, objective, and going moment to moment). Then I began to study sensory work; that is, the technique he was teaching. I was like a sponge, absorbing everything he taught. I also studied directing with him.

I began to teach scene study and sensory work for Lee and then I auditioned for The Actors Studio with my wife, Ann Wedgeworth, and I became a member. I taught for Lee until 1977, when I started to teach on my own.

How is your approach to the training of actors different from Lee's?

First of all, I believe that I must continue the teachings of the past, but through my personality and understanding, and that I must add creatively and constructively to that foundation. I never felt that Lee believed sensory work was the end of the game, was all of it. He talked about and encouraged actors to do improvisations also and taught them to adhere to the logical and proper through line of the play. Every teacher has a forte. Lee's was sensory work. He was a specialist in it.

I believe sensory exercises are a way of disciplining your concentration and expanding and opening up the imagination; a way to learn how to use yourself and how to come into contact with yourself (this is called personalization). I call them an emotional gymnasium. All the sensory exercises are geared toward experiences in your own life. The first homework you start with is a cup of coffee or any nonalcoholic-flavored liquid. In this exercise the student approaches the tangible object as if he had never seen it before in his life, as if he were a child and had the openness of discovery. He hears it, smells it, tastes it, explores it with his five senses; he finds the weight of it, the texture of the cup, puts it on different parts of his body because different parts are receptive in different ways. Then he sets it aside and re-creates it. This teaches students, right from the beginning, that they must go moment to moment when they try to re-create from their imagination. They practice this exercise at home and then they bring it to class. I tell them it's not the result that counts for now. It's their growth in the adventure toward that result. From the beginning, through scene work, improvisations, and sensory exercises, I keep emphasizing that it's always moment to moment. Never go for a result. An actor's focus has to be on the moment.

Lee had a certain procedure, certain steps in the sensory work that you had to take. I agree and follow the same procedure, but I always keep in mind that everyone is an individual and the procedure can be altered or changed. I always start students with nonemotional exercises such as creating a drink, creating three fabrics, or putting on makeup. Slowly we go into emotional areas. The first emotional area is creating a physical pain, one that students have actually experienced for themselves. From there we go on to create personal objects that the student is emotionally attached to. Then we go on to various other exercises. We finally end up with the student being able to create and alternate up to five different emotions while reciting a memorized monologue. He is to ignore all punctuation and meaning, but let his emotions from the exercise color the words. He is not to let the unrelated words control him. This teaches the actor that it's *how* and not *what* he says that affects his acting partner. Lee never used monologues that I know of. If a student can do this exercise—that is, make sense of those unrelated words by giving them a life—imagine how easy it will be for him once he has the intention that is suited to the words of his character. It's going to be a breeze for him.

After a while I will ask the student to create a neutral physical activity like making coffee. Then I have him engage in that activity while he is doing three, four, or five emotional sensory exercises. Then I ask him to add his memorized monologue. After that I may ask him to address that monologue to me and to members of the class. This gets him to deal with other people. He has to take from and react to the person he is giving his monologue to. If the students in the class react, it is the actor's doing.

The way some people interpret Lee's work it would seem that sensory exercises are the predominant force. They believe that a student creates an object or event sensorially, works with it, is stimulated by it, and should never forget that he or she is doing a sensory exercise. I disapprove of that. To me a sensory exercise is only a catalyst. It's like the booster in the rocket. The exercise is the booster and the rocket is the emotion. But the booster has to fall off while the rocket keeps going. Many people believe that those exercises are self-indulgent. That's because students are trained to continue working with the sensory exercises to such a degree that they are no longer relating to the actors they work with. And that's what happens when you don't know how to apply sensory work correctly. I believe that the best craft is a well-rounded one that develops the intellectual, spiritual, physical, vocal, and emotional life of the actor.

How do you prevent students from becoming self-indulgent with sensory work?

When I work on sensory exercises and I see that a student has already created a personal object and is being affected by it, I encourage him to go on to the next moment. If other feelings are stimulated, I encourage him to let them come up. For instance, if you are working on a personal object and suddenly your father comes to mind, don't get Freudian, don't analyze. Go with those feelings and that image. I might encourage the student to talk to his father in the middle of a sensory exercise, if that's what comes up. I want him to deal with it. It may bring the actor to another level of work. You have to let students do that. If they get an impulse, they should go with it and not let somebody tell them they can't. This is one way they can find the uniqueness in themselves, and once that happens, they can find the uniqueness in a character.

Do you teach relaxation?

Like Lee I believe that relaxation is a very important step in the process and must not be overlooked. There are two types of tension—physical and emotional. Before approaching sensory work I teach students a specific way to release both forms of tension because if they aren't free of tension, it will definitely obstruct the flow of creative energy and block inspiration.

Another way I differ from Lee is that I use his Song and Dance Exercise only occasionally, whereas he emphasized it. Lee designed this exercise to help the student become aware of hidden areas of tension. Doing the Song and Dance Exercise forces the student to become emotionally vulnerable and overcomes his defenses. It also encourages the interaction between the student and the class through movement and song. I feel I can get the same results through sensory work because I train students to interact with the class during the sensory exercises.

Do you teach your students the Affective Memory Exercise?

Yes. An Affective Memory Exercise is one where the student goes back to a traumatic event that happened at least seven years in the past and one that he has never confronted or dealt with, an event that was denied. When it crops up in memory, the actor doesn't deal with it. To do this exercise I take a student through the following steps: he closes his eyes, he relaxes, and through prompting I take him back to that event by having him remember the day it occurred, what month, what year, what he was wearing, what the room was like, the color, etc. What I do is take a person back and have them relive the event. To feel comfortable with this confrontation, a student has to continue working on it under supervision over a period of time. Soon he will be able to use it when needed.

In 1973 I remember doing an Affective Memory with a fifty-five-year-old student. She went back to an event that had happened when she was five years old. Her mother left her at a friend's house, which this actress had always resented. I had her do that Affective Memory for six weeks because it tapped something very emotional in her. Five years later she told me that she was still using that exercise when she needed to get that emotion. Unlike the other sensory exercises, an Affective Memory is a bottomless pit and it just keeps on feeding the actor. Students have to be with me for quite a while before I let them do this exercise.

I also find a Private Moment Exercise helpful. It helps students overcome their fear of exposing themselves in front of others. It is designed to counter their natural embarrassment onstage. I ask them to perform an activity onstage in front of the class that they only engage in at home. Once students overcome their embarrassment, they become comfortable onstage and feel free to make personal and, therefore, interesting choices.

How do you teach your students to use an Affective Memory Exercise in a performance?

Once the student has learned to elicit an Affective Memory properly it is no longer just an exercise. It becomes a normal extension of his craft, and he is now so flexible and emotionally receptive that he can respond from an emotional point of view and not an intellectual one. There will be scripts that an actor will be able to relate to, and others that he will not. When the actor can relate to material personally, his emotions will come to the surface. It's when he can't relate personally to the text that he needs something to help him do so, something that is dependable. Affective Memories are dependable.

Another way actors can learn to relate to a script is through the use of "as if." A lot of people who teach sensory work seem to avoid this term, but I believe that an actor's craft should be a combination of both sensory work and "as if" work. There will always be aspects of a character that the actor cannot relate to. An actor can use an "as if" to help him as well as an Affective Memory. "As if" is fantasy, something that never happened, whereas sensory work (Affective Memory exercises) is personal images of events that did happen. I believe an actor should use both these tools in his work.

What techniques do you teach students to help them learn to relate to each other on a moment-to-moment basis?

I find the Repeat Exercise helpful in this area and I do my interpretation of it. I believe in using various schools of thought if they are useful in achieving a clear, productive, and creative craft. Improvisations and Repeat Exercises are ways of getting students to interact and stimulate each other.

I ask two students to sit onstage opposite each other and I ask them to relax. Then I give them a word to say, any word—"peanut butter," for instance. The person who starts is the one who first gets the impulse to start. The other person says the word back in a way that is colored by what he or she feels at the moment and by his or her reaction to the other person. What happens is that as the student responds on a moment-to-moment basis, he begins to trust the feeling that it's all right not to say anything unless the impulse to say it is there. You can see the actors begin to go with their feelings and respond to what they are doing to each other. When I see a strong impulse in a student I tell him that he can say what's on his mind and not just stick with the words we started with. He can change the word when the feeling is strong. At other times I let students start by themselves, using a word or a short sentence. A typical sentence might be, "That's a nice shirt." I steer students away from making personal comments as part of this exercise. I also have them use a Repeat Exercise as a preparation for a scene using neutral words, then expressing their feelings, then going back to neutral words, and so forth. I let students get out of their chairs and do whatever they like during this exercise—if the impulse calls for it.

I also do improvisations every week. A student may come into class believing he is going to do a sensory exercise, but will get an improvisation instead. I like to surprise students because I don't want them to work on improvisations at home. I want them to be spontaneous. Improvisations are usually based on a simple situation. For instance, I tell a student that he is a doctor who is happily married. He is going to a convention and his secretary is going with him. He has to catch a plane and is packing. I then proceed to tell the actress in the improvisation that she suspects her husband is having an affair with his secretary. Her objective is to stop him from going. I tell the students that it's not whether they accomplish their objective, but what happens to them in trying to accomplish it. If they believe the situation, they don't have to keep focusing on their objective.

I believe there are two kinds of objectives: passive and aggressive. In the improvisation I mentioned before, the doctor has the passive objective because it has nothing to do with his wife. He is going to catch a plane in five minutes and is late. It's his wife who wants something from him, and that makes her aggressive. She's the one who is making the scene happen. Too often actors will make choices that are strictly from an aggressive objective when, in fact, they have the passive objective. Then actors wonder why the scene is not working for them. It's usually because their choices are unrelated to their objective in the scene.

How do you advise a new student to approach working on a scene?

From the very beginning I teach my actors to ask, "Who am I? Where am I? What do I want? Why do I want it?" I never teach them how to get it. There are a lot of teachers who work on the "how" of acting—the execution. I don't. I encourage students to discover the "how" themselves. If you are very specific about your objective and really understand it, if you understand your prior circumstances, prior life, and relationships to the other characters, and if you have a preparation, the "how" will come. That doesn't mean you haven't made choices. It just means that you haven't predetermined how you will execute your choices. Then you can be spontaneous.

I don't like to talk at length about beats either. The reason I don't stress breaking a scene down into beats is because it prevents students from living out the scene on a moment-to-moment basis. They may map it out too carefully, which could prevent them from responding to the unexpected, from going with their impulses. Beats are transitions and I don't want students to get conditioned to them and wind up waiting for them.

An elementary thing I like to teach is what an objective is. I will ask a student to pick up a chair and walk across the room. Then I will ask him to bring a chair across the room with the objective of making someone else feel comfortable. Now the present objective is to carry the chair across the room, while the overall objective is to make someone feel comfortable. There is a big difference between those two and how someone will execute each one.

I throw in one other thing. I ask students, "When a character achieves his goal, what is he going to do with it?" This question teaches the students about the future. I do believe that both the past and the future enhance the present moment. If you can understand the future, you will know why your present need or objective is so strong.

How do you instruct students to begin rehearsing their first scene?

I assign two people to a scene, and they go home and read it. But the partners don't contact each other. They come in and read the scene together. Usually actors already have ideas about their character and what's going on in the script. If I see that an actor is responding from an idea instead of responding to the person in front of him, I will stop him. I tell him that this is the first time that he is hearing those words coming from his partner's mouth. I want the actor to speak to the person in front of him, not to the character, because we don't have that character yet. The actors should be talking to each other as themselves. This teaches students to have the patience to learn how to use each other without the obligation to play an idea of the character. This process should continue until impulses arise in the students that will take them to other levels. That's the first rehearsal. Students always have a pencil with them and take notes on ideas that come out of rehearsals.

What other exercises do you use?

There is one I call Entrance with a Preparation. After an actor works on an emotional preparation, he comes on stage alone to present a story or scenario he has worked out. He is not allowed to speak unless he has a strong impulse to do so. The class and I then have to determine who that actor is, where he is, what he wants, and why he wants it just by how he comes on stage. This teaches the actor how to come into a scene or enter a stage with a preparation, how to drop the preparation and go on to the next moment.

That's Variation 1 of Entrance with a Preparation. In Variation 2 the actor has to come on stage having prepared himself with one emotion; by the time he has finished his improvisation or scene, he will have gone through a transition into another emotion. In Variation 3 of this exercise he has to use three emotions.

I also use an exercise called a Personal Story. There are three variations: (1) The student comes on stage and relates a personal experience to the class. He gets involved in it and allows emotions connected to that experience to come to the surface. (2) He creates an emotional preparation that is *unrelated* to the personal story that he is about to tell the class. This is hard to do, but it teaches students how to separate what they were doing offstage from what they will do onstage, and how *not* to come on stage anticipating feelings. (3) Students do a combination of variations 1 and 2 and add something to the story that is not true, that did not happen to them. The class is not supposed to be able to tell which aspect of the story is true and which is fiction. This teaches students how to use themselves, how to be personal and allow a fantasy to be combined with truth.

I also do script analysis, but it's not a separate class. I do it when I critique a scene. I talk about tempos and rhythms, time periods, colors of characters, what the through line of the play is, and what the playwright is saying. This leads a student to interpret a scene for himself on the basis of logic. I try to get students to be as truthful to the author as possible, but I will not impose my interpretation. When they are way off base, I will give them a direction, an adjustment, but I will tell them that now I am directing them, not teaching them. I only do this to get them back on the right course.

How is your school structured?

My acting classes are technique classes with scene study. Beginners study sensory work and improvisations before they are given scenes to work on. I do have an intermediate class where I introduce cold readings for auditions. I also have an advanced technique and scene study class where, for example, we do Shakespeare, Ibsen, and Chekhov. I have nightclub and musical performers who study with me as well. I help them understand that there is no difference between acting and singing a song except that singing is speaking on pitch. I also coach actors privately for auditions and performances. I have a teacher who teaches the Linklater voice technique for any student who may want to take it. There is a speech teacher and a class in movement for the actor as well. The movement class is taught by a dance teacher who studied acting with me and who understands my work. This class combines movement with acting techniques such as emotional preparations and improvisations.

We also have the Actors Creative Theatre, which consists of an Ensemble Company and a Playwright/Directors Unit. The Actors Creative Theatre produces Equity Showcases. We develop a script in the Unit, hold a reading of it before an invited audience, and, if it's good enough, the Actors Creative Theatre will back it for production. All students participate in the readings, and auditions for the Ensemble Company are held once a year. I encourage my students to audition for it.

How do you help students learn to create a character?

Earlier we talked about learning to distinguish between the areas of yourself that fit a character and those that don't. I use animals to develop the physical aspects of a character, and I also have my students observe people. When I was in *Serpico* I played a derelict. In order to prepare for this part, I went down to the Bowery and watched derelicts on the street. I took an old pair of shoes and sliced the heels on an angle to make them wobbly. I also created the feeling of prickly heat in my groin and I created the feeling of being drunk. I never forgot the way those derelicts walked. Those who were no longer drunk had drunk so much that they would wobble even when they were sober. They had lost their equilibrium and could never really walk straight again.

I have one exercise where I tell students to observe a person carefully, someone they either know or don't know, and come back to class and act that person out while telling us about him or her.

They start out as the actor telling the class about a person, and all of a sudden they start to behave like that person. After that the student has to create a fantasy life about that person and tell it to the class as if he or she were that character.

Animal work will enhance the physical side of character and that can trigger the emotional life. First the student has to discover the strength of the animal, its muscles, the feeling of its fur, how it looks at objects, etc. Then, if the actor gets impulses, he can move like the animal, but he has to be careful not to imitate the animal—just to understand its rhythm. Then the student as the animal stands up and slowly has to do a neutral monologue. The animal begins to disappear and the character emerges. This process takes three weeks or more to accomplish. Recently a student worked on a monologue from *Kennedy's Children* in class. This student was very shy about her sensuality, so she created a cat. This made her feel sensual. Then I told her to stop working on the cat and start working on her character and to allow the sensuality she had discovered when she worked on the cat to come to the forefront.

If a student is having trouble getting at certain aspects of a character I often will give him what I call an adjustment to help him overcome the problem. For example, if a character needs to have an edge of hostility, I might tell the actor privately that I want him to do the scene again, but this time with only one thing in mind—that his fellow actor raped his sister. This adjustment may have nothing to do with the scene, but it helps him achieve that undercurrent of hostility.

Another adjustment I use is to tell an actor that he or she has a secret in a scene. For example, I might tell an actress that she is pregnant, but that it will never be divulged in the scene and may not have anything to do with it. This teaches actors that there is always a part of the character that they are going to keep to themselves. Also, having a secret makes an actor interesting to watch.

There is an interesting story about George M. Cohan. A play of his was about to open and he thought it was going to be a flop. On opening night, just before the play started, he walked across the stage and put a gun in a drawer. The gun was never used in the play, but you can bet the audience didn't leave its seats until the play was over.

Too many actors think that ranting and raving is what acting is about. So I created an exercise to demonstrate how expressive you can be without talking. I pair off people, usually four couples at a time, onstage, and I have them relax. I tell them to create a personal image. This can be anything from the beach to a dance hall, to clouds, whatever. They then start to send out their personal image to their partner while they are all sitting quietly without speaking. I want them to relate to each other and pick up each other's vibes. In the course of this exercise students find that one image a person is sending may be stronger than another and they will be drawn to it and begin to receive it. I have found that people become receptive to each other's images when they are in a relaxed state and that their own original images may change because of this. They learn they can be alive and send vibes without words. If the impulse is strong enough, the actors can touch and explore in this exercise. Inevitably actors wind up sharing an event, and that's what acting is really all about.

John Hart

Alice Spivak

Alice Spivak teaches a private professional workshop in New York City. She is also an acting coach for feature films and has worked on miniseries and TV movies for the major networks. She is a professional actress as well and has appeared in feature films, on TV, and on the stage.

Ms. Spivak received her primary acting training at HB Studio with Herbert Berghof and Uta Hagen. After approximately nine years as a student, she was asked to join the faculty. She taught at HB Studio for fifteen years before devoting herself to her private classes and coaching.

Ms. Spivak feels strongly that the actor should not isolate "emotions from conflict because when we play the play we never do. . . ." Her approach to actor training focuses on freeing the emotional life through "the conflicts, the conditions, and the circumstances" of the character.

*   *   *

How did you get started teaching acting?

I grew up in Brooklyn and when I was sixteen I enrolled in a summer course at the Fagin School of Drama because I read that Susan Hayward, who was my favorite actress and also came from Brooklyn, had gone there. While in high school, my friends and I became "autograph hounds," chasing movie stars, and one night we went to see Jack Palance in *Darkness at Noon*. It was the first "live" theater I had ever seen, and, in a flash, I decided that that was what I really wanted to do—act!

Right after I graduated from high school I took an acting course at NYU for one semester and a young man in my class told me about the HB Studio. I joined Herbert Berghof's class, and when he gave his first lecture about acting, I was enthralled. I knew right away that I was in the right place. Of course, I wasn't at all ready for his class, which I soon learned after some very discouraging criticism. You see, I thought I was a star because at NYU and at the Fagin School, where the training was very external, I had been a great success. Then I came to HB and heard about Stanislavsky for the first time. I was fascinated with Mr. Berghof and this "new" approach to acting, but was told that I needed to get a better foundation before I continued to work with him.

I began basic technique courses with Anthony Mannino. He had a very graduated kind of course in which we did various exercises and improvisations. We learned about obstacles, objectives, and so forth. They were very well-thought-out exercises. I took three technique courses with him. Then I got into an off-Broadway show. I was eighteen at the time.

Mr. Berghof was the first big influence on me, but it was difficult for me to understand him at first. When I went back to him after Mannino's classes, he complained that I kept everything in my head, that I was too intellectual. I didn't understand why or how I could "forget" what I had chosen to do in a scene. I became more and more frustrated, until one day his wife, Uta Hagen, took over the class, and suddenly I was excited all over again. She made us feel that we were all colleagues; plus her precise approach to teaching was just what I needed. I decided to work with her and she became the second most profound influence on my acting and eventual teaching. I studied with her for almost six years and stayed at HB Studio for twenty-three years altogether as a student and a teacher.

When Ms. Hagen had to go to Europe in the winter of 1961, she asked me to take over two of her classes for three weeks. I was nervous, but she convinced me I understood enough of her approach to help other students with it. When she returned from her trip, she asked me to stay on as a teacher at HB.

Over the years I have become a coach for Broadway, movies, and TV, and I teach groups privately when I can—usually two eight-week sessions a year. Currently, my classes are in advanced scene study with professional students only because I don't have the time to teach beginners technique. For fifteen years at HB Studio I did teach technique as well as scene study courses.

Unlike Lee Strasberg, Ms. Hagen always focuses on the play as the primary source for all of the actor's choices. She believes in analyzing the script and the character and in using "particularization" to free one's emotional life. She discusses substitution and using personal choices for the events in the play and for the relationship. We never did sense memories, Private Moments, or Affective Memories. She felt, and I certainly feel, that actors shouldn't isolate these things from the play. They have to be woven into the script. Whereas the Strasberg technique emphasized the actor's freedom, Uta emphasized freeing the *character's* behavior.

What we did in Uta's class was a series of object exercises designed to help us solve certain problems in the script. In scenes, we dealt only with the material, paying great respect to the author. She had a series of clear steps to help an actor create the life that the author intended. So our attention wasn't focused on how *to feel* or what's wrong with the actor or whether the actor has a block. As a teacher, I continue to believe in the same approach. I coach students using the material of the play rather than making a public display of their personal lives. When personal choices are made, I encourage them to "keep it a secret." I prefer that they keep private choices private because once exposed they are no longer usable. I talk to them about the system of using Affective Memory Exercises, when it comes up, as "'crutches"—tools to use when the actor needs them. In some acting classes, there is so much emphasis on these personal tools that actors are made to believe that that's what acting is all about. An actor should go to a conscious substitution or conscious memory source only when he has to.

I also felt that Uta's approach to the craft of acting was very refreshing, very healthy and sane. Most students think there is some kind of mystique, some mystical area that they have to get into in order to develop a character, whereas I feel, as does Miss Hagen, that acting is a craft, not something mystical. There is a point, however, at which the character does start to take over. I stress that the actor is not to have preconceptions about the character, is not to look for emotional results or look at the externals first.

The technique course that I developed and taught at the HB Studio embodies all my thoughts on acting. It is a very systematized approach.

Would you describe it?

I begin by telling my class what Herbert Berghof used to say: "If you really want to know what acting is, you look it up in the dictionary." The dictionary is the source of all definitions and acting requires a lot of definition. Now, the first definition of acting is "doing." To act is "to do." When you describe it that way, it unburdens the student, because "to do" is something he can control. But if he has "*to feel*" or "*to be*," how is he going "to do" that? *Feeling* and *being* come out of *doing*.

Then I assign each student to *do* a task, a simple task, and to do it as if he were in a room or a place that he knew very well. This is similar to Uta Hagen's basic Object Exercise. Students are to use at least three objects in order to accomplish a task and they are to be themselves when they do it, not a character. Tasks can be routine or something they do only once in a while. They are to use three or as many real objects as needed to accomplish their chosen task. In the following class, after each exercise is completed, there is discussion defining place, objects, and objective (or task). Suggested tasks are cleaning up a room, preparing to go out, writing a letter, etc.

For the second assignment I pair up two students and tell them that the following week they will do their Object Exercises again, but this time in conjunction with a partner. The place has to become a mutual one, as does the time of day and day of the week. They must also decide what relationship they have. For now the relationship doesn't require any emotional judgment—just a factual decision. For instance, they may be siblings, friends, lovers, roommates, married, or something else, as long as it is logical to them; therefore, neither can choose to be "parent" if both partners are about the same age.

The students are requested not to rehearse this joint object exercise, just discuss it. There is to be no speaking or very little. They are simply involved in their physical tasks as before—only this time in the same place at the same time. However, if one trips over the other person, each might feel an impulse to say something. By limiting speech to the impulse of the moment, they begin to discover where dialogue comes from. I instruct them to avoid the most common trap in improvisations—too much unnecessary talk. Instead, the goal is to be occupied while in the physical presence of one another, the first step in relationship experience.

In the third week I add a conflict. One student will have a need of the other and he will be what I call the *objective*; the other is the *obstacle*. The same physical tasks are respected but now become the *secondary life* or *ongoing activity*. The activity may get stopped, however, because the *primary objective* (i.e., to borrow money, ask a favor, or get the partner to leave) is more important. The actor who is the obstacle has agreed in advance why he will not or cannot give in. This creates a conflict. The obstacle still has his physical task to carry out as his main objective. Therefore, his talking is still limited (he may have to say no, for instance) unless he is forced to respond to the other person's need. There are two objectives in this first conflict improvisation: one is psychological and the other physical (the obstacle).

Now a lot of interesting things happen. For instance, I point out to students how blocking occurs, how a great director couldn't have blocked this improvisation any better than they did because all their physical moves came naturally out of impulses. By the way, there is no chosen ending to these and the following improvisations. I just stop them after five or ten minutes. The actors are told to discuss in advance all the reasons the objective wants what he wants and why the obstacle will not or cannot give it, so they won't suddenly spring some unexpected "fact" at each other. At the same time, they are not to preplan any dialogue or endings.

The following week I add a psychological need to the other person (the obstacle) and I call it a double conflict. Their physical life or tasks continue as *secondary life* for both. Both need something from each other and both are obstacles to each other's need. At this point, they have built a scene comparable to a written one and I describe to them how it came about: they decided (1) who they were to one another; (2) where they were; (3) what they were doing in this place and time; and (4) what they wanted from each other in this place and time.

Now I begin to add specific acting problems to their improvisations. First I assign *inner objects* to their existing scenes. I explain inner objects as things that weigh on their minds, preoccupations, inner conflicts. They should be unrelated to their outer conflicts (primary objectives) and usually come from chosen events in the previous circumstances. They should not take over, however, but remain part of the secondary life. The primary objectives are still to go after what they were going after to begin with. I point out in retrospect how inner objects (and events from the past circumstances) can influence or condition behavior. I then introduce *conditions* in the room: i.e., it can be quiet, hot, or cold. These conditions also affect behavior. The actors begin to grow more vulnerable to one another.

As we continue I introduce further "problems": an overall *physical state of being* they must create in themselves. It is usually at this juncture that I assign them a new partner and they build a new improvisation using the basic steps. They decide what their relationship is, where they are, what they are doing in that place and time, where they have come from and where they are going, and, finally, what they want from each other. They must also decide in what way they are each other's obstacles. But now they must add a *physical state of being*, which they do not discuss but which obviously affects their behavior. Examples of a physical state are a headache, a fever, being drunk, and having a cold. To accomplish the feelings of such a state of being, I describe Uta Hagen's steps of sense memory plus muscular adjustment (1) Remember a time you had your chosen affliction. (2) Pinpoint the area most affected. (3) Describe the symptoms (to yourself). (4) Find your own particular muscular adjustment to *relieve* the symptoms. This ought to bring about the sensations without distracting one from the primary objectives in the scene but still having an effect on behavior.

For the next "problem" I add an *emotional state of being*. For example, I tell them that they have just received terrible news or very good news, though they are to keep this information a secret from each other. This is an extension of the inner objects tried earlier. Again, it is meant to affect behavior and effect greater vulnerability while not weakening the main conflict in the scene (why they are there to begin with).

Is the dialogue set at this point?

No. It's still an improvisation, although the framework is very well conceived. I tell students, "You will remain spontaneous no matter how often the improvisation is repeated if you maintain the primary objective. Always begin with attention to your goal." I stress this point over and over.

The next two assignments are meant to further relationship. First, I introduce *endowment*, a secret investment in the partner to create more vulnerability in the relationship.

Is it the same situation, the original one, that is repeated in these improvisations?

Yes, with all these additions. But after students have built one improvisation through my guidance and before I add the states of being, I assign them new partners and they build fresh situations to improvise on. They do the preparation at home with their partners. They decide on the past, the relationship, the place, the time, and the conflict, and bring these in as they keep increasing the number of elements in the situation.

Of course, many things occur and most of my teaching comes up in retrospect. In other words, I don't know ahead of time what is going to happen or what their objectives are, but in retrospect I might say, for instance, "You see, your objective changed. It's gotten deeper because the more conditions and obstacles you put in the scene, the deeper your objective becomes." And when students eventually approach written material, the first objective they see is usually obvious (i.e., the text), what I consider the *Author's Objective*. As they begin to add the objects, place, conditions, etc., to the situation and are on their feet working through the relationship, the original objective changes and deepens and becomes more subjective. So I call the first objective they see in written material the *Objective Objective*. As they grow personal and more familiar with the scene they begin to discover the *Subjective Objective*. The process is one of personalization.

What exactly is "endowment?"

Endowment is an imaginary addition to the relationship. The student might choose to have his partner speak in a foreign language, or be bald, or belong to the Nazi party. Each student grows more alert and more vulnerable to the other because each now holds a secret about the other. It could be a physical secret or a judgment. This prepares them for the next step, when I ask them to make a full *substitution* of their partner. I describe a substitution by saying, "Pick someone from your life, your past, whose memory is special to you in some way, and believe that your partner is that person—but transform that person back into your partner. In other words, it is 'as if' your partner were your Uncle Joe, but Joe is now a young woman who is your sister in this improvisation and she wants something from you and you want something from her." At this point, substitutions are conscious on the part of the actors. I tell them that when they use a substitution in a rehearsed scene, it will be forgotten before they actually perform, but during this technique course we are watching the process of substitution as it would be used in a first rehearsal.

Do you take students through the steps of learning how to create a substitution?

I tell them the theory and how to do it and let them do it in front of us. I describe it as fully as I can and then I watch them go through the process. I tell them that a substitution is imagining that your partner is someone from your past life who was an important person, someone who changed your life in some way. Students are not to look for a result; they are not to look for fear or hate or love. They are not to try to fit a feeling into the improvisation. I say, "Pick a substitution of somebody you would like to see again; for instance, someone who changed your life. Then I want you to replace your acting partner in your mind with that person from the past, but don't stop there. Continue this replacing or substituting all through the improvisation—meaning that it is that person from your past 'as if' he or she now looks like your acting partner, sounds like him, acts like him, wants this of you, and is factually in this relationship."

So rather than telling a student to look for the similarities between his acting partner and the person in his substitution, you want him to believe that his substitution now looks and behaves like his acting partner.

A big risk with substitution is that it can set up a wall between actors because the one doing the substitution is looking at and behaving with his partner as if he were someone else. I believe that a substitution or an endowment should only increase the actor's awareness of his partner, not the person from his past. As a matter of fact, the actor using the substitution can even be surprised at how his "Uncle Joe" has changed. I try to open up the process of substitution as a way for the actor to respond more sensitively to behavior from the person onstage with him, not just a way to have a great emotional experience that has nothing to do with the person in front of him or the play.

During the 1950s when the Method was very popular I would see how the playwright suffered because the actors were so busy with the emotional life based on their own private histories that Chekhov might as well not have bothered to write the play.

When I introduce substitution I also point out to students what *actions* are—the moment-to-moment doings in a scene. At that point they have gotten to the most sensitive stage of making a fictitious situation real for themselves. I now make lists of all the various actions that they used during their improvisations and I read it off to them afterward. For instance, I might tell a student, "You began by 'stating your case,' then moved on to flattery, then you warned, then you bribed." Students are usually quite surprised. I emphasize to them that this moment-to-moment behavior grew out of facts and choices and was not preconceived.

Now, ready to do so, they move on to their first real scene. I assign everybody a partner and a scene from a play, usually a contemporary American play, and I give them a series of steps on how to approach the scene, at first creating an improvisation based on what the author has written. I give students eleven steps to follow that include all the terminology they are now familiar with.

Students begin by reading the scene, closing the script, then discussing the place, inventing the place, deciding on the circumstances and the activities, deciding on the prior relationship that brought them to this point in the play, deciding what the conflict is, and breaking the conflict down into actions. Now they do an improvisation based on the choices they've made about the script.

Do they use the actual dialogue of the scene?

Not yet, but some of the text will creep in. Students are not learning the text, but breaking it down. Usually the improvisations are longer than the scene itself. Then, for the following week, when they actually learn the lines of the scene and do it, most of them are pretty awkward, and I say, "Now you understand why you have to take Technique 2." I've brought them to the point where their work really looks amazing in an improvisation and then I've handed them a scene and they begin to see that there is much more to it. They have not learned scene study yet, but are developing habits that will eventually serve them in approaching material.

The procedure I describe in breaking down a script is the same procedure I use with a professional actor in private coaching. It's the way I approach all material.

In Technique 2 we work only on a very personal and emotional level. Substitution was the beginning of self-exploration and now we continue to work within that framework during the first part of the second term. I call Technique 2 "character work."

What techniques do you give students to help them create a character?

What I do at the beginning is ask students again to do an Object Exercise, only now I use another variation of one of Ms. Hagen's exercises that focuses on different behavior. The students start by doing a task in a familiar place, as themselves, using at least three objects, and add an emotional state of being, a physical state of being, and a room condition. Then I ask them to do the very same task in the very same place, but now to change the circumstances, meaning the time of day, what they did before, etc., and have a different emotional state, a different physical state of being, and a different room condition, causing different behavior.

And then I play a game with the class. I will say to a student, "You noticed that the behavior changed and the student may feel like a different character. So how would you describe the character in the first task and how would you describe the character in the second task?" The student is now becoming aware that certain elements, such as conditions and emotional states, can result in behavior that could give other people the impression of a different character. The same student doing the same task, but under different pressures, may seem ambitious in one and lazy in the other, or depressed in one and optimistic in the other. We define and label character traits or characteristics as coming out of vulnerabilities and needs.

It is important to note at this point, however, that characters in plays are made up of standards, values, wishes, and a point of view, not just behavior. An actor can behave outwardly in any way he imagines the character does, but if there is no source, no justification, then he's not really the character—just an impersonation.

For the first exercise in character, I ask the student to choose three *negative* traits. Negative traits can be shy, neurotic, withdrawn, aggressive, domineering, lazy, bigoted, etc. I ask for negative traits because positive ones are generally what each of us feel we are (i.e., sensitive, generous, patient, etc.), and the student doesn't have to stretch as far. I tell the student that in certain situations, in certain relationships, any of us can be any of these things. For example, I might ask a student when she has felt like a bigot. She may have felt like one when a drunken person stepped on her toes or spilled whiskey all over her dress and, for that moment, she despised all drunks.

Now I explain the use of endowments to arrive at these feelings all over again. For their three chosen negative traits they are to find three endowments to invest in their partners. These personal endowments are meant to cause feelings and opinions (all unspoken) that should emerge in behavior. So, for bigoted, the student endows her partner with drunkenness. Then I want her to choose two more negative traits. Has she ever felt lazy? Perhaps she has when she has been with someone highly organized. I tell her to endow her partner with the attribute of being highly organized. Now her partner is—in her imagination—someone who has spilled liquor all over her dress and is very organized. For the third trait, she might choose paranoia. Her endowment for this trait can be imagining her partner to be carrying a loaded gun or bugging the room. The improvisation will have nothing to do with these secret imaginings. The endowments chosen are in her mind only as she goes after the primary objective in the conflict. With the use of endowments, the concentration in the relationship grows stronger and causes peculiar behavior (i.e., a character).

By the way, it is not that I believe this is required in every play or every scene they will ever do, but it is something students can go to when they need it, and, more importantly, when they are training it proves to them that they can do and be all those things. I am basically sensitizing students to the kind of observation and concentration that makes them freer emotionally and very volatile.

So it is the actor's point of view that influences his behavior.

I believe that the character comes alive based on the way we look out at the world. To use an outrageous example: a stranger hits you over the head with an umbrella and you have done nothing to provoke it. That person "saw" something that made him hostile. I'm showing students how they can arrive at character—not through behavior per se, but through the feelings that erupt due to what they see, hear, sense, and believe.

I have students do the endowment exercise several times, choosing different negative traits, before they move on to substitution. Now I discuss how we "become" different characters with different people from our past. As an example, whenever I'm with old friends from school days, I "feel" and act like a giggly teenager. And if I imagine myself in previous times with a friend or a sibling or a parent, I might revert back to the feelings and perhaps my behavior in that earlier time. I ask the students to make a list of the character traits—how they felt whenever they were in the presence of their "Uncle Joe"—and to bring me the list. Then they do an improvisation, forgetting the list, just using the substitution incorporating the surprise element when their acting partner does something that their substitution would never have done. As before, discussion in the scene is limited to the circumstances of the chosen situation.

During this substitution exercise I keep their lists on my desk face down. I write my own list of the traits I see in the "characters" in the improvisation. (I ask the whole class to do the same.) Then we match up the two lists, the actor's and mine. Students begin to see if they were "right" about what they felt or if they were way off the mark. If their lists do not jibe with mine or the class's, I look for what might have caused the change—their feelings might have changed toward the substituted partner or their perceptions been inaccurate.

At this point in character work students are beginning to discover what traits feel like, not just what behavior is. We can all imagine what certain characters sound like or how they stand or move. But we don't want to jump to these externals. We want to go to the source, which means why they do that. The Stanislavsky system introduced actors to the cause of a person's behavior, not just the effect. The actor finds causes from the facts given by the playwright and this interpretation of facts (what Uta Hagen calls "particularization"). To this I add illusions such as endowments and substitution, which help the actor arrive at the behavior. I make a major point that students should only use substitutions when they need them, because if they choose to use them before they have fully understood and realized as many of the facts as they can, their personal substitution choices will be intellectual ideas and may isolate them from the play.

For the second half of Technique 2, I choose written scenes that require a real analysis of character. These are usually from plays by very great writers like Chekhov and Tennessee Williams, writers who created strong, particular characters. I start with breaking down character using a *character chart*. The first part of the chart has vital background statistics: where the character was born, how well educated he or she is, what family relationships existed, what the marital status, vocation, and avocations are. No psychoanalytic judgments—just like filling out a personnel form. Students do their first improvisation on the scene with only this background information.

Before they repeat the improvisation the following week, they work out the second part of the character chart—a list of ten to twenty-five traits that make up the character. From that list, I ask them to choose two or three that they feel they are furthest away from, and use their endowments or substitutions to achieve those traits. Kim Stanley once stated that first she listed all the characteristics of her character and then crossed out all the ones that she already had and worked only on the ones she didn't have; reading that inspired this exercise.

The third and final portion of the character chart is what I call the "tying up" of the character, the *life drives*. I ask students to choose two or three *character objectives*: What drives them? Is it power, love, control, peace, harmony? These may not appear overtly in the events of the play, but they are the underlying source. They constitute the *spine* of the character.

How do you advise students to work with directors?

In class students do nondirected scenes, but they learn how to break down and translate scenes into motivations and actions through a clear and basic procedure. A director will never describe these steps for an actor. He will say, "Learn the lines. Speak louder and faster." An actor must be able to take that kind of direction and translate it into the actor's vocabulary to make it work. For instance, a director might say, "I think that the character is more ambitious than you are playing it." The actor might need an endowment, a substitution, or a condition. The actor should know what to go for. That's what the technique courses are for. I call knowing what to reach for the actor's "tool kit."

The actor must also be able to define the subjective objectives that I talked about earlier from the character's point of view. In some cases the actor is aware of needs and motivations that the character isn't and buries them in the text. The character, and eventually the actor, is unconscious of what drives him. Character is derived from the conflict and the surrounding circumstances. One's character is growing and developing all along in rehearsal and yet when it finally comes about, it sort of comes upon you. I have called it "giving birth to the character."

Are there techniques that you use specifically for film or TV work?

Working with actors on movie sets with all the pressure of time and tensions, etc., I have had to learn little tricks of the trade. For instance, in order to find the objective, I read through the scene a few times, then, with the actor, look at the character's opening lines or bit of behavior and at his closing or exit line, and decide whether or not he's failed or succeeded at whatever it was that he, the character, wanted. Then I ask the actor what was it "he" wanted? Whatever we come up with we choose as the first premise. This "trick" is particularly helpful with movie scripts because scenes in movies are so varied in size. Some are very short; some are as long as a play scene; some are only description with no dialogue.

When I have the time to go through a script from beginning to end before we get to the set, I break down each scene the character appears in (looking at the beginning and the end), and find one single objective for each scene. It gives us a greater sense of the progression of the character through the script and a greater, more definite sense of the character himself. We find out if at the end of the entire script he failed or succeeded at what he wanted and, therefore, what his destiny was. I think that all material is based on the ancient Greek classical idea of destiny. The character was headed toward the end from the beginning. On the set and for the "takes," we are more involved with moment-to-moment decisions than would be true in live theater—again because of the very brief scenes. For instance, thinking is never a good choice for an activity on the stage, but may be a necessary one in front of the camera.

I believe in acting as a craft as well as an art. Practicing the craft of interpreting and personalizing a character should be aimed toward simplifying what may seem complicated at first. I believe in clarity because my memory of my early days of confusion is painful. I meet many actors from various training backgrounds who are in terrific pain because they have grown confused about what they have to do, and my job becomes one of nursing them back to the simple reality of a craft process. Considering the very real struggle of building a career in this business, the acting experience itself had better be a joy or why act at all?

ON THE
WEST COAST

Eric Morris

Eric Morris teaches acting in Los Angeles. He has developed a number of new procedures that he has described in three widely read books: No Acting Please, Being and Doing, *and* Irreverent Acting. *He has sought to develop a comprehensive acting program that, while rooted in the Method, delves more into the behavioral aspects of the individual actor. Along with his studio in California he teaches workshops on a regular basis in New York City. He is the founder of the American New Theatre, a company of bicoastal actors, and has served as chairman of the director's unit at The Actors Studio West.*

Eric Morris is also a professional actor and director. After graduating from Northwestern University he appeared in plays, motion pictures, network television episodes, and television series.

How did you get started teaching acting?

By accident. The circumstances were interesting. I'm an actor, and I've been an actor since 1948. I was in Hollywood studying and

I was very dissatisfied. I was about ready to go to New York when I met Marty Landau, who invited me to join his class. He opened some doors for me that had never been opened before, and put me on a good, honest, truthful track. He was a disciple, if you want to call it that, of Lee Strasberg. This was in 1959. I had never studied with Lee. I studied with Marty for about three years and during that time I grew a lot as an actor. Actually, Marty was teaching the work he learned from Lee, with his own additions and interpretations.

And then he got a picture called *Cleopatra* and went to Rome for a year. Again, I was left without a teacher. So I started to look around and ran into the same problem. There weren't any. A fellow actor, Ann O'Hara, said, "Why don't you start teaching a class? I learned as much from you in class as I did from Marty when we worked on scenes together." So I began. At first I had two students, then I had four, and then I had three, and then I had five, and so on. I taught for seven months and fell in love with it. Contrary to what I thought, I found that I wasn't just an actor, but that I had a real feeling for teaching people, a real empathy, a real understanding of the actor's problems. And my class built quite well. I started teaching in 1961 and I've been teaching ever since.

Did your work as an actor affect your approach to teaching?

Yes. I'm still an actor, and it still affects the way I teach. You see, I have an understanding of the actor's problems and the actor's obstacles, and what the actor has to deal with in the profession because I am an actor. I have that experience firsthand. A lot of directors separate actors like labor and management. They relate to the actor as if he were labor and they were management and there were a line between them. When I direct I always approach the actor, particularly people I've worked with, as a "we" thing. I give direction from an internal place and whenever the actor is having a problem I relate to it as "our" problem. When I communicate with the actor he knows where I am coming from in that I have experienced that problem and understand it. As a result, actors open up to me and communicate with me on a level that they are unlikely to do with directors they feel are alienated from them by a lack of understanding.

How do you advise your students to work with directors?

Actors who work with me over a period of time and not just for a six-week course discover that preparation is an ongoing process. It's not just a way of working, it's a way of living. You can't separate life from acting. Now, I don't want to sound like Rajneesh or some self-styled guru because I'm not. If you talk to any one of my students they'll tell you that I'm one of them.

The way I prepare my actors to work with a director is to train them solidly to learn how to push their own buttons. I train them to know their instrument and to know their craft so well that a director can make any kind of demand on them, and they will know how to accommodate him. I also tell actors that I train not to let their method show. That's their own private business, and as long as the director gets his results, he doesn't have to know how they work. Don't parade your process in front of people. That's your business.

On the other hand, if an actor needs to prepare and he can't prepare privately in his dressing room, then I tell him to take a moment on stage, and do his preparation as unobtrusively as possible. If you need to do it, you need to do it.

Which elements of your own training do you retain and which do you reject?

I reject all of my early Northwestern University acting training. It took me ten years to unlearn the crap that I learned there. I don't think that there are too many universities today that prepare the actor for the profession of acting. Universities prepare actors for community theater, for academia, and for teaching other actors in an academic environment.

Let me digress for a moment. I was exposed to many different approaches to acting. I rejected any representational style of acting instinctively, right from the beginning. I was attracted almost immediately to anything that smacked of reality, anything that seemed to be the truth. And I was intuitively attracted to the Method, Stanislavsky's system, because the underpinnings of that approach are that, if the character feels something, the actor has to find a way to feel it also. That made sense to me.

I was an avid movie fan and I would sometimes go to as many as six or eight films a week. The actors that I was most attracted to were Montgomery Clift, Geraldine Page, Kim Stanley, Eli Wallach, Karl Malden, Rod Steiger. These were the actors I would go to see because they touched me more than others.

Now, flash, cut, we spring ahead. When I was watching these actors I had no idea of a method or a system of acting. I didn't even know who Stanislavsky was. Many years later I found out that every one of the actors I had admired so much was trained by Lee Strasberg. They were all members of The Actors Studio or had attended The Studio. So, actually, I had an instinct for that type of acting right from the beginning.

When I started studying with Marty Landau, these techniques began to open up to me, and my acting changed. I grew, became more honest and real, and for the first time I had a process, the beginnings of a solid process, which I had not had for the first twelve years of my training with other teachers. So I would say that my training really started with Marty, and through Lee's work.

Is there any aspect of the Method that you've found doesn't work or that you have adapted?

Yes. That's a really good question. Stanislavsky said that his system was incomplete and, by the way, he never called it the Method. Lee called it that. Even though Stanislavsky was a genius, an innovator, a man who came along at a time when there was nothing like this around, his system was incomplete. Then Lee came along and took his system and clarified it a lot. But a lot of teachers are still haunted by things that Stanislavsky said that were countercreative.

For instance, I've eliminated the notions of objective, superobjective, actions, and activities. I got rid of that section of the Method because I think it's counterproductive. It's cerebral and intellectual, and the minute an actor deals with an action—"What am I doing? How am I doing it? And why?"—the moment an actor tries to confront or plan the "How am I doing it?" part, he's being premeditative, he's being cerebral, and he's cutting off his own organic impulses. So I feel that's a countercreative, counterproductive part of the Method and I got rid of it.

Let's talk about your particular techniques. How do you train your actors to cope with stage fright, for instance?

That's like opening a Pandora's box. I have a whole chapter on tension in my first book and I have both complex and simple exercises that deal with the elimination of tension. Now, Lee was very big on the elimination of tension. He said that creativity begins where tension leaves off, and I agree with that totally.

Which of your exercises do you consider to be the most beneficial? Which one do you use when you have a new student who is very fearful?

I do Relaxation, Sensitizing, and Personal Inventory with everybody before I start all my classes. Students come in and lie down on the floor and we all do all three of these. These three exercises are designed (1) to eliminate physical tension, (2) to elevate your sensory accessibility, and (3) to help you get in touch with how you feel on a moment-to-moment basis.

In the Relaxation Exercise students become aware of their own body weight and exaggerate that weight until they feel much heavier. Then they try to move their limbs and let them fall of their own weight, feeling the pull of gravity on each part of their bodies. What this does is force the release of any muscular tension. Along with that I ask students to make an aspirate sound, like a yawn. It helps to open up the voice box.

Sensitizing is a process that heightens the actor's sensory availability and stimulates all five senses. This helps the student use his instrument on a much more organic level. Both individually *and* in groups, students are made more aware of their senses so that they can be more responsive to the environment of a scene and to the physical aspects of their acting partner. I will ask a student to focus on one sense, one that he is least in tune with—sound, let's say—and tell him to concentrate all his energy on just listening for some period of time. Nothing else.

The Personal Inventory Exercise helps the student to penetrate to her real feelings and express them on a moment-to-moment basis. It starts with a semiaudible stream of consciousness monologue in which the student asks herself, "How do I feel right now?" then expresses those feelings, and then repeats the question. Another exercise is called "What do I want?" I ask the student to answer this question for herself in the same way as in the Personal Inventory Exercise. Both exercises can be done alone or in groups, with the answers given out loud.

To answer your question about stage fright: tension and self-consciousness or self-involvement creates stage fright, whereas selfless involvement prevents it. I have a slew of exercises dealing with selfless involvement. If the actor can get out of himself and make things in his environment more interesting for himself, he is home free as far as being self-conscious or tense goes.

A good exercise for getting out of yourself is called Observe, Wonder, and Perceive. It helps actors get interested in the people and objects around them. For instance, I'm waiting on line at the bank and I see a pretty lady. I wonder if she's married. She's carrying a philosophy book. I wonder if she's a teacher, or perhaps she's a student. Then I perceive that she's a bit fidgety; she keeps looking at her watch. You see what I mean? Maybe she's late for her class. Then I notice she's all dressed up. Maybe she's going on a job interview. Who knows?

When an actor focuses on another person it helps him get out of himself. A student will practice this in class with an acting partner. Two people will be onstage alone and they will do this exercise in the natural course of conversation by asking each other questions. Or one student will ask another these questions and the second won't even know that it's an exercise. For all intents and purposes, all that a student is doing is being interested in another person. He can do it in conversation, or he can do it by first thinking of the other person. In either case, the actor is taken out of himself and into the other person.

An actor can ask himself the same kinds of questions about the environment. He can simply look at something—a tree, say—and observe its height, color, shape. He might wonder how old it is, if it grows elsewhere, who planted it, etc. By practicing this in his own life, an actor gets good at it and can do it with ease on the stage.

When an actor is working on a character do you have him ask these questions as that character or as himself?

Now you're opening up a can of worms with me. There is *no* character. You see, when the actor separates himself from the character, he's creating a chasm. He is saying to himself, "The person in this play is not me." Well, of course the person is not him. But he's going to step on that stage and represent that character, correct? He's going to be that character. Essentially, the actor must never separate himself from the character, even by using the expression "the character" or "myself," even though he knows it is the character. I'm not Willy Loman, but in the creative process I will find personality facets in myself, from my own frame of reference, to stimulate the life of Willy Loman or whatever character I'm playing. And I absorb the character in me. That's a very important statement.

Some people believe that the actor invests himself in the character. Jane Fonda once said, "I inhabit the characters I play." You see, I think it's just the reverse. The character is not alive, but only described on paper, and there are a limited number of words that describe human behavior. I believe that as an actor, I do not inhabit the character. It inhabits me—the personality facets of myself with which I can give the character dimension. You see what I mean?

How do you help a student work on a character who is very different from himself?

First of all, I would never take a new student and turn him loose on any piece of material, not until I started to deal with his or her Instrumental Obstacles or blocks. That doesn't mean I wait years before I let people work on material. If a student has been trained prior to working with me, he can work on material immediately. However, I will begin to persuade him to use my system and techniques. But with new students I deal first with breaking down their obstacles to being who they are. You see, if I have made any contribution to the world of acting, it's first and foremost that I deal with getting the actor to a place of being who she or he is. It sounds simpler than it is. You cannot create truth on the stage unless you come from a place of truth. And you would be shocked at how many actors don't even know what their own truth is.

How do you help an actor get to his or her own place of truth?

Through what I call Instrumental Work. I use about 300 exercises that actually work. How do I do it? It all depends on the individual. I ask people to do in the instrumental area the most difficult things first. Once they gain confidence that they can do those things and expose those parts of themselves, we go on.

Let me give you an example. Say I get a student from the South who's been raised to be a lady. She would never use curse words. She might think them, but she has been properly educated and conditioned, and she is a lady. In addition to that, let's say that she is somewhat conflict phobic: she doesn't like conflict, she doesn't engage in it, and she will either quit or walk away from a conflict situation. Now this actress has decided to go into a profession that is based on conflict. There has never been a theatrically worthwhile play written that doesn't have conflict.

I'll take this conflict-shy person and I'll have her do an Accuse and Indict or a You Never Gave Me or a Dump Exercise to get into her anger, frustration, and conflict areas. I'll do this slowly. I wouldn't ask a new person to do these exercises. I will do this in stages until she overcomes her fear of conflict.

Could you describe these exercises?

They cover a lot of bases. These are not just conflict exercises; they also stimulate vulnerability.

I say to an actor, "I want you to pick somebody in your life who you feel didn't give you what you need. It can be anyone, a girlfriend, a wife, a lover, an aunt." The actor then stands on the stage and talks to someone who isn't present as if that person were there. And he indicts and accuses the (imaginary) person of his choice of not giving him the things he needed. For example, he might say, "You never gave me any love. You were never there for me. You gave me money, but you never gave me any understanding. You never touched me. You never even put your arm around me."

And this builds in intensity as the actor takes it from there and gets in touch with these hurts.

The Dump is an exercise that helps a student expurgate all the emotion that he has locked up. I tell him to begin by expressing all the feelings of frustration and suppressed anger that are blocking him and to keep on making big, forceful statements ("I'm angry. . . . I hate feeling this way!") until he feels his emotions flowing out with no obstructions.

I have another exercise called The Deathbed Exercise that is paticularly good for stimulating vulnerability. It can be done in two ways. I tell a student either to talk to someone he loves who is dying or to imagine that he himself is on his deathbed. I tell him to talk to the meaningful people in his life, saying the things that he never had the chance to tell them.

What these exercises do is open the door to expressing conflict, anger, and hostility as well as vulnerability. As the actor experiences things that he heretofore was afraid to (not in just one exercise, but repeatedly), he gets less and less afraid to expose that part of himself. And once I perceive where an actor is coming from, I structure exercises for him in particular. Everybody has his own problems or, as I call them, "obstacles." When I can pinpoint them I'll structure a whole series of exercises that will ultimately move an actor to a new place of freedom.

Once you get past an actor's "Instrumental Obstacles," as you call it, how do you instruct him to approach a particular character? Let's say that he is working on someone very different from himself in physical type or in background. How should he begin?

First of all, I think that as human beings we all share a fabric of common realities. I think that I am the way I am because I have emphasized, or been influenced in certain ways that stimulate, certain facets of my personality. You can call them subpersonalities, if you like. They are personality facets that represent how I function in the world. But I have inside of me every personality facet of every character ever written for the theater or film. I am the composite of everything. For instance, I have a deep reverence for life. I pick up spiders and put them outside my house because I won't kill one. But I also know that there is a part of me that, under certain circumstances or with the proper provocation, could, but for the grace of God, be a killer—or at least have every impulse that a convicted killer has had.

What I advise the actor to do through my process is something ongoing and quite elaborate. I ask him to find parallels in his own life that can be worked for and that will stimulate the internal emotional areas—the thoughts, impulses, feelings, concepts, belief structures, etc., that will create a character.

I have students develop the physical side of a character through animals, inanimate objects, or even insects. This will help them change the way they use their bodies and the way they relate to the world. I do tell actors to observe others, but not to imitate—to get an organic sense of another person through a specific process.

For example, say I have to work on a character who is very introverted, shy, frightened, hard to relate to publicly on a one-to-one basis. Personally, I'm not that way. I'm outgoing, outspoken, and gregarious. I can function in almost any environment fairly comfortably. But what if I had to play someone like that? I would start by asking myself under what circumstances and in what environment and in relation to whom I would feel shy, introverted, or frightened. Right offhand I know that whenever I'm involved with people I respect, I become very quiet. If I feel that they know more than I do in an area and are extremely accomplished in their knowledge, I get nervous. So, if I imagine that I am surrounded by people who intimidate me because of who or what they are, I can completely change my personality. And creating that kind of a situation would be the first thing I would do to fulfill the obligation related to being introverted, shy, or insecure as a character.

You use the term "obligation." What do you mean by that?

What I have done over a fifteen-year period is develop a system of acting that separates the craft into three simple and practical areas: Obligations, Choices, and Choice Approaches.

Every piece of theatrical material contains seven obligations (responsibilities) that the actor must define and fulfill: the emotional obligation, the relationship obligation (the relationship between him and the other characters in the play), the time and place obligation (where in time this takes place), the character obligation (what kind of person this character is), the historical obligation (when in history this play takes place), the thematic obligation (the statement the author is trying to make), and the subtextual obligation (what the essence and ambience of the play are).

A Choice is an object, a person, or a place that an actor will use to help him feel what the author tells him the character feels.

A Choice Approach is how an actor will go about fulfilling a choice, such as using sense memory to stimulate an emotion that he has decided is appropriate. If I were going to work for my mother sitting at this table I would have to create her so that I could believe she is there. I would have to create her so that I could see, feel, taste, smell, hear her, and then I could be affected by her.

Being, irreverence, and ultimate consciousness are the philosophical underpinnings of my system. It may sound a little arrogant to say *my* system, but it is. I don't feel arrogant, I feel blessed. "Being" is the state you want to achieve, "irreverence" is a philosophical and pragmatic responsibility of the actor (while working with material he must be "irreverent" toward it in order to find the elements that will fulfill the material). "Ultimate consciousness" is that state that the actor achieves when he crosses the line between conscious and unconscious inspiration. It is the point when actors will say, "I don't know what happened. Something happened to me and I took off." It's the magical state in which an actor consciously sparks an unconscious response. It's a never-never land of experience and I'm working on ways to get there consciously, repeatedly, consistently. It's not easy. That's my fourth book, *Acting from the Ultimate Consciousness.*

I was excited about doing this interview because I will talk to anyone about my work—someone on the subway, if he asked me. And I'll tell you why. The public relations aspects really don't interest me. I have a successful school. But I was anxious to do this because I want to make clear and get out to the largest number of people I can what I am doing and what this system is, not so they will come to me but because I found something I think is very important for the actor and I want to disseminate that information all over the world.

When my books were first published someone asked me why I was giving my secrets away. But they are not secrets. I wrote books because I want to share what I've discovered for myself with everybody. If there is anybody who wants to teach this work and is qualified to do so, I encourage that. I'm just anxious for more people to start using the work.

I don't want to sound like a messiah, but you see anything that improves the work of any actor anywhere in the world makes us all richer. We all profit from it. Whether I get credit for it or not is a secondary consideration. I want to go to the movies or the theater and see people function from a creative, organic place. And whoever is helping them do that makes us all richer. Good theater is good theater. Good film is good film.

I want to tell you one other thing. Over the years people have told me that coming to my classes is very interesting because there is a total absence of competitiveness. Everybody seems to want everybody else to succeed in his or her work. Nobody makes any comparisons like "I can do that better," or If I got up there I could do it." The atmosphere is that way because of the philosophical underpinnings of my work. I believe that everybody is on his own journey. Everybody is as individual as his fingerprints. So how can you be competitive with somebody that you're not? You have to be everything that you are. And that attitude permeates the work in my class. If, after my time is up on this earth, I can feel that I have contributed something in the time and place I took and the air I breathed, I will feel that I have had a successful life. It won't be measured in dollars and cents and it won't be measured in recognition. Although those things are both nice, having material objects has never been my first consideration. Neither is being famous.

Getting back to techniques, are there any specific exercises you give your actors to help them when they have to speak directly to the audience?

No, because it would all depend directly on the choice they were using. We would identify what the impetus was to speak at all, what impels the actor to talk to the audience. I directed *The Glass Menagerie*, and the lead, Tom, talks to the audience a lot. And what impels Tom to talk to the audience is his intense need to tell people about his life. I believe that was Tennessee Williams' motivation in writing that play.

When talking directly to the audience, the actor can make substitutions, make the audience different people—whatever will stimulate the inner circumstances needed to speak to those people. If it was the audience at large, the actor would have to give himself an adjustment, would have to give himself a reason to talk to this collection of people. But the reason would have to be an organic one.

You use the term "impetus." In your acting vocabulary, is that the same as "objective"?

No. Objectives are something else. Also, an objective is what you want to accomplish. Here's why I don't believe in objectives. They are all based on what I want to do. Let's say my objective is to get you to lend me money. I've got to pay my rent, I'm destitute, I'm here in this restaurant, and I want you to lend me $300. That's my objective. You see, the objective is after the fact. It's countercreative. I, Eric, have got to create a reality that stimulates a *need* in me to have $300. I have to stimulate the impetus, the need to get that money. If I just decide I want the money, it's bullshit. I, personally, don't need it. But I do *need* you to put on paper what I believe about my system of acting. So that's what I might choose to work on. The audience hears $300 because those are the lines of the play, but internally I'm working on my need to tell you about my acting system and how important it is for you to understand, not to get $300 from you.

So you are saying that you will substitute a real need from your personal life for the one you need as the character in the play?

Exactly. That's always the impetus. The word "objective" relates to what I'm doing, not what impels me to do it. Actors start at the tail end of it, not at the beginning.

Do you feel that actors need to approach comedy in a different way from drama?

No. Comedy is funny reality. The character most often doesn't know he's funny, doesn't know that the material is funny. Let me give you an example. Let's say a script says you and I have been friends for many years. We are in a restaurant and we're having a cup of coffee. The check arrives and you say, "I'll pay for it." And I say, "No, you won't." This leads to a violent argument and we end up destroying the restaurant—over a sixty-cent cup of coffee. The audience may be rolling in the aisles, but I'm totally determined that you're not going to pay this check. You got the last one. You know damn well this is my turn and I can prove it. We're into it fully. It has to be total, on-the-nose reality. The circumstance makes it funny. Comedy is funny reality. The actor approaches the material as reality. It's up to the author and the situation to make it funny.

Of course, there is an amendment to that. There are things like a comic facility, comic timing, comic intuition, riding a laugh, knowing what a punch line is. These are techniques the actor absorbs and can integrate into the creative process. But he can't make a process out of comic timing, out of creating a laugh. He can't make a process out of mugging and punching a line. He has to know that those are technical elements in the comedy so that he can absorb them into reality. In film an actor cannot make a career out of knowing how to hit marks and how to match close-ups with master shots. Those are things he learns to do, but he must integrate them into the creative process.

What about different styles of acting? How do you help actors work on Shakespeare and classical theater in general?

That's covered in the seven main obligations. The historic obligation carries with it the relationship to the morality, customs, dress, behavior, religion, and superstitions of the time the play takes place. The actor has to find parallels in his or her life that will help to fulfill the stylistic demands of the piece.

For example, during the Restoration period there were a lot of plays dealing with cuckolding. Today's sexual morality has changed considerably, so an actor who is not particularly fearful of being cuckolded will have to find something from his own experience that is as important to him as a Restoration character's fear of his wife cheating on him. When an actor makes the choice that will stimulate similar responses, feelings, and thoughts, he creates that reality.

What about the physical aspects of working on a Restoration character—the walk, the posture, the speech? How do you help actors achieve those?

That's not very difficult. You see, the physical behavior is often governed by the dress of the period. In Elizabethan drama they wore tights and ruffs. You can't really bend your neck or hold your head the same way if you wear a ruff. They wore billowy sleeves. They had a rapier and wore bodkins, and when they sat, they had to make way for the rapier. When the actors deals with costumes of the period, it naturally promotes the posture, movement, and other physical aspects of the period.

Also, I use animals to deal with certain kinds of physical manners; that is, animals translated into human behavior. By using animals an actor can affect and change his own rhythm, tempo, and aspects of movement. Studying an animal's mannerisms and working to re-create them through the body can help create character. I ask my students to go to the zoo and observe carefully, looking for the ways in which an animal's center of gravity, tempo, mannerisms, etc., can be translated into human behavior.

Years ago I used a leopard to create the character of a stealthy killer I played on a two-part "Kraft Suspense Theater." The killer was someone who did his work swiftly and silently, unseen and unheard. I'm not a particularly awkward person, but I certainly wouldn't describe myself as stealthy. When I used the leopard's movements as a starting point, it changed the way I moved and affected my behavior and thinking. Everything around me became potentially threatening. My reflexes became sharper, and I even felt like a predator. So working on the leopard helped me create the character and the emotional realities.

As far as speech is concerned, the technique for dealing with an accent or period speech (like iambic pentameter in Shakespeare) is one that an actor can and should learn. But once he has perfected his ability in this area, he must fully support the reality of the character as well. I say an actor should learn how to speak, learn the demands of style, and once he's learned those aspects, he must integrate them with the rest of reality.

Do you work with your actors on those aspects of character?

No. I send them to people who are much more qualified than I am. However, if an actor comes to class and serves us the technical demands of Shakespeare and not the reality, I say, "Put the icing on the cake after you've baked it."

Do you have any particular exercises to help actors deal with their physical environment?

The time and place obligations in every piece of material are among the first things I encourage actors to work on. Wherever a playwright sets the piece, he sets it there for a reason. The place has an impact on the character, and the actor must honor that. A setting will affect the way a character behaves; i.e., a husband and wife will argue quite differently on a city street than they would in the privacy of their own bedroom. I ask the actor to identify the impact of the place on the character and choose a place of his own that will make him feel the same way. Then I ask him to create it sensorially.

Let's say that as the character I'm supposed to feel very safe in my study. It's my private place. Well, in reality I don't have a study, but I do have a den where I go when I'm finished teaching and my wife is asleep. It's my sanctuary. I unwind, get comfortable there. I can take off my clothes, I can relax. If I wanted to feel like the character does in his study, I, Eric Morris, would sensorially create my den for myself onstage. And you have to create it so that you can see it, feel it, taste it, hear it, smell it.

Is there a particular technique that you feel helps actors learn to relate to each other on a moment to moment basis?

Yes. I have what I call Involvement Exercises. For example, one I call Telepathy. Two actors face each other and look into each other's eyes and beyond into what lies behind them. They try to respond to what they perceive to be there. They try to pick up things about the other person that they have never seen before or things that particularly interest them. This exchange forces a deep involvement with the other person.

A variation on this is for two seated actors to try to relate to each other without words, gestures, or mime, just allowing whatever is going on in the moment to happen. For example, an actor feels something for the person he is relating to, and expresses it (without words or gestures). They both respond to each other in an unbroken chain of emotional responses until both actors are ready to go into a scene they have been working on.

Another, the Inner–Outer Monologue Exercise, is very good for stimulating a moment-to-moment expression of feeling. An actor starts with the words of a monologue he has memorized. He says three or four lines and then uses his own personal words to express aloud what he is feeling at the moment. He alternates the memorized lines with his own words.

Is there anything you do to help actors prepare for TV and film as opposed to the stage?

If the actor becomes a solid craftsman, he can make the medium adjustment on his own. For the stage you have to be bigger, etc. If you're solid, you can do it. Some teachers build their careers on the froth of teaching medium technique. In my opinion that's nonsense. That's not really where the actor's involvement should be. Once you're a craftsman you can adjust to any medium very quickly.

Are there any specific techniques you teach your actors for auditioning purposes?

Only to do the work, to relax, to get to be who they are, to be honest and willing to expose themselves. I warn them against any ingratiating behavior. If they do the work, that's the best audition facility they have. When I hear about audition classes and cold reading classes or scene study classes I have to chuckle to myself. I see ads for scene study in the trades all the time. You can't teach an actor to do scene work until he is instrumentally ready.

Also, if you teach an actor how to audition by reading properly or understanding the material so that he can intellectually deliver a good reading, he won't be acting from an authentic place.

How do you use improvisations?

I do use them, but I think that the indiscriminate use of improvisations is a better playwright's technique than an actor's. Indiscriminate use teaches the actor how to write the circumstances as he goes along. The way I use it is to improvise material using personal realities from the actor's life parallel to those the actor will use in the final production (play or film) that he is preparing for. When you give an actor the freedom to paraphrase the lines and improvise around the circumstances, he will feel freer to use the technique until he becomes solid with his choices and choice approaches. Then he can go on to the words. I never hold improvisations for general use.

How is your curriculum structured? Is it divided by levels?

I don't have separate classes. I mix working professionals with beginners. A lot of people frown on that.

First of all, I don't audition people who come to my classes. I think that's more for the ego of the teacher than it is for the benefit of the student. I don't think people should audition for the privilege of learning something. An audition says "Prove to me that you have talent," or "Prove to me that you know how to use it." I don't believe in that.

I have a weekly master class. It's not for master actors, but for mastery of the work. We only do scenes and monologues in that class and that's only open to people who have been with me long enough to have gotten far enough in the instrumental work and far enough in their understanding of the craft so that they can work directly on the material without worrying about blocks.

I mix my other classes with beginners and working professionals for this reason: Everybody is on his or her own journey and I deal with people so individually that it doesn't make any difference where they are in relation to anybody else. The seasoned professional can learn as much from somebody working on his first exercise as he can from other professionals. And the beginner can learn as much from the professional struggling with the process. I've never had any problems in mixing the levels. It works out wonderfully.

Do you allow students to critique each other?

Always. It's part of the learning process. Actors need feedback. Also, learning how to critique the work is a growth-producing process and lets me know where a student is in her understanding of the craft. It also gets an actor to articulate what she sees; later, she can use what she has absorbed on herself. But I always ride herd on criticism. If a criticism seems to be coming from the wrong place—which is very rare—I will jump in. I don't allow subjective, hurtful, or destructive criticism.

What techniques do you use to help an actor create a physical state like drunkenness or pain?

Drunkenness and pain are approached sensorially. You can approach drunkenness on two levels: you can work sensorially for the alcohol as it goes down your throat and into your body and for the process of getting drunk. Or you can work sensorially for the physical manifestations of drunkenness (how it feels to be drunk), which produces the same effect. It depends on which side you want to approach it from. I prefer using getting drunk. I think it's a more creative way of doing it.

What do you think makes some actors better than others?

One thing, surely, is the amount of talent and instinct they already possess, their innate ability. You might say because someone is more endowed. But given two actors with equal endowment, the thing that makes one better than the other is his commitment to developing his talent. You see, I think talent is very common. What's rare is the development of that talent. There are, of course, some exceptions to that. There are some very gifted actors, some naturals who have never had an acting lesson. But they are very few and far between.

Do you want to mention some of the people you've trained?

I'm reluctant to mention them. There are a lot of teachers who have made careers as a result of the success of the people who have studied with them. Some teachers claim responsibility for actors who came to only two of their classes. But the fact is that actors study around a lot and I think that most actors become a composite of many exposures. I've had a lot of famous actors work with me, but I don't want to claim responsibility for them.

Do you feel that contemporary actors approach their craft differently than their predecessors?

Oh, yes. I think that today's audiences are so psychologically sophisticated that their demand for reality in acting has created the necessity for today's actors to dig deeper and to be much more authentic in the life that they produce on stage.

Who are your favorite actors?

Geraldine Page, Anne Bancroft, Jack Nicholson, Al Pacino. Clift was my favorite. I'm not a fan of Brando, but I feel he's a talented man—a little schticky, maybe, but talented. I like Robert Duval, Rod Steiger. People like Meryl Streep, who I think is very talented, come from a much more technical place than from their own reality. There are many talented actors, but there is something I admire more than talent, and that's truth. Talent has got to be married to authenticity.

What do you think of the English actors?

Which ones?

Let's start with the old school: Gielgud, Olivier.

I'm not fond of them, and particularly Olivier. I think he is an extraordinarily talented trickster. He choreographs his voice. He marks his voice and knows when it's going to peak and valley. He choreographs his whole vocal delivery. People in life don't do that. Did you ever see him play a Jewish person? I come from an immigrant Jewish family and I know what they sound like. This man plays a Jew like he read it in a Sears catalogue. He's got as much affinity for the soul and heart of a Jewish person as that coffeepot. In my early years I saw Olivier play Hamlet and I was impressed. I saw it again and was not nearly as impressed. I do like someone like Richard Harris because he has moments of authenticity.

The English theater and its actors (with some exceptions) leave me cold. They are impeccably trained and get a chance to develop their facility better than American students by acting in the provinces all the time. They work so much more. But, then again, it is a facility. If my son or daughter wanted to study at the Royal Academy of Dramatic Arts I would tie that child up and lock him or her in a closet until such a foolish notion disappeared.

Now the Method is creeping into England. I'll say this and risk a raised eyebrow, risk sounding egocentric and pompous and maybe even arrogant. The system that I am developing and have developed is the acting of the future. What is now controversial (and I have been known as a controversial teacher) is becoming less so as I've become more successful. I'm still considered avant-garde and out of the mainstream, but I think that in the next ten years or so my Method will be more widely accepted and used. I'm convinced of it.

What aspects of your approach were considered controversial?

People used to say that I was practicing therapy without a license. They used to call my class a couch class.

Does your approach involve probing your students' private lives in some public way?

Of course. Acting is the most personal form of art. And I get into personal areas with the students. I ask them to express how they feel and who they are. Not the things that they hold private, but their personal views, their relationships. Lee Strasberg avoided that. When an actor would begin to tell him something about his work that smacked of being too personal, Lee would throw his hands up in the air and say, "No, I don't want to hear it. Save it for your therapist." I think that was a horrific mistake—and I dedicated one of my books to the man, so you can see that I respect him. But that's a mistake. That's the missing link in the Method. Stanislavsky wouldn't do it and nobody else would do it either. I am not considered controversial so much anymore, but there are still people who come to my class and say that it's a little bit like group therapy, because they don't understand. Of course it's therapeutic. All acting training is therapeutic. But it isn't psychotherapy. I don't deal with psychotherapy. I deal with Instrumental Behavior Modification. There's a big difference.

Instrumental Behavior Modification?

In psychotherapy one of the roles of the therapist is to get a patient to understand his problems and find tools for coping with those problems. I don't care if the actor understands the origin of his problems. I only care whether or not the actor is aware that his problems are an obstacle to his freedom of behavior and expression.

Would you give me a concrete example?

Let's say an actor feels physically inadequate because of his size, feels that he is not accepted by people. Let's say he even imagines that people are talking about him behind his back. First, I begin to work on the expression of that fear or belief structure ("I feel inadequate; I feel short; I feel that people don't like me"). I have the actor expose his feelings in front of the class so that he doesn't have to redirect anything or hide his feelings. They are out in the open. Then I start working on building the actor's self-esteem through a series of Ego Exercises.

Can you give me an example of an Ego Exercise?

I might do several of them. For instance, in the Count Your Blessings Exercise I ask a student to list all the good things in his life. This can be done audibly or in silence. I would start by saying, "Okay, you've already said you feel inadequate, especially with women. Now, what's good about you?" Then the student might reply, "Oh, I think I'm smart. I think I'm talented. I think I'm a really good person. I care about people. I have a lot to give. I feel I have good parents. I feel I've had a wonderful education." As the actor's esteem builds in the areas of his strengths, the other areas become less important and less hurtful. I have seen actors do a total about-face and actually look different when what they are inside becomes visible. They become more attractive because they are exposing who they are. That is an example of an instrumental problem and obstacle that can be overcome through instrumental Behavior Modification.

Another exercise, which is an Ego Craft Preparation, is called the Magic Pocket. In this fantasy the actor imagines he has anything in his pocket that will fit there: a contract to do three pictures a year for the largest studio in Hollywood; a cashier's check for $10 million; the keys to a brand-new Ferrari—anything that stimulates elation and a sense of specialness that will help the actor give his best to a scene.

What advice would you give new actors starting out in the profession?

Don't act unless you must, unless you have to, unless it's the primary passion of your life. And if you must act, train yourself to become the most complete craftsman, the best actor, that you can be.

Laura Zucker

Allan Miller

Allan Miller conducts private acting classes and coaching sessions in Los Angeles, where he works with singers and actors for Broadway and feature films. A director and actor as well as a teacher, he—with his partner and wife Laura Zucker—founded The Back Alley Theatre, which has presented Are You Now or Have You Ever Been, Slab Boys, The Journalists, The Fox, Duet for One, Feedlot, *and other productions. He also maintains a career as a professional actor and appears regularly on TV, in feature films, and on the stage.*

While on the East Coast, Mr. Miller was on the faculty of Yale Drama School, New York University School of the Arts, and Circle in the Square Drama School. He was an early member of The Actors Studio, and continues his association with that institution by conducting special exercise classes when he is in New York.

Mr. Miller's concern with the source of the actor's inspiration has been an ongoing focus in his teaching. He believes that "if you only prepare yourself for the expected, you only do the expected." How to

prepare an actor for the unexpected "so that inspiration can strike" is
something he continues to seek through new and innovative
techniques.

How did you get started teaching acting?

Basically, I was an actor and still am. As a young actor I became
a member of The Actors Studio and as a member of The Studio you
are always asked for comments and critiques. I became quite a
commenter. After a while Strasberg recommended me for a teaching
job at The Dramatic Workshop, which is where I initially got my
training in acting. Erwin Piscator is the man I originally studied
with. He was Bertolt Brecht's mentor and had taught him "epic
theater." As a fledgling, I had gone to him to study, and Piscator has
been in the background of my mind ever since. Whenever I doubt
my own abilities or perceptions, I go back in my thoughts to Erwin
Piscator. His vision of theater was so marvelous, so human, and at
the same time so theatrical. Everything that Brecht used at the
Berliner Ensemble came from Piscator originally. His use of stage
devices and media—talk about multimedia! He was a great innovator
and as early as 1948 was using slides, projections, scrims, turnta-
bles—you name it. I was on crew for a lot of those productions and
took classes as well. His vision of what theater could be was very
inspiring.

What was his approach to acting?

Although he taught acting, he was mainly a director. Like
Stanislavsky, he would use all sorts of combinations and a variety of
ways to get actors to arrive at certain things that are not in the acting
books. He used all the *principles* of the acting exercises when he
directed, but he didn't literally use the exercises themselves. Piscator
would say to an actor, "Green, green, darling. Think of green.
Growing. Things are growing here." And the actor sometimes got it
and sometimes didn't. He would say, "You have to see life growing
inside, like fields." I thought I understood what he meant. I
remember Toscanini saying the same kinds of things in order to
inspire people. Stylistically, the productions that Piscator did at The
Dramatic Workshop were just wonderful—from Shakespeare to

Robert Penn Warren. This was 1948. Then I studied with Uta Hagen and then I got into The Actors Studio.

So my first job as a teacher came because I became more incisive and perceptive about other people's work and Strasberg recommended me. Then I began to become more of a teacher. I held private classes and I coached and taught at four different universities. Yale brought me in as a troubleshooter and so did NYU when the professional theater program was started. I stayed there two years. I was a professional coach to the directors at Yale because at the time Robert Brustein had begun to perceive that a lot of the third-year directing students were not well enough equipped to know how to work with actors.

When CCNY got the single largest private donation for a cultural complex, it started a new professional theater program. I helped start the acting program. I taught classes there and also continued my own private classes and sometimes took acting jobs. Doing all that helped me realize certain things about teaching. In 1964 I was hired to head the acting program for Har-You-Act, the Harlem Youth Act that was intended to teach acting to young black teenagers and eventually to develop a black theater. In two years time we did build one, The New Lafayette Theatre, which was well known during its time. I found that I had to use very different acting devices to teach these teenagers—they were not conceptual thinkers. So I began to devise ways to deal with them and I began to incorporate the new ways back into my earlier ideas about how actors learn their craft.

How has your own training influenced your teaching techniques?

When I was studying I learned sensory work, sense memory, etc., and I got good at them. In fact, when I studied at Uta Hagen's there was only one person who mystified me, and that was Geraldine Page. I began to perceive that Geraldine was doing something else besides working on the actions, the beats, and the objectives that we all did. There was something else going on with her that was not quite as nameable. I began to realize that there was another area of acting that was not being talked about or explored and that was one of the reasons I left Uta and moved elsewhere.

We had been told over and over again what we were supposed to do. We had to have a subtext, for instance, and so I would write it out carefully. But every time I tried to do it, there seemed to be other text beneath it that I couldn't keep out of my head. I couldn't figure out how any human being could think only what he told himself to think. It's impossible. All sorts of other thoughts used to come into my head. Then I began to remember Geraldine Page and I thought, "Yes, that's what she was doing. She was letting other thoughts in besides the ones she was supposed to think." That became a key element. I was so taken by these ideas that were going around inside me that I thought, "This time when I do a scene at The Actors Studio, I'm going to list all the things that I think I'm responsible for—like, my character is a writer so I have to do something about his being a writer." The man carries around his wife's will in his pocket, so I wrote an imaginary will for this character. As a writer I took a pen and pad and jotted down things that were interesting to me that I thought might be good for a writer to use. There were a whole series of things like that.

So I had this list of things that I was going to do, but I decided not to do them in any order. I wasn't going to try to do them simply so that they paid off for the scene; I was just going to make sure that I carried out some action for each thing on my list. My partner couldn't figure out what I was doing, but she agreed to do it with me. A lot of different experiments were going on at The Studio at the time.

We came in and did it and at the end, Strasberg, for one of the few times I worked there, was beaming. When the scene was over he suddenly swung back to me and said, "Allan, I thought you were doing one thing with a lot of variations." And I said proudly, "No! It was a lot of different things." He said, "Like what?" I pulled out my piece of paper and started going over the different acting choices I had made. He kept nodding and nodding as I told him. He said, "What were you working on when you started to shake?" I said at that point I was in between subjects and that's just what happened to me. He said, "Next time let more of what happened in between happen. And there is only one thing you left off this whole list." "What?" "You didn't do the scene." I said, "Oh, my God, I didn't do the scene." So next time I came in and tried to do "the scene" and it was terrible. He didn't see a structure for whatever was supposed to be happening dramatically in the scene in terms of the totality of the play. But that wasn't my goal in the work I was doing. I was trying something else.

A while later I came back to The Studio and tried a scene again. Lee got a little tough this time. He said, "Allan, I really don't know what to tell you. Let me try to express what I perceive about your work. One part of you strives mightily to arm yourself with all the things necessary to act the scene—actions, sense memories. And it's all good. But there is another part of you that seems to want something different, something else. You aren't quite there. You're a teacher. Maybe you do something in your own classes that would help you find your way."

I began to define the problem. If one part of me is striving to do what I think should be done to accomplish a scene and another part of me is trying to do something different—I don't know what—how am I ever going to find out what this other part is if I'm busy trying to do what I think I need to do in order to fulfill the scene? That's the conflict. It seemed to me that the only way to find out what this other force was *was not* to do the scene.

So I tried another scene at The Studio. But this time I didn't learn the lines. I read the scene once. I didn't make any choices or do any sensory work, any actions, anything. I decided that I would act out in sound and movement whatever happened to *me* during the scene, moment to moment. I was trying to locate this other force so I took away the opposing force.

Three days before I was scheduled to do the scene I went into absolute panic. I couldn't eat, sleep, or control myself.

I went to do the scene at The Studio and found myself screaming backstage, "It's not a scene. . . . It's just an exercise." And this strange voice came out of me and I proceeded to go ahead and act out whatever I felt was going on in my body. A little way into it I was deeply involved with sensations and feelings and, suddenly, I was overwhelmed with the need to look at the audience. When I looked up I saw every single person in the room riveted and I started to cry.

What I learned was that when you prepare yourself for the expected you do only the expected. How do you prepare yourself for the unexpected so that inspiration can strike? That's what I have striven to maintain as part of my work.

How do you as a teacher help your students achieve that?

If a student can use his own devices to get there, I don't interfere. I just build on what's there. But if somebody has obstacles I do different things. For instance, I have students pick three different physical movements—one for the upper portion of the body, one for the lower, and one for the whole body, such as bending forward and coming back up. Then I show them how to open their voice box while they do that. I try to stress that their goal is to try to get their voices open. But they must do it in rhythm no matter what happens to them. So there is a structure there all the time regardless of what impulses occur. They have to stick to the rhythm no matter what they are doing. Then I will say, "Sing a little song like 'Row, row, row your boat.' " And they have to do that while they are moving in rhythm. At this point it's all very innocent, it's all very simple, it's all very familiar.

Then I'll give them the second movement—a kick for instance, which has to be executed in a totally different rhythm and to be vocalized with the throat open. They do one movement in rhythm, like bending forward, bending backward. Then they hold it. The second rhythm, with the legs, is different; and the third rhythm, with the shoulders, differs from the first two. Now when they sing it has to be in time to each rhythm. So there is this physical rhythmic structure. Then I encourage them to speed up the rhythm toward the end. And then I tell them, "Each time I say, 'Hold,' I want you to let all these physical forces gather within you. Don't release them."

By now they are engaged in three movements. When they end the three movements, I say, "Hold. Stay where you are. Close your eyes and make only sounds that reflect whatever is happening inside your body right now. It can be prickles, changes in temperature, a kick in your stomach, whatever." They can only make noises with their eyes closed to help them get in touch with the various sensations they are experiencing. Then I'll say, "Put your arms out and add in anything you now feel in your arms." Then I tell them to keep making those noises, but to go into a monologue while they are vocalizing.

A monologue they have already prepared?

Yes. I do this exercise after they have already done a monologue in class, one that has not come to life for them and that they are having trouble fulfilling. It's just incredible what can happen after this exercise. The monologue becomes so wonderfully infused with thought, feeling, and sensation, that you cannot imagine the difference until you have seen a "before" and "after." There is no way to describe how students unconsciously make connections with the material when they get in touch with what is happening in their bodies.

I'm now going back to the story about The Actors Studio. The unconscious is where all our real impulses lie, every day. Ninety percent of the day our reactions are surface reactions—they are typical, habitual, and conventional. Most of the time, to locate our real selves, we have to separate ourselves and give ourselves over to something else, something physical. I found that this exercise helps cut into those areas where students connect with material unconsciously. You see, once you have read a piece of material, it is already stirring somewhere in your mind. You just don't know the code for it. If, after reading a script, you wake up the next morning and feel sick, for instance, how do you know it isn't because of what you've read? How do you know it isn't because of some association to the material? The point is to use anything that is going on inside you that may be connected to the material to see if it is associated.

What are some other exercises that you have developed?

Let's say I just saw a student do a scene and it wasn't very good. I will take a hat and say to the class, "Will the first five people in this row just write down a subject, any subject, like 'My Happiest Vacation' or just one word—'Money'? Write a title or subject." I tell the students who have been working on the scene, "Here. These people have given us some topics. Reach in the hat and pick out two. But don't tell us what they are." Then I trick them a bit and tell them to pick out a third. "Now you have three subjects. Remember when you were in school and you used to have to do an essay on a subject? All you are going to do as you go through the scene (which you are going to repeat) is try to think of and behave in any way that is like an essay on these three subjects. Do anything that occurs to you about, for instance, chocolate candy (if that was on one of the papers you picked), including licking your lips or moaning. I want you to act out any impulse that occurs to you that is related to any of those three subjects, while you go through the lines in the scene." Some people find that very difficult to do because they are stuck in what they are used to thinking of when they say the lines. In no time at all these same people are thinking and feeling and behaving in the most extraordinarily different ways you could possibly imagine during the scene.

After they have done the scene using the three subjects in their heads I tell them, "Out of all that, not everything was right for the scene. That's not why we did this. But, if you liked *some* of those things"—and there are invariably lots of things they did like—"try to duplicate them. Remember what you were thinking of when you did such and such? What did that come from?" And students always know what sparked a particular moment. But they have no idea of how it would fit into the scene. That's the whole point—to free them, to get them to stop trying to make the scene fit their preconceived notions so that other kinds of impulses can flow into it. I have not yet seen a single scene that didn't gain by this exercise.

Let's say someone does a scene and it's just okay. I will often ask the person if he or she has ever gone sailing. He or she might say yes. I will then ask, "How do you get a sailboat to go from one place to another when you can't go in a straight line? It would be no fun or adventure if you could just go straight. It's all that tacking that makes sailing fun. *That's* the pleasure. If what happens to you while you are going from one place to another isn't exciting, isn't a pleasure, simply having arrived at your destination in a straight line doesn't make any difference. Now please try doing the scene again as if you are sailing and you don't know whether you are going to get to your destination right away or not, but there is a little time to enjoy the wind and sun."

Sometimes a student will look at me without understanding, and then I might say, "Look at your scene partner. Do you like the color of her hair? Why don't you take a couple of moments to enjoy her hair, like the sun and the sailboat?" Then he will understand. I say, "Try to commit yourself to incorporating any other things that you may be thinking of and do something about them." Invariably, the person will reach out in the middle of the scene and touch the hair of his partner, which wouldn't have occurred to him before. So impulses are encouraged to emerge that are not in a "straight line."

How are your classes structured?

I gave up scene classes about twelve years ago, when it occurred to me that prior to that time I must have seen at least 3,000 scenes and I couldn't remember more than about ten—because only ten were memorable. The rest were either poor or fair—or even good—but not illuminating or evocative or stirring. So I asked myself why this is. Am I contributing anything to scene work? Then I thought, "There is no one right way to do a scene and I, like all other teachers, tell students how the scene *should* be done." But I'm just giving them the solutions I think are best. If I weren't able to be in class on a particular day and another teacher were brought in, that teacher might see totally different things about the scene. I've seen too many different productions of the same play not to know that that's true.

So I said to all my classes at the time, "From now on anybody can do a scene, but I will only talk about it after I've seen it done in three totally different ways. I want the scene done with three totally different interpretations, each done well. For instance, I want a scene done as if it had been directed by Ingmar Bergman, Fellini, the Marx Brothers, or Kazan. In other words, if a particular director gives you an interpretation of a scene and you can't carry it out well, that's one problem. But if you do carry it out well, that doesn't mean you've played the scene right. It just means you've done what the director wanted. There is no right way to do the scene, particularly for most TV and movie work nowadays. But for your own sake why shouldn't you enjoy the idea of 'Well, gee, suppose I had the chance to do this scene with Fellini—I wonder what he might ask me to do,' and then try to do the scene with those attitudes in mind? After that we'll talk about your scene work." Needless to say, I don't get a lot of scene work anymore. Most actors, I find, are terrified they won't be able to carry it off.

What do you do instead?

I do improvisations on scenes and, most of the time, I do exercises.

You see, in the last fifteen years I have found a huge change in the way actors think about parts. When I taught in New York most actors I was dealing with were stage actors. Discussions of how a director worked with you or what you were doing in rehearsals would go on for hours. In California, TV and film actors don't discuss their rehearsals with each other because they don't have any. There is a paucity of thinking about the different ways to deal with a piece of material because nobody is given the opportunity to do it. My own experience in the eleven years I've been in California is that out of the 150 TV and film jobs I've done, if I've had a total of ten rehearsals, that's a lot. Four of them were on *Barney Miller*. That show was famous for letting actors work on a scene while it was being taped and letting the actors see the tape so they could go back and try something else to improve it. That was as close to a real rehearsal as you are going to get in TV. Most of the time all a director gives you is blocking. That's not rehearsing and you can't give your imagination free rein.

What I do in California is different from what I would be doing in New York because the emphasis there is still stage work. Now I give eight-week courses that break the actor's work down into five basic areas.

(1) Text. You should be able to deal with text separately from character work. You should be able to find what the *text* says before or besides engaging in how a character may deal with the text.

(2) Character. You should be able to work on the character separately from the text. Suppose a playwright changes the lines. Often different drafts change the plot line, but leave the character the same.

(3) Personal Habits. Everybody has personal habits. We don't

regularly break habits to do a part; we bring our habits to the part. Some habits keep an actor from using himself creatively. So there is a whole area of improvising and exercise work that I call working on one's personal habits.

(4) Emotional Areas. I'm open to anything here.

(5) The Material. What does a particular piece of material call for? If you are doing *Summer and Smoke*, it's not the same as working on *Long Day's Journey into Night*. There is a different quality. I don't mean just culturally. If you only had to deal with the title, *Long Day's Journey into Night*, you would get totally different images than you would from something titled *Porky*. You have to be free to let yourself conjure up images and sensations from a quick reading of the material before you go into the details.

Let me expand my text analysis a bit. I explain this to students by asking them if they know the song "Row, Row, Row Your Boat" well. Of course, most say yes. Then I ask them how and why, given the song, I am supposed to row the boat according to the "text" of the song. Invariably, after going over the words by rote, a student will say "gently." Then he will correct himself and say, "gently and merrily." I will say, "Okay, that's how I'm supposed to row the boat. Now tell me why. It's in the text." He will say, "Oh, because life is but a dream." Then I will ask him to repeat how and why I should row the boat. "Gently and merrily because life is but a dream." Then I say, "Okay, now that you all know that—it's in the text—take away the last three lines and just say the first line." Everybody just does it the same way again instead of letting his or her new knowledge of the song affect the way the lines are said. Then I remind them all that the boat is supposed to be rowed gently and merrily. "Why don't you at least say the line gently and merrily?" Then I will ask them if "life is but a dream" is good or bad. And I get them to say the last line on the basis of their answer and then tell them to say the first line again exactly like that. What I am looking for is what the *text* says. It's a way to get students to focus on what's in the text, and not on their habitual reaction to material.

Next, I will ask a student to tell me what he thinks is the dirtiest, sexiest song that was ever written, judging from the text alone. You'll never guess. It's "Night and Day." The students look at me with disbelief. But if you repeat the lyrics you will hear a person talking about making love night and day, and wanting to spend his or her life making love day and night, night and day. Has it ever been sung that way? Never. Maybe it wasn't written to be sung that way, but the point is that nobody has ever tried. I've coached a lot of singers and very few sing the text. They sing an arrangement of the text, not what it *says*.

I feel the same habits apply to dialogue. Most actors immediately read in some reaction to the text or interpret it in a way that doesn't reflect what is really in it. When an actor has to get down on his or her knees and say to another actor, "You are my lord," he can be ironic or whatever. But why not just try to live up to what he is saying and actually give someone else the power to be a lord over him? I want to see actors do that first. Then we can discuss other variations and interpretations. I find that 99% of the time nobody does what the text says.

I also ask students to use the lyrics of songs as a way to learn this because lyrics are instantly available. If an actor works on "God Bless America," he has to do what the text says, invoke God to bless all of America. I don't want to know about his personal prejudices or his personal reactions. It's tough to do that, but incredibly wonderful. And it brings up emotions and insights and all sorts of wonderful things in the actor that he never gets a taste of when he is only trying to figure out how his character is trying to react to the text.

Another exercise I like I use for personal habits. Most of us are used to the obvious relationship between expression and thought and feeling: when you are feeling good, you behave that way. I like to change that around a little bit. I will often ask a student to repeat a scene (or a monologue). If he was feeling good the first time, I ask him to do something hostile or aggressive when he repeats it— punch the air, hit the table, growl, whatever. I tell him to use his body or his voice to express something negatively. If he was feeling angry or depressed, I ask him to do a celebratory thing, like clapping hands or shouting with joy, the second time around. And if he was not sure how he was feeling, I tell him to do a little soft shoe. But

I insist that he stay with the impulse for a while, even if it changes. Whatever action he picks, he does it only once in a while. It's amazing what the scene looks like when it is based on what is happening to the *actor*. I mean, after all, who is making the adjustments to the part—the actor or the character? If an actor is doing something habitual in a scene and it feels really good, I tell him to add another thing that gives the scene an unexpected wrinkle.

Everything I do is based on trying to trap and trick and encourage inspiration. And inspiration is unexpected, unanticipated. So if an actor only does what he is supposed to be doing, he can't get inspired.

What other exercises do you do to help students break personal habits?

Going against the lines is an exercise I like. Say an actor is supposed to like another person a lot in a scene. I suggest that he behave as if he doesn't—as if he has the opposite feeling—just to see what happens. That can help the actor move in and out of his accustomed habits.

But there are also physical habits that need breaking. If you are accustomed to using your hands, tie them down. I've hung a sheet across the stage while a scene is going on and told students to act the whole scene with only their feet showing. It works miracles when students get the bottom part of their bodies involved in what they are doing.

What about character work?

Character work is totally misunderstood. One of the reasons I got angry and left The Actors Studio is because Lee never worked on character. He only worked on the actor's problems and I found that didn't help the actor use his talents in character work.

Let me give you an example. Some years ago I was in a production of *The Country Girl*. The actor who was playing the part of Bernie Dodd was not doing well and I came in to read for it. I came in like gangbusters because I was dying to do it. I got the part and was thrust into short rehearsals and then, suddenly, I had to get down to work. I began to flounder and the director was not helpful at all.

One day I was sitting there trying to puzzle this all out and nothing was sparking me. So I decided to go out on stage and act everything I *wished* I could do for the role, and it just took off like a sizzler. That's all I did in production. I acted what I wished I could do in the part, and I must say the response was good. Strasberg came back and said it was the best Bernie Dodd he'd ever seen.

So I adapted what I learned from my own experience and use it as a principle. If somebody is having trouble working on a scene I may say, "Do what the character has never done before, and do it well. Do it the way the character wishes he could do it." Or if somebody is having trouble with a monologue I will say to him, "How do you think the character would *wish* he could do this? Now try to do it like that." Invariably something gets sparked. What I'm saying is that as any good actor reads a part he gets ideas about his character, but these begin to wear down or be overshadowed by the actor's own proclivities or habits.

An actress was doing a scene in class from a play she was in out here in California. Her character was somebody who was hired to sing at funerals. Everybody wanted her to sing because she was so good. The actress thought of herself as a terrible singer, so I said, "Okay, you're a terrible singer, she's a wonderful singer. You can't get to be a wonderful singer by tomorrow, but what kind of singer do you think she is? Dramatic, wailing, blues? The character probably thinks that most other singers can't touch her. Instead of you, the actress, singing, why don't you instruct everybody else in the class on how they are supposed to sing?" At first we did this as an improvisation to get the other students to sing, and the actress started to make them sing very well. Then I said to her, "Now you sing like that." And she took off. That scene stopped everyone in class.

Sometimes an actress can't do it as herself. Doesn't the *character* want to do this to be seen in a certain way? I will say to someone, "You are working on a part now. If you had to write an epitaph for this character, what would you want to have written about him or her? Now act those things." She'll put down things like "wonderfully compassionate." I'll say, "Then behave like that. Never mind if you don't feel like that, behave like that. Practice it in the supermarket, in the bank; live up to that epitaph for that character." Then I see people beginning to do character work. That's different from having special quirks for a character.

I had a part in *Are You Now or Have You Ever Been*. The character I was working on had tics and I wondered when I was supposed to tic and what it was based on. Well, tics are physical short circuits that come from anxieties or whatever is going on in the person. So I decided that whenever I felt any sensation in *my* body I'd tic. When it's based on something that is true, it is done truthfully. When it's just an idea of something, it stays an idea.

A good example of that is Olivier's performance in *Becket*. Originally, he was playing Becket and Anthony Quinn was playing the king. Quinn was very well cast for the role—he was crude and rough, and he was good. And Olivier was good too. But in one sequence when he had to change from his Becket robes to those of the archbishop, he became luminous. He had no words and he just lit up the stage. When I heard he was going to switch roles and play the king, I went to see it again. He was brilliant but totally unbelievable as the king. He was brilliant because his choices of behavior were astoundingly rich and theatrical and moving, although he wasn't believable doing them. He did a drunk scene that didn't convince the audience that he was drunk, but the behavior that emerged was extraordinary. Quinn never could have imagined doing such a thing. At the end of the first act when Olivier has to scream, "Becket, Becket," he lay down behaving as if he were drunk at the edge of the apron of the stage, upside down, screaming. As the curtain was coming down, he was dragged off by his feet just before it touched the stage. Any other actor would have been shot for daring to do that, but he did it wonderfully.

Olivier's behavior throughout was so much richer than Quinn's, although Quinn looked the part so much more, that it confirmed some things for me: If you behave like the part, if you carry out something wonderfully, you create behavior for the character. So if you are playing a boxer, you work on the behavior of a boxer. How you relate to that behavior makes the difference. If an actress is playing Laura in *The Glass Menagerie*, she has to ask herself whether a person with a brace wants to have it or not. The actress has to put one on her leg and behave as terrifically as she can and create something for that character. If she acts out the externals of the character, she can give a nice accounting of the part. But if she adds in the desires, the hopes, and the dreams around that brace, that's a whole other matter.

I will often give an actor a physical characteristic to incorporate into a character. For example, I may instruct a student to behave asymmetrically. I will say, "This character is not in charge of her life, so whatever you do you have to behave so that she's never in symmetry. You can't use two hands on the same level at the same time. This is for a character who is out of balance, so you are going to make a choice, right or wrong, but you must carry it out well. Whatever happens you can't hold your head straight or have both arms even." All sorts of other impulses come up then.

Character work to me is a combination of physical choices that help express something about the part that is based on things happening to you. If you want to create a character who is very pinched, for instance, and concerned about his life, you can make a physical choice like wearing tight underwear. Then you play that you are wearing tight jockey shorts. That's got to make you shift around uneasily. You don't have to *be* uneasy, you don't have to make believe you are uneasy, you just have to pick something that creates uneasy behavior.

Let's say you want to play someone who behaves as if he were on top of everything all the time. Imagine yourself wearing a cashmere outfit. That's all you are doing the whole time you are playing— wearing cashmere, as you drink, as you eat, whatever. And suddenly you are behaving luxuriously. If you want to behave sensuously, do the same thing. If you enjoy stroking a cat, stroke your partner as if he or she were a cat and you *are* behaving sensuously. You don't have to feel sexual to do the part. Just pick behavior that creates the feeling. I find that helps actors begin to find character.

Then there are attitudes. If I say to you, "Everybody who comes in through the door from now on is a leukemia victim," your attitude toward anyone who comes in, even if you don't like him, changes dramatically. So, as the character, you walk around thinking everybody else is terminally ill. It's an attitude. It doesn't mean you have to like everyone, but you begin to give off some sort of message that communicates deep feelings for everyone. So I give students physical choices that I think may be conducive to or guide them to character behavior that they can then assimilate for themselves.

How do you help students in the emotional areas?

I use places. Now remember, all of these things are basically to warm the actor toward working on the material more openly, more intuitively. They have nothing to do with th actor's interpretation of a given part. The director may have an interpretation that is different from the actor's or the actor may not have an interpretation for the whole play anyway. He's just doing pieces of the part and leaving the director to shape the entire interpretation.

Anyway, I tell students to pick a place suggestive of friendship, for instance, from their own experience. It could be a schoolyard—anyplace. Now I ask them to describe that place physically and sensorially. How big is it? What does it smell like? And after they are clearly focused on the place, I ask them, every once in a while, to make a sound that is expressive of that place. Less often, I ask for a sound that doesn't have anything to do with that place, like the sound of a dive bomber or something else. So when they start to talk about the place they chose, a sound will emerge and I see them start to light up. Then I ask them to pick somebody who occurs to them, even if that person doesn't belong in that schoolyard, and to put the person there. And I ask about that person. What are his physical characteristics? As they begin to describe the person and I feel them tune into that person, I say, "Now sing the first song that pops into your mind and sing it to that person." They always start getting emotional at this point. It never fails. All sorts of mixed feelings from the schoolyard through friendship come up.

Then I change. I say, "Let's pick a place suggestive of business or service—a bank, for instance." And we go through the same sequence again and I'll say, "Pick a person." Sometimes they will pick their grandmother, for instance, and I will ask them to sing the first song that pops into their head to their grandmother. Then I ask them to sit quietly for a little while, think about that person, and imagine that person is singing a song to them. Then they get emotional all over again.

Of course I use affective memories, but very often, right in the middle of one, just before a student gets to the climax, I will ask her to tell me a joke. The emotional fires that are cooking inside will make the joke explosively funny. So to get somebody to be very funny, I will get him to work on a very warm, soft, emotional environment with somebody in it and then, right in the middle, I will make him move to material that is funny. I always get emotional qualities that way. Sometimes it helps to do an Affective Memory right to the end to get the so-called climax so that if somebody needs a kickoff to get emotional, he or she will know how to do it.

I happen to believe that an Affective Memory takes the most skill of any acting exercise I know. The person doing it begins to feel very skillful after a while. I use it quite often.

Do you prefer actors to use their own experience or that of the character when they work on a role?

It's always a mixture of their own experience and the imagined. I will not rely just on personal experience. Anyway, most people's personal experience is so colored so much of the time, to find out what it was really like can be almost impossible.

Do you recommend that your students observe people for character work?

I recommend that they observe everything, even inanimate objects. I was once in a production of a Russian play in New York in which the director said very early on that I had to imagine I was in a concentration camp. At that time in my life, the last thing in the world I could get myself to believe in was that. It was just too horrible and I couldn't focus on it. One day I was walking along Madison Avenue after a movie with my wife and I walked past a shop. All of a sudden something went off in my head. I was standing in front of a lamp store and I saw all these lamps full of dust, some with their wiring pulled out, some with no bulbs in them. I just stood there and started to imagine myself as one of the lamps. All those pictures of concentration camp victims started mixing with the lamps for me, and the next day at rehearsal I started acting those lamps.

What similar kinds of exercises do you do with your students?

Well, I'm very fond of reminding my students that Sid Caesar used to act inanimate objects on the "Show of Shows." And I would demonstrate his famous gum ball machine routine. When he did it, I saw the whole life of a gum ball machine humanized so wonderfully and believably that I often ask the class to pick any object around the house, like a washing machine, and give it a story title, like "The Life and Death of—," or "The Marriage of the Washing Machine" to a dryer. When students do this, all sorts of areas of innocence and vulnerability and dreams that are not literal open up. They all bring their own experiences to it. I will tell them to keep making their object more human. Now, instead of washing laundry, the washing machine is having lunch with a blind date, and the students have to create the situation. The people who don't try to do these exercises, who get scared, invariably are the noninventive actors.

How do you instruct new students to begin on a scene?

When I work with beginners I will lay out a set of circumstances for them and talk about prior events, objectives, etc. But I won't tell them what the objective is. I will ask them to find that through the situation of the play. I don't ask the actor what his objective is. I ask the actor to tell me how he is going to accomplish what his character is looking for.

The best thing that ever happened to me was in one of my private acting classes. There was a very plain girl from upstate New York who came to audit. At the end of class she said she would like to study with me. Usually I ask people a lot of questions to find out what they are like, but there was something just so honest about her that I let her in. She was in class about four months. It took her at least two months to get up and do an exercise, but I never pushed her. She was well liked and attentive. Finally, she got up and did a simple sense memory exercise. Then she tried a scene, which was okay. Then she disappeared. I thought that was for the best. Four or five months later I got a wedding invitation from a family in upstate New York with a note on the back. It said, "Dear Mr. Miller, You probably don't remember who I am and I know you didn't think I did much in your class, but I really learned a lot about myself and by the time I got back home everybody noticed how much warmer and more open I was—including the boy I have always had a crush on, whom I am now marrying. I want you to know that I think your class was responsible."

To me it doesn't matter whether or not people pursue acting careers. If acting class makes their lives richer and gets them to open up and lead warmer emotional lives, it's worthwhile.

David Groh

John Lehne

John Lehne is a California-based teacher, coach, director, and actor who has been training actors for more than twenty-five years. He has also served as acting coach on many major feature films. Along with his ongoing professional classes, Mr. Lehne recently directed the world premiere of Lyle Kessler's Orphans, for which he received the L.A. Weekly and Drama Logue awards as best director.

A member of The Actors Studio, Mr. Lehne studied with Lee Strasberg and Elia Kazan and was selected by them to teach at The Studio for three years.

Mr. Lehne believes that his major contribution to the teaching of acting is "forcing behavior to be part of the training concepts. . . . There has been too much emphasis in the past on what actors say and feel, not on what they do." Also, focusing solely on the actor's own experience "isolates him, makes him more concerned with creating his own world in terms of his personal experience and less concerned with how that world relates to the situation and character of the play."

232

*   *   *

How did you get started teaching acting?

I was in The Actors Studio in the late 1950s. I became a member in 1955. Lee always asked for comments from members and I always had something to say. Then Frank Corsaro, who had his own classes, was about to go to Spoleto to direct *Night of the Iguana* and he called me aside and asked me if I would like to teach his class for the summer. I said, "Are you crazy? I don't teach. I don't know how to do that." He said, "Just do what you are doing. Come to my class and just speak up like you do at The Studio and we'll see." I went to his class and taught all summer, and by the end of that summer nine people decided to stay with me. That was the nucleus of my first class and I found that I enjoyed teaching. I liked working with people and I particularly liked problem solving. That's really what I do as a teacher and a coach.

I started to take teaching seriously, so I went to Lee and said, "I really want to be a good teacher and I need help." He said, "Okay, come to my classes and observe what I do and take notes, and if you need help, I'll talk to you about it." I did that for three years. I went to every class he taught and every session at The Actors Studio. I was so impressed by him that I even began to clear my throat the way he did. I wanted to be exactly like him. At the time my career as an actor was starting to level off after a very good start in the theater and leads on TV. I became more and more involved with teaching and the challenge of it. Lee made his library available to me and pointed out the books I should read. My mind began to expand tremendously and it helped me in my teaching. That was really the basis of my teaching.

Years earlier, when I first came to New York, the person who influenced me most was Erwin Piscator at The New School for Social Research. My mother was a socialist and she believed strongly that we all have a social responsibility in life to fulfill more than just our own pleasures. Piscator brought that right into focus for me as an actor. He believed that the theater is a teaching tool, that it educates and leads people, and that by illuminating their lives, the theater will help people grow and improve life for everybody. He had narrowly escaped Hitler in Germany, had been head of the Folkstheatre and worked with Kurt Weill and Bertolt Brecht. He developed the "epic theater" concept and he made you see yourself as an actor in the perspective of the whole theater. Theater was a force for him, and the actor was a cog in the wheel of that force. So the actor's individuality and need for stardom was never encouraged. Instead, actors were encouraged to be part of the ensemble and illuminate the ruling idea of the play. We did plays like *The Flies* by Sartre and *All the King's Men* by Robert Penn Warren. Piscator had a theater on Forty-eighth Street and another on Houston Street through The New School. We really got a chance to work.

Then I started working with Bret Warren in New York. He was a man who believed very much in the responsibility of the actor to the playwright and he believed that everything serves the play. All of his teaching was in terms of that, and the kind of work he did, the improvisations and character exercises, all focused on serving the play. Then I worked with Thelma Schnee, who was one of Lee's protégés, and she introduced me to (and Lee later reinforced) the concept that without the actor's personal experience there is nothing in the play. The actor needs to create his own real experience every time he works. What's important is not just the play and its ideas, but the process of welding your own experience with that of the character. So the actor's personal experience became the most prominent part of the training.

When I got into The Actors Studio and began to work with Lee I saw that he was a further extension of the work I had begun with Thelma Schnee. It was then that I got deeply involved in the actor's personal experience. Lee's emphasis was really on the instrument. Training the actor had less to do with performing the role and more to do with the actor developing his instrument so that he could do whatever he wanted to. Then everything becomes possible. That became my emphasis, too, and I spent long, long months just harnessing relaxation and concentration, simple sensory exercises, working with real objects, observing them sensorially, then putting them aside and working with them from memory. I took beginners and put them through these sensory exercises, which started simply but led up to very complex inner–outer exercises and body response exercises.

These sound like variations on Lee's sensory exercises.

They were all variations on Lee's progression of learning how to create the real experience for yourself. Each step got more and more complicated. I really tried to emulate Lee because I believed in it so much.

After eight or ten years of that I began to notice that things were often missing in the work when it was used professionally. The actor's experience, if used to the exclusion of other things, isolates him, makes him more concerned with creating his own world in terms of his personal experience and less concerned with how that world is related to the situation and character of the play.

For example, there is the Affective Memory Exercise. In that exercise so much time and effort were placed on the actor's ability to express his emotion freely that some actors saw the emotion as an end unto itself. Actors who already had a background in Sandy Meisner's technique, for example, understood that sensory work was also supposed to serve the play. But those who only worked with Lee often misunderstood sensory work. Some actors would do an Affective Memory and bathe in the resulting emotion. They did not understand (a) that the emotion was to be used logically within the situation *as the character* and (b) that emotion, as Stanislavsky so clearly defined it, is the motive for action and if you don't carry the cycle of the work far enough, you create a passive expression of emotion. The emotion must create a desire, a need, and that's what you're acting. That's what makes drama: the tension created by two or more people struggling to overcome whatever obstacle prevents them from getting their needs met in some way.

So my work began to change. I saw holes in the application of the sensory work and I began to look toward other people's ways of working. Then I read *The School of Stage Art* by Vakhtangov. He opened my eyes further because I saw another way to use the Stanislavsky system. Stanislavsky's premise was "What would I do if I were in this situation?" Vakhtangov's premise was "Under what conditions would I do or get myself to do what I perceive the *character* does in this situation?" It's a different approach and I began to see that sensory work itself could be used to accomplish Vakhtangov's premise. I began to train people that way and still do because, in my opinion, every actor, if he is really an actor, is a character actor.

There are performers who use their personalities to gain popularity and notoriety, and it is their personality that draws and attracts people regardless of what they are in; therefore, they maintain that personality at all costs regardless of what a script calls for. Then there are those actors who understand that they need to go through a process to become what they perceive the author wrote. Even as a young actor I was always drawn instinctively to the latter. To me the joy and challenge of acting are to totally become someone else, to use moments of my own life and experience to create a character's life. In my teaching I work very hard to make young people aware of the life of the character prior to the play. I do a great deal of work around that.

You mean you put a great emphasis on understanding prior circumstances in your teaching?

Yes. All the time. Without a thorough understanding of the character's life prior to the play or film, the actor has no specific starting point from which to act. We all act in life according to our histories, and since a play or film is "life interrupted" the actor must know his character's prior life much like a spy must be totally familiar with all aspects of the person's life he is about to assume. I use inner monologues, improvisations, Affective Memory Exercises, Private Moment Exercises. The Private Moment Exercise was really something that Lee embellished on from Stanislavsky's notion of public solitude, but he carried it further. Lee turned it into something pragmatic, something the actor could really experience and use professionally. Stanislavsky describes it as the moment in the play when the writing stops, but the experience and the life of the character go on.

Lee said everybody has moments in private when they behave unlike themselves. So he began experimenting with it. It was always fascinating to me, not so much as a release mechanism for the actor,

but because I saw actors become different characters, become totally
different from the people I knew. I use it as a character exercise,
explaining that it's organic to the actor because he is acting out of
very specific given circumstances from his own life that make him
behave in a way unlike himself, even if it's only for a moment. If
that moment or the stimuli that led to that moment were carried
further, that person would change and become a character. Let's say
someone is very self-effacing and quiet. Suddenly, under certain
conditions, he becomes a potential killer. When I see that I say, "If
you have to play a killer, do it by creating those circumstances,
whatever they were."

How do you use the Private Moment Exercise in character work?

What I do first is get the actor to do a number of Private Moment
Exercises—to re-create a situation in which he does things that he
doesn't do when others are around. Sooner or later the actor hits on
something that is very strong and brings out a unique side of his
personality. I then ask him to take that same exercise and try to
extend further the impulses that came up during the Private
Moment. I get the actor to extend them for about ten minutes even
though he may originally have had just a fleeting impulse, perhaps
only a segment of the original Private Moment Exercise. I ask him
if he remembers what that specific moment was connected to—not
the result, but what motivated it. I tell him to use that. Then I get
him to do the Private Moment as a preparation for a scene, and to
carry all those impulses right into the scene. That can be very
hit-or-miss, because the actor may lose it somewhere in the middle
of the scene. Then I have him work on the images or the sensory
aspects that motivated those quixotic impulses, that gave rise to that
specific behavior. We work together in a stop-and-go fashion on the
Private Moment within the scene.

We work on an Affective Memory in the same way within a scene
when he is first learning how to use it. I interrupt the work and
alternate it with reminders of the sensory images from the Affective
Memory. It's the same thing with a Private Moment. It creates a
tremendous impact not only on the actor, but on the other people
watching, because they see that person become a totally different

human being. I mean totally. I say, "There. That's a character. You don't have to fake and perform. That character is coming from you."

To go further with a character, you need to change some of the externals, add things that shape those impulses differently, and go even further with the physical behavior, letting the impulses come out in different parts of the body—the muscles and so on. You can, by partially stifling the impulses, channel them into action. That's the part of the work that has fascinated me. I've become, over a long period of time, a behaviorist, and when I coach that's what I do. I work out the behavior.

What do you mean by "work out?"

Well, when I'm coaching someone for a specific role in a movie, I direct the performance using both acting and directorial techniques. First, I work out the character's arc or growth through the film. I visualize that performance for the actor and then make it concrete by directing him moment by moment through the film. Then I work personally with the actor to truly motivate and justify all those moments. It's a complete process, starting from a vision of what the character is like to the personal motivation for all the actor's behavior, emotions, objects, etc.

I worked with one famous actress on and off for nine years. The major change in her work came through Private Moment Exercises. When she started she was very "Sarah Lawrence." She was working on a soap opera, but was very talented and dedicated and wanted to become a different kind of actress. She immediately took to the Sensory Memory work and was very risible and free emotionally right away. However, physically she was very controlled. I told her she needed to do Private Moment Exercises because her concept of acting was verbal and emotional, but she had no sense of the physical life of the character. And this would be a source of characterization for her. My instincts about her were that she would take to it very well.

We started on Private Moment Exercises and she said, "I don't have any private moments. When I get upset I sit down and read a book or go to sleep. I get away from it somehow." I asked her if she had impulses. She said yes, and I asked her, "What if I told you that you have permission now to act out all the impulses you didn't act out at the time?" "Oh, that might be fun," she said. And that's where we started. We did two years of Private Moment work and she blossomed. Her whole understanding of the work was that she could do anything now. That's what this work gives you: a sense that you can do anything that is asked of you, because it taps all the different sides of you.

Over the years what have you discarded or altered from your own early training?

As far as sensory work goes, I no longer do that because I found that it took so much concentration and repetition that I was beginning to get bored with it. And I don't ever want to be bored teaching. So I made the decision not to take any real beginners. But I still believe in sensory work and recommend my students to teachers who do it.

As far as Relaxation Exercises are concerned, I still find them valuable, but I don't believe in turning anything into a ritual. Taking everything to excess becomes ritualistic and serves no purpose except to indulge those actors who get attention by continually failing in the work. I have very little patience with that. I feel that relaxation is an important starting place, but that's all it is. If you need an hour's relaxation before you work, do that on your own, before you come to the studio. It gets so ritualistic that the preparation for doing the work is longer than the work itself.

It's very important for an actor to learn how to relax while he is working, rather than before, so I will often prompt actors to relax parts of their body that seem tense while they are doing a scene. I don't want them to spend a half-hour chasing tension because it will come back anyway. It's better to teach them how to relax while they are working. So I don't spend a lot of time with relaxation—perhaps two or three minutes.

Aside from the Private Moment Exercise, do you have other techniques for helping students develop a character?

I use animals, observing them and really creating them through the imagination: how an animal relates to his environment and the other animals in the zoo; the psychological makeup of the animal—

whether he is aggressive or passive; how he relates to food, sex, all the basics. After students bring the animals they are working on into class, we put them on their feet and do a two-legged version. I work with one person at a time. I don't believe in group work. It's not beneficial. I nccd all my attention on the one person because I may see one minor moment that can be the key to everything that actor is doing wrong—or right. With thirty people on the stage, I would be bound to miss it. So I work one person at a time.

I want students to create an animal totally, inwardly and out-wardly. I really am tough on people in terms of turning their hands into paws, for example, and feeling the claws come out of their sheaths, and what the tongue does when the animal licks itself, that it lifts hair and lays it back down; the muscular rhythm of the body and trunk as it moves across the floor. After the actor as the animal has moved around in his own environment, I put him into a human environment to see how he moves around in a human home. All the elements that have been generated in the first exercise, all those drives, need to be carried over.

The next step is to eliminate those aspects of the animal that are recognizable only as the animal's way of doing things, but to retain anything that might also be appropriate for a person.

Next, we create a simple human event—getting ready to go to work, for example—and the same aggression or nervous energy that was the animal's is carried over into that event. Ultimately, instead of hitting the phone with his paw, the actor may pick it up with a slight hit. And I tell the actor to make the sounds of the animal during this exercise. You can find a great character voice; it's exciting to see students find other voices this way. Then the man-animal, instead of the animal-man, is put into a situation, either an improvisation or a scene, with other people. I believe in using improvisation within the structure of the scene. We put this man-animal into a series of improvised situations prior to the scene to get him to understand how this man-animal functions in *any* situation. The actor's imagination, together with the permissiveness of the animal, releases a lot of inhibitions that the actor would normally have in a variety of situations, like picking up a girl in a bar or entering a party. So I use both Animal Exercises and Private Moments to help students create characters.

Sensory Exercises can also be used as roots for characterization. Fear of suffocation can become a character element. There are many sensory things, like a person who is itchy and can't scratch or has to go to the bathroom but can't.

My work over the years has led me to try to see what I call the actor's language. The playwright has a language and even implies what emotions are required by the actor. Partly what separates one actor from another, and has throughout history, is the ability to deal with the emotions, but the real difference is his or her *behavioral* vision of a character.

Could you explain that?

It's the balance between what seems to be and what the actor perceives really is. It's the subtext. Behavior illuminates the subtext, what is really true about that person.

For example, in *On the Waterfront* Marlon Brando's character had to ask Eva Marie Saint to go and have a beer with him at a local pub. An average actor would have looked at that scene and said, "I can play that. It's about a guy asking a girl out to a bar, and I should probably try to sweet-talk her and be nice to her, be gentle with her because she's a very naive girl, and get her to come to the bar." Brando must have thought, "This character is a punk. He has sold out as a human being to Johnny Friendly and his own brother. He's betrayed Eva Marie's brother by setting him up for the roof so that he could get pushed off. He didn't know that was going to happen, but he does whatever he is told by Johnny Friendly. There is a very basic, deep-seated lack of self-esteem in this character; therefore, how am I going to try to make a date with this girl who is pure, and beautiful, and from another life-style? I can't openly ask her out. I don't feel entitled to that as the character because what could she possibly see in me? I'm a bum. I *expect* her to say no. But if I play it as if I expected her to say no, how will she know I really want her to go with me?"

Eva Marie was wearing a pair of white gloves. Brando went to Kazan and asked, "Could you get Eva Marie to drop one of the gloves?" His subtext for that scene was that he would not let her leave until she agreed to go out with him. The objective of the subtext was that he would take her glove and not let her have it back until she had consented. So his behavior was an assertion of his real need, which liberated him as an actor to then play his expectations with fear and indifference in the text. He didn't look at her, but every time she went for the glove, he moved it out of her range, put it behind his back, put it on his hand in a very sexual manner—a big hand in a small glove—very sexual. All of that was the subtext of what the character really wanted coupled with the logical behavior of what the character expected.

Now the average actor would try to show you the subtext in the *text* and wind up acting illogically, behaving illogically. I've read about moments like Brando's in theater books. Edmund Keane, Duse, Sarah Siddons, all of the great actors who serve as role models for actors had moments like this. Duse was called "Duse of the beautiful hands" because in one famous scene over a child that had died she tried to bring him back to life with her hands even though she was mourning his death. So the hands created one reality—the behavior of how much she wanted him to come back—and her grief was revealed in how much she accepted the fact that he was gone. The balance between the text and the subtext, between the logical behavior and the unconscious emotional need of the character—the balance of all those things—makes for great acting. There are numerous examples in the history of the theater.

How do you help your students to think along those lines when analyzing a script?

I constantly remind them to do it in rehearsal. Last night in class two students did a scene from *The Real Thing*. Rather than act the subtext, they basically acted out the text. I asked them, "What does it mean for a man to believe that his wife has been unfaithful to him? What does it do to him?" I told them that for their next rehearsal to play their subtext out in the open, forget the text and scenic behavior, and play the subtext out in the open: that is, what the character would *really* like to say and do. They could use other words in addition to the author's, and physically do anything they wanted to that might come up. I don't encourage actors to use their own words too much because then the scene becomes just another discussion. I don't want another discussion. I want the actor to get in touch with organic impulses that will make him want to act or behave in a different way, act out of the impact of finding his wife's passport in a drawer and knowing that she couldn't have gone to Europe and then living out the nightmare of his imagination. I want him to experience that first and *then* put a cover on it.

Other students were doing a scene from *Beyond Therapy*. When the woman in this scene said to the man, "You have nice chest hair," the man was using something in his subtext that made his hands leave the table and start running over his chest. Suddenly, he reached for his nipples. It was hilarious. It had nothing to do with words.

The one thing I have really focused on more and more throughout the years is behavior. And it works for comedy and drama as well.

For example, I recently coached a well-known actor and actress who were having a problem in a movie they were making. The very talented young director of the movie was having trouble exacting comedy from the situations. First of all, when you work with people, you have to size up what their natures are. These actors are both very strong people. When you try to motivate two very strong people with given circumstances that serve to intensify those strengths, there is little room for comedy.

So I worked with them in terms of different motivations. I said, "I want you to try to tease her," for example. When they tried that I could see what their impulses were, and then I made suggestions about how to do the scene. Out of that came the behavior that I was looking for. The ultimate stage of the work is always nailing down moments. We did a whole improvisation based on a scene in which the woman hires the man to help her in the jungle, which is really a very funny moment. I told them that their behavior has to go on beyond the moment when they talk about hiring, and I asked her what she expected from him now that she had hired him. She said, "Well, I expect him to help me out of the jungle. I guess I expect him to be my porter." I said, "That's it! So leave your bag on the ground and walk away and expect him to pick it up like a porter." She did that and noticed that he hadn't picked up the luggage and wasn't following her. She turned around, looked at the bag, then looked at him. He looked at her, walked up to the bag, picked it up as if he were going to be her porter, walked up next to her, dropped it, and kept going. It was hilarious. All of that came out of the kind of work that I do. I want the actor to be motivated to behave.

I also ask my students to observe people as a way to teach character. I tell them to pick a person, someone from their family, someone they know very well, and bring in every detail of that person: the voice, the way he moves, objects that belong to that person, the way he deals with people, and so on. Then they present that person in a very simple situation—visiting for tea, cooking, whatever. First, the actor is alone on stage. Then two actors work on characters together. As their characters, they meet at a dance or a restaurant. If it works well, I'll put them into a scene together. That's the process. It's taking the actor's perceptions and observations of life and putting them to work in a distinct way so he or she can become another person. To me that is the legacy of acting. The four basic areas of characterization are human observation, animal observation, Sense Memory, and Private Moment work.

On one occasion I worked with an actor who asked for help in creating a character for a movie. He didn't want me to work with him directorially on the script. However, he wanted to find his character before he began shooting. It was a huge stretch for him. This actor is a deeply religious man, very gentle and very spiritual. I said, "You are going to have to turn yourself around 180 percent from where you are, and you can do it through Affective Memory work." At the beginning of the movie his character has no regard for life, including his own. For this actor to create that we had to find something in him under the old principles of "Under what conditions would I think, behave, do, and perceive as this character does?" I started asking him questions and he came up with something very strong from his personal life. We worked together on the character using that.

On the last day of working he asked me why I thought he had

been cast instead of someone else. And I said, "Maybe because you are more unpredictable and you bring dimensions to this character that others might not bring. You are a warm, loving person. There needs to be a moment of that somewhere in the film, when life comes back to you." I told him to study all of Kurosawa's films, and study the samurai, his inner intensity, how this kind of warrior loses himself inside and comes back to the outside and then makes a decision—the moves samurai make that are so deliberate. And that came across in the film. He accomplished it brilliantly through the work. I believe that this is what most actors should do.

How are your classes divided?

I have two levels of work foundation: intermediate and advanced. Those in the intermediate class have already had a year or two of training. The advanced class is for people who are experienced and have worked professionally. Many of these professionals are burned out—been on soaps a long time, for example—and want to go on to a different level.

Do you have any techniques to help students work on comedy?

Just the basic one. The forces in comic tension are the same as those in dramatic tension. It's just that in comedy there is a sudden unexpected change in direction of some kind; either verbal, emotional, or behavioral. Comedy is based on one of those three. The emphasis on reality is just the same as in drama; it just depends on how you define the character and the trouble he gets into.

I love behavioral comedy; Chaplin, people who are great at situational humor out of which behavior arises that demonstrates the fallibility of the human being. I'm not mad about stand-up comedy; I tire of it quickly. Most of what is called "sitcom" today is not situational comedy, but a series of stand-up routines, setups for gags and punch lines. There is no behavior at all—with a few exceptions.

How do you advise students to rehearse?

In order to find where your work is as an actor you have to understand how much of you automatically connects to the script. The first thing to do when you read a script is nothing at all. Try to appreciate it like a member of the audience. Read it appreciatively. Approach the work on the first reading as if you were just going to see the play. Then read it simply, without any obligation to play anything, but just to see, based on what the character does and says, how you feel. Allow yourself to see how much you don't know. Read it as if you don't know anything about the situation. If your character has the line, "You frighten me," and you don't know why, react that way. Go through the script allowing your real perceptions about yourself and your partner to flower, and don't impose any scenic realities. Just be yourself to start with.

Then you can start to invest things from your own experience that are similar to those of the character. If the character has been on a train for ten hours, try to make it real for yourself, using something similar from your own life. Then rehearse using those sensory elements: hot, sticky, smelly, thirsty. In the next rehearsal allow yourself to act out any impulses that come up from the previous exploration. Then start using personal objects in place of any that might be in the script.

Early readings are like first meetings: if you are busy impressing your acting partner with how attractive you are, you never see him or her. The same is true with a play. When an actor starts working I can see quickly whether he is content to explore the experience or is merely concerned with presenting his solutions to that experience. What I get actors to do very quickly is understand that rehearsal is not a process of presenting answers to solutions. It is a process of reworking the same problem over and over again. I don't want actors to bring me a performance of their answers to a problem. I want them to bring me their work on that problem.

How do you help students work on the moment-to-moment life of a character?

It's not a concept. Once you learn how, it becomes a way of working forever. I make it clear that what students are learning in all the exercise work sets their way of working throughout their lives. You learn to work moment to moment in an exercise so you can do it in the scene or in a play or movie.

I often work with students on a moment-to-moment basis. One student was doing a play about two people in a hospital. One character was injured in Vietnam: his genitals were shot off; the other had gone slightly crazy and repairs radios all the time. The injured one always needs to test his present masculinity on someone. That's the situation. The injured fellow gets the radio fixer to play a girl so he can pick her up in a bar. It's both funny and very moving.

The actors compromised the situation. They accommodated each other. If you accommodate the other actor, give him what he wants, you are doing him a disservice. If you provide the other actor with an obstacle, you are servicing him. I told one actor, "You are play-acting a girl because he asked you to. What about your history based on your character's prior circumstances here? What do you expect from the other people in this hospital?" He said, "I guess I expect to be humiliated." "Yes, you do. So what is your first instinct when this other guy asks you to play a girl?" "I would expect to be humiliated and resist it, and hide more in my radio." I said, "You got it." The next time they did it he presented his acting partner with a real obstacle, moment by moment, and that partner had to work hard to pull him out of his shell. By challenging the actor to deal with the moments you get dramatic tension.

Do you permit your students to critique each other?

Yes. I believe in it. It is a means of maintaining the language we all need. Other art forms have a language. Musicians can talk about their music in an articulate way. Some people believe that the most talented people can't talk about what they do. Well, tell a musician that. The truth is that there is a language in the art of acting and it needs to be transmitted so that more of us speak it in relation to our craft. There is so much available information about the craft of acting that when actors see things, they should see them as practitioners of a craft rather than as members of the audience. Part of testing whether an actor knows the craft himself is asking him to critique other actors. And I learn very quickly how an actor thinks. It helps me to teach the actor faster when I see what he goes for in his criticism.

What do you feel has been your special contribution as a teacher?

People say two things about me: (1) that I'm very clear and

articulate and that I understand Lee's work well, and (2) that I have a passion and excitement for the work. What my students have said is that they feel safe in my class as well as challenged.

In terms of the work, I think that my major contribution is forcing behavior to be part of the training concepts. A lot of people today are using some of the work that I started in the 1960s and making it part of the actor's training—which I love to see. To me the actor's way of working is clear in statements like DeNiro's when he said he had to go off and learn to be a fighter in order to play Jake Lamotta. That's the way to work. That's always been my premise. You are taking a person, an actor who has had a life, and asking him to be another person with another life. How does he go about doing that? Part of that is imaginative, part intellectual, part emotional, part behavioral.

Acting is the art of communication, and people communicate in three ways: in what they say, what they do, and what they feel. There has been too much emphasis in the past on what actors say and feel and not enough on what they do. The concepts of behavior have been overlooked, in my opinion. It's only recently that I see the concepts of Vakhtangov that I've been pushing since the 1960s emerging. I think that's my main contribution or addition, because so much has already been said so well by various people. That's why I've never tried to write a book; it would be presumptuous of me to claim to have a great insight into something that has already been well defined. However, as in all things, what separates one teacher from another is the application of the information available and, in the theater especially, the teacher's perception of human experience.

After thirty years as an actor, director, and coach, what advice would you give someone just starting out in his or her career?

I feel that the actor has a basic responsibility to the world as an artist. You don't do certain things. You don't do trash! You have to have standards. Those standards have to be encouraged by the teacher, and ultimately they have to be embraced by the actor. Every acting teacher I ever had had standards. I may have either accepted or rejected them, but they were standards. I want to pass those on to my students.

The impotence you feel as an actor is painful and takes a terrible toll because you are always at the mercy of someone else's decision about whether or not you are desirable. That's very hard on the ego. For young actors who believe they will make it in two years, that doesn't bother them too much, but for those who have been in the business for twenty years and still have dreams of success, it's a terrible price to pay. The theater can be the most exciting and rewarding profession, and it can also be the most devastating. All I can tell young people is, if you want it badly, you will withstand the rejections. You have to be able to say yes when everyone else says no. That will force you to be good, possibly to be great. If all you have is a drive to be a movie star, you may be in for a lot of heartache. The truth is that a lot of people come to the profession wanting to be movie stars and end up being actors. And that's good.

When you go into the theater, think of it as entering the Olympics. Figure on putting in a lifetime of work for maybe one or two shots, and maybe then a possible chance for the gold medal.

Jane Hunt

Darryl Hickman

A California-based teacher, Darryl Hickman has conducted a professional workshop for actors for many years. He believes that acting should convey "a sense of life being lived right now, a sense of immediacy, a sense of unpredictability." His approach consists of dividing the acting process into two parts: the scene work, "which deals with the thinking part of acting, and exercise work, which involves the intuitive, spontaneous part of it. As we go along, the idea is to put the two parts together."

Mr. Hickman's own acting career started at the age of three and he has appeared in more than 100 motion pictures. He went on to TV and stage work, and was later a producer for CBS and developed TV series, specials, and miniseries for Paramount Pictures.

What was your own acting training like?
In 1963 I was in New York performing in How to Succeed in

Business Without Really Trying. I had never had an acting class. I started in the movies when I was three years old and I had done more than 100 movies and TV, but I had no formal training. While I was in this show I wanted to study, since I knew I would be in New York for a while, and Milton Katselas was recommended to me. I worked with him privately and in class for a long time.

In 1970, after I decided to leave acting, I was working for CBS as an associate producer. During that time Milton was going off to direct a movie and needed somebody to take over his class. So I did it while he was away. I really enjoyed the teaching, and decided to start my own class when he came back. I gathered together about fifteen actors, rented space, and started teaching. I had a very clear idea of what I wanted to do. I didn't know if I could do it, but I had a very strong sense that there was something missing in the work that I had seen in class and on the stage. I had done a lot of investigating into the acting process from 1963 to 1970. I had spent a lot of time at The Actors Studio and at HB Studio and I had sat in on Uta Hagen's classes and Warren Robertson's classes. I also taught at HB Studios for a while. When I started my own class I had a very clear idea of what I wanted to get at so I set up a format that I have not changed till this day. There was an original point of view that I think has been maintained throughout.

What is that format?

The best I can do is give you a brief genesis because there were so many elements that went into it. In the 1960s I worked with Paul Curtis at The American Mime Theatre in New York for a while. He was an enormous influence on me, as were the things I heard from Mr. Strasberg and the experimental work I saw at the Open Theatre and The Living Theatre. When Grotowski came from Poland, he was an influence. Harold Pinter was very much on everybody's mind at that time. I was going through a seeking period and I felt that my own work had gotten kind of stale. I had been acting for so long—since I was a little boy. I guess I can sum it up in one example. I remember seeing Michael Moriarty in a play sometime in the 1960s and thinking that what he was doing in that play was giving a sense of life being lived right now, a sense of immediacy, a sense of unpredictability. He was exuding a kind of life energy that was flowing and seemed new and unplanned.

Paul Curtis had an exercise he called Conditions. Much of his work was very formal and technical, but in this particular exercise he had everyone stand up in the class and told us simply to call out all the things we were feeling at the moment as they were happening to us. We would call out all this life energy that was coming up from the inner self. When I started teaching and was searching around for a way of approaching it, I divided my work into two parts: I did scene work, which I considered the formal and technical part of acting, teaching the mechanics of putting a form together. And I did exercises. I took Paul's exercise, conditions, and started with it as a seed. After students identified an impulse, whatever it was that they were feeling at the moment, with words, I asked them to do the same thing with sound. Then it seemed like a natural extension to ask them to put that impulse into the body. Conditions was the basis for all of my exercise work, though as time went on new exercises were added. I was trying to see if I could isolate that living thing that I had perceived in performances that was so unique, if I could isolate it, could identify it, and then find a way to help people recreate it.

Later I realized that, without being aware of it, what I had been doing was trying to identify the left brain/right brain dichotomy and then trying to find a way to integrate both sides of the brain so that it worked in a balanced way. That is really the basis for my approach. There is the intellectual part of the work that has to do with the thought process, and then there is this other thing that has to do with the nonthinking part of the process, which I call, for lack of a better word, intuition. The nonthinking, unconscious part of ourselves is constantly flowing with energy. A lot of it is emotional, but there are other energies that are constantly coming out of our inner selves, and they are changing so fast that most of us are not even aware it is happening and don't even identify what is going on. Subsequently I have discovered that because we are all so dominated by our thought process, we don't know how *not* to think for a moment and instead to allow the intuitive part of ourselves to send up spontaneous information. We're just like babies who haven't learned how to decide what to do with their impulses.

The first thing I do in the exercise class is ask people to define for themselves what thinking is and what intuition is so that they can distinguish the difference. Most people can't make that distinction and most of us are not that aware of the difference.

As human beings, the closest thing we have to control is thought, and we believe that as long as we have that power we can control our feelings and feel safe. That's what we have to get away from in the exercise work.

I have three classes and all of them are divided into scene and exercise classes and they are all mixed. I have new people with more experienced actors because the way I teach, everybody starts in the same place no matter how much work they have done. You still have to ask yourself, "What am I feeling right now?"

I always start with a group exercise that I call a "prep." It involves a lot of stretching, producing sound that is connected to feeling and impulse. We work a lot with emotions, especially in the beginning. In this exercise I ask students not to make any sounds unless they are connected to an impulse because then they are just empty sounds and don't reconnect their instrument in a way that I want it to.

I do the same thing in the physical exercises in order to get students to take the same flow of energy and connect it to the body, and get the body to move as freely and fully in a nonstructured way. Then we put the sound and the body together so that the whole instrument is connected.

What kind of instruction do you give a new student?

I still call the basic exercise Conditions. A student will call out what he is feeling at the moment and I constantly prompt him to reconnect to the feeling only. When I ask what he is experiencing, a student may say, "I'm wondering if you are going to let me sit down pretty soon." I say, "No, that's what you're thinking, not what you are feeling. Tell me what you're feeling." Then he might define it and reply, "I'm afraid." Depending on the awareness of the person I'm working with, he or she will begin to distinguish what I am asking for. Once a student can identify the feelings directly, I ask him to put the feeling into sounds. Most people find it easier to connect their feelings to vocal rather than physical expression. Once I get the sound, I ask him to put it into the body and allow the body to go with the impulse as it happens.

Do you do Affective Memory Exercises?

One thing I have found since I've been teaching is that most actors don't have a problem reaching emotions, but they do have trouble allowing the emotion that is already there to come through. I've found that even with people who are not trained actors, with just a little help in getting them to become aware of their momentary impulses, an enormous amount of emotion is ready to come out. The problem is not so much to dig down to get at it, but to reduce the barrier that exists to releasing it, to do away with the need to control that emotional energy.

Some students find out that they don't really want to do this kind of work because when one lets go of one's control, when one stops thinking and controlling and organizing and watching and just lets out what is going on in one's soul, one is very, very naked and vulnerable. Most people don't want that vulnerability to come out in front of other people, if at all. It's something that we have learned not to do. Newborn babies come into the world without the behavioral characteristic that we call thought and don't know what to do with all the energy, so it comes out spontaneously in the voice and body. Since I have been teaching I have watched very small children. Usually within the first thirty days of life they begin to get feedback from the environment. The environment says, "Don't cry," and if the infants do, they get a frown from mother or father. Spontaneous behavior is not acceptable; I've seen that flicker of recognition that they will only get approval if they stop that natural flow and do something else. Then they begin to control spontaneous behavior and all those barriers start getting built.

What is your favorite exercise?

I have one called Numbers. A student is onstage alone and I say, "Isolate the emotion that you feel when you say you are happy, and feel it for ten counts, while you are counting aloud. Then feel it and give it a sound for ten counts. Then feel it and express it with your body for ten counts." We do this exercise with happy, angry, sad, and other emotions.

Your exercises seem to focus on getting students to be more expressive.

I am trying to get them to isolate the intuitive part of themselves, to let that flow through their voices and bodies in the same way that it did when they were two days old. That's the essence of these exercises.

How do you help students work moment to moment?

I get three actors up on stage. They all have a monologue they know very well, but have learned only mechanically. I ask them to stand onstage and simply be aware of the flow of energy among the three of them, and, at the same time, to be physically in touch with the class and to allow the flow of energy to go around the entire group. When they feel that the energy of the class is directed toward them, that they have the focus, they are to give their monologue. When they feel the energy leaving them and going to one of their fellow actors, they are simply to let it go and stop the monologue. When another actor senses that the flow of energy is with him, I want him to pick it up and do his monologue until it leaves him, all the while staying in touch with where in the group the energy is emanating. It's incredible to watch students learn about the life energy that is flowing around a group of actors and to be able to work with it in this way.

In all the years I was in workshops and studied, I never heard anyone, including Mr. Strasberg, deal with the psychological implications of standing on the stage—with what is really happening when you walk out onto a stage, with where the energy is. Is it in your body? Where is it in the room? How are you connected with it? I try to get students to get as close to an existential base as they can, to start from absolute ground zero to see where they are in every part of themselves before they even deal with the acting process. I want them to deal just with *being* there.

The exercise I just described to you convinces me that there is an incredible flow of energy among people that is ignored most of the time because it's so subtle—but it is there. If an actor is smart, he will get on that wavelength and ride with it rather than try to force it to do what he wants it to do.

How do you advise students to approach scenes?

I have a very detailed approach that I suggest new students follow. I give each of them a six- or seven-page distillation of the mechanics of putting a performance together. I also have a clearly defined approach to the rehearsal process that I advise even those who have studied before to explore. One of the problems that I have noted in my own and other actors' work over the years is that there is no real systematic way of starting work.

Could you describe your approach?

The first question to be answered is what statement do I want to make with the material. To me everything that an actor does in rehearsal ultimately will be decided on the basis of whether it relates to the statement to be made. The answer to the question is in the performing and the actor can't answer this question until the end. All the actor can do is keep asking whether what he is doing is consistent with his intention. Let me restate this. The first thing an actor has to ask himself is what he wants to say with this role. The key is to keep asking.

I then tell students to read the material nonjudgmentally as many times as possible without analyzing what they want to do, then to allow the author's words and subtext to get into their blood in a way that is primarily unconscious, and then, before they even start to work systematically on the material, to allow that part of themselves that is unconscious to feed them with ideas. They are to try to listen to whatever that inner self tells them to do and explore the impulses and ideas that begin to come up from the inside. That's the basis of all the mechanical work that I do.

Then I suggest that they decide on a place for the scene, the furniture, a floor plan. I advise them to learn the text before they rehearse for the first time. I believe that an actor can't rehearse properly unless he has memorized the text. That's the opposite of the way I learned to rehearse, but I found out that holding on to a script was a crutch. Then I tell students to read the scene they are working on together and get up and do some sound, movement, and communication exercises with the text.

Could you describe these exercises?

Students simply get up on their feet, get in touch with one another and send energy through their voices and bodies, and allow themselves to feel what they are sending each other. Once that is happening, I want them to add the text in a free form.

I then advise them to start with character. I think that everything comes down to "Who am I?"—and that's character. Once you start working on character you are automatically thrust into your relationship with the other characters. All drama is about relationships.

Do you use terms like prior circumstances?

Yes, only I divide my procedure into character, relationships, place, event, action, prior event, beats, and blocking. I explain to students why I feel this basic progression works, and I ask them to make choices, one step at a time, in each of these categories. If they follow it, there is a very good chance that they will get where they want to go when they are in performance.

How do you help students develop a character? Do you have them observe people and animals?

Everything. A really good actor is essentially an observer of human behavior, and everything feeds that. I do different exercises. We sometimes work from an animal, or I ask students to work from a photograph or a painting or people they know. I tell them to take an image from one of those, an image that they think is in the direction they want to work, and to see if they can extract the essence of it and get it into their own bodies. I recommend that they start with how the character walks and talks. I think that's as good a starting point as there is. Anything they can do to get the beginnings of character work out of the cerebral part of themselves and into something they can feel and work with physically and organically, the better off they are going to be. Often actors get hung up on character work because they have all kinds of marvelous ideas. But they are just that—ideas. The purpose of the entire rehearsal procedure is to find behavior. If an image a student is working with doesn't give him specific, clear behavior, it's no good to him.

If something is not working in a scene, how do you proceed?

I tend to stop students a lot and work with them on the aspect of their work they are having a problem with. I try to demonstrate what it is I think they are not doing. Before students do a scene or monologue I ask them what they are working on. They might say they are working on character, or a place, or an action.

So you ask them what specific problem they are trying to solve with that piece of material.

Exactly. I am forcing them to be specific, to be clear about what they are trying to do. Each time they get up to work, they are trying to solve a different aspect of the work. If it's a piece of finished work, which I rarely see, at least to my satisfaction, they say, "We are working on the whole thing." Then I judge it on that basis. If they say they are working on character, I don't judge whether there is a subtext or not, or whether the blocking is good or not. I watch what they are doing with character. If they are doing something that works for character, I will leave them alone.

What do you mean by blocking being good or bad?

Blocking is the schematized movement that the actor uses. Blocking is determined by the set and is formalized. Once students have done some amount of overall investigation on a piece of material, they have to build a form. Toward the end of the rehearsal process, when it's time to do run-throughs, it's time to block. I also think that they should have made some choices at this point about the structure and progression of the scene that are based on changes in the relationship between the characters. Those changes I call beats. I don't think it makes sense to work on beats without blocking—nor does it make sense to block without having worked on beats.

A new actor will block a scene without taking into account where he is on the stage, who can see him, or if he has been in one spot too long—mechanical aspects with which new actors are not familiar. With a more experienced actor, if the blocking isn't working, invariably it's because his choices or beats are not clearly defined and he doesn't have a clear reason to be where he is or to move where he is going next. If the blocking is not right, there is probably a problem in the subtext. Blocking is really an external manifestation of the internal form of the scene, and the internal form, I believe, is the subtext.

How do you advise students to work on subtext?

The subtext has to do with all the choices that are made along the way. The subtext is the internal motor of the scene, the spine of the scene upon which all of the externals rest. It's the invisible core of the scene. I don't mean the inner monologue, because I try to get actors not to think at all while they are working—to let go of the thought process.

I try to get actors to build subtextual form, build in their beats, work out the relationship, etc., and to put all that into their unconscious clearly, without ambiguity, and then to let go of it—to forget it and allow the spontaneous energy that is flowing from the moment to tell them step by step how it's going to play, how to make it as new as it can be every moment. That is the hardest part of what I try to do: to get someone to trust the fact that he doesn't need to know how it's going to come out, that he can build form into the inner computer that will keep him within the guidelines that he has very carefully laid down in the rehearsal process, and that it will give him the structural elements that the scene needs, like beats and blocking. Then I want him to let go and to trust that his inner mind will give him those guidelines as he is working—to let it play as if it had never played before, as if it's the first time. That's the ultimate.

Let's say you stop a student because you see that something is not working. What do you do?

If it's character he is working on, for instance, I ask him to tell me about the character. I ask a lot of questions because that's how I find out where he is. Most of the time I find that he is very unclear about what he is trying to do. A student might say, "My character is from Michigan and had an abortion when she was sixteen." Whenever an actress tells me the facts of her character, I always ask her, "What kind of behavior does that give you for this scene? Play for me that you had an abortion at sixteen." I've made my point that that information isn't going to give you anything. That doesn't mean it isn't a valid element of that character or that at some point it won't trigger something that could give you behavior, but by itself it doesn't give you anything to play. Then I would ask, "What is your central image for the character?" The actress might say, "Well, I'm working on somebody I knew when I was in college." I ask, "How does that person walk? I want you to do it, to show me how that person walks." Often, once the student has done it for me, it tends to have real clarity and be something that she can get into her body.

I also do an exercise I got from Paul Curtis that comes from mime. You take a word like "crybaby," for instance, extract the essence of what crybaby means to you, and start putting it into your face. Once you have created a mask, you begin to get it down into the body, into movement. When that happens, you can then begin to find sound from the body, and you can get a walk. It's a tough exercise to master, it takes a lot of work, but it's a marvelous device for character work. Again, you are using a central image, taking an idea and getting it into your body.

What other words do you use in this exercise?

I give students a sheet with nouns: bully, kleptomaniac, seducer, anything that will give an actor a clear concept from which to work.

I believe the most important thing to start with when working on character is how he or she walks and talks. Then, what does he or she wear, and what kinds of personal objects does this person use? Olivier starts with a nose or a physical mannerism—anything that gives a clear image of the character.

Do you have any techniques specifically for film acting?

My feeling is that acting is acting, and it's a big disservice to say you are learning how to act for film. But there are technical adjustments, not acting adjustments, that actors need for different media. I do the sound and energy exercise that I described earlier. I use a simple text and I call out ten, fifteen, one hundred. What I want is for students to give me 10% of the energy, 15% expression of the energy, and 100% of the energy. I keep calling out different numbers and it's amazing to see how they can adjust the energy flow. The amount of the energy flow remains the same: it's simply the size of the aperture through which the energy is flowing that changes. When Robert DeNiro or other good film actors work, their energy level doesn't diminish, but the aperture through which it flows expands, and shrinks.

I ask students to bring in TV material and we work on it as it would be worked on for a TV performance. I tell them that they should do one hour's homework on it the night before, and that they have thirty-five minutes on the set to put it together. I'll block it, give them last-minute adjustments the way a lot of TV directors do, often telling them I want the opposite of what they planned to do, and see how far we can get to a really finished performance, taking into account where the cameras are. I do things like that because I work with a lot of people who act in film and on TV and it's essential that we work on the technical aspects of film and TV. Although my orientation tends to be stage, I try not to shortchange the technical needs of the film medium.

Do you work on Shakespeare?

Oh, yes. I also tell students that they should all be working on something from Restoration comedy, Oscar Wilde, or Noel Coward as well as Shakespeare. If you can play Restoration comedy, you can play any comedy; if you can play Oscar Wilde, you should be able to do anything that Neil Simon has written. That's where an actor can really stretch with comedic ideas. So I suggest all the classical work, including Shakespeare. You have to deal with it if you want to be an actor. When students first come to class I tell everyone to learn the prologue from *Henry V* and then we work with it in a variety of ways.

How do you work on it?

We will do sound exercises with it. I will have students do this monologue as different musical instruments or sing it in the highest part of their register, the lowest, and the middle, and then have them play it up and down—anything to explore the musicality and their own vocal instrument with that language. I ask them to learn about iambic pentameter and to investigate the range of vocal demands that will be made on them in this classical writing.

What do you think has been your special contribution as a teacher?

Distinguishing between the thinking part of the work and the intuitive part of the work and putting the two parts together. I would hope most teachers are doing that in their own way, but I try to do it formally through separate exercises and scene work. I'm told by students who have studied with other teachers that this is unique. But how much of a contribution I've made, I have no way of assessing.

Do you feel that today's major actors differ from their predecessors?

Things are different today. When I was a kid in the movies I worked with Gable and Tracy and Hepburn and John Wayne. They were movie stars. Some were good actors; some were only fair. But they were people with enormous charisma. Then there were actors who worked in the theater and tended to stay there, like Helen Hayes. They were a separate entity. Nowadays, we have a third medium, TV, which is a thing all its own, and everything has opened up. I think the actors I admire tend to work interchangeably in film and theater, like William Hurt, Al Pacino, Dustin Hoffman. They are people who came out of the theater, work in films, and go back and work in theater. A lot of good actors today stretch their ability. They don't just go back and do what they have already done. That's very important for the serious actor.

Have you noticed a change in the kinds of students you get?

What surprises me is that there is so much real passion for good work. I'm surprised by the number of young people who want to do something more than TV and commercials and who really want to give some time and energy to learning.

The most discouraging thing for me as a teacher is to have a student come in, work a while, begin to open some doors, and then disappear and not stay with it. He or she reaches a certain level that is probably okay, but nowhere near as high as it could be with a little more dedication. That's very discouraging, because I guess that there is nothing that I admire more than wonderful work, and I would like to be able to contribute to that as much as I can.

What advice would you give a new student just starting out in acting?

Try to figure out if you are doing it for the right reasons—

although I am not at all sure any reason is the right reason, since life is a learning experience and it's by making mistakes that you usually learn. I would like to think that a young person wants to act because he or she has a tremendous need for self-expression rather than a need to be a star or rich. I have found that even those who become stars, if they don't have a passion for the work, are guilty of pretty empty acting. The only reason to be an actor is because you really love it and feel it's something you need to do in order to express the things inside of you.

Charles Marinaro Photography

Joan Darling

Joan Darling is a teacher, actress, director, and writer who holds professional classes in New York and Los Angeles. She has taught acting at The Actors Studio West, and Circle in the Square in New York.

Ms. Darling began her acting career with the improvisational theater group The Premise, and over the past twenty years she has continued to appear in stage productions, on film, and on TV. Her directorial credits include pilots and series for ABC, NBC, and CBS, and she is the recipient of an Emmy and a Director's Guild award for outstanding direction. She has also developed and written scripts for TV specials, serials, and feature films.

Ms. Darling believes that her early and extensive experience in the improvisational theater has been a major influence on her teaching because "in the improvisational theater there are no lines so you have to go moment to moment with yourself in the here and now." This ability is crucial for the actor and is acquired after dedicated study.

However, "After you've learned all the technique, you have to come back to the problem of how to walk on the stage as if you were alive." Only then can you affect the audience. "That's what great actors do. And that can be taught."

What was your own training in acting?

I went to Carnegie Tech for two years and then to the University of Texas for one. Then I went to New York to become an actress. I got into an improvisational group in New York called The Premise.

I always wanted to be an actress and I had dreamed about going to a real technical college, so when I went to Carnegie Tech and discovered they knew nothing about acting and couldn't teach me anything, it made me nuts. So what I did was I started directing people's scenes and fighting with my teachers all the time, saying things like, "How can you give me an A− in acting when you haven't given me any notes, you haven't told me what's wrong with my acting, what to do about it?" The way they were teaching me made me very crazy in a very specific way. They would say, "Write your objective for the scene in your margin—I want to get him to love me, for example"—and I felt that was insane because writing it in the margin of my play did not help me solve the problem of walking onto the stage and wanting him to love me. And I knew that was the bottom line in acting. Also, Donna Krochmall could cry real tears and I couldn't, and if she could cry real tears I was going to learn how to do that somehow. There was one other thing. I felt in those two years at Tech that there were some people who were just magical and I was afraid that I wasn't magical enough. I couldn't stand the idea that charisma, star quality, all of that stuff, couldn't be taught. If I didn't have it and it couldn't be taught, what was a young, ambitious person to do?

Do you now believe it can be taught?

Totally. Absolutely. There is no question in my mind. I don't audition actors for my class, I don't interview them. I don't care whether they are lawyers, doctors, swimmers, actors, whether they have had one acting job or twenty, whether they are sixteen or fifty. All they have to do to get into my class is want to be in it. I've discovered, through both watching people in other classes and my own teaching, that anybody who wants it badly enough will do all the work necessary to become magical on the stage.

When I came to New York I first studied with Michael Howard. He started to answer the questions for me about what steps to take. I studied with him for a long time and I learned a tremendous amount of basic information from him. Then I studied with Milton Katselas, who was equally wonderful to me. Now he disowns a lot of the things he taught then, like relaxation and sense memory, and how to use them in scenes. He, along with George Morrison, was a strong influence at that time of my life. George, interestingly enough, was more on the track of what I do now, but I didn't quite understand what he was doing at the time. Through George I learned that you never know what an actor can do. He had one actor he was very excited about and I couldn't understand why. You couldn't even hear him. Now, as a teacher, I've been in that same position. I will say to a student, "You are an incredible actor, and not many people in this class will believe that." George's actor turned out to be Gene Hackman.

Michael Howard was in touch with something that I teach explicitly called the "here and now" part of acting. He never explicated it at that time but it was always there in his teaching and it's a very strong basis for the difference between someone who has star quality and someone who doesn't.

How do you start with a new student?

The first thing I would say to you is that acting can't be explained because it's an athletic sport. I would say that it is going to be your experience in class that is going to teach you to act. Not that I don't have information for you; however, you won't understand a lot of it until you get up and get it into your body and start trying to do it. Until then, you won't be able to understand it fully.

My class is constructed to address the unconscious of the actor and, because of that, there are a couple of things that I do. First, I tell all my new actors that they have no responsibility to know anything. If they don't understand something, it's my fault. If they aren't solving a problem, it's my fault. If it isn't my fault, they shouldn't be paying me. I take the responsibility.

Second, I say that the rules in this class are that there are no rules. The best reason not to come to class is because you don't feel like it, because you want to go to the movies. If you come to class for five minutes when you want to be there, you'll learn more than you would sitting through four hours of a class that is boring you or that you don't want to be in. I don't ask actors to criticize other actors, because that's a different job. On the other hand, they can say anything they want any time they want. I do suggest they don't say it when the other actors are working because it might piss them off. There is a method to this madness. I do literally mean it. What I am beginning to create is an environment in which what it takes to be a good actor is accepted by everyone.

The improvisational theater has influenced me because in the improvisational theater there are no lines so you have to go moment to moment with yourself in the here and now. So part of what happens to new students is the climate in class. I will begin to create a climate that will relieve them of those things that might keep them from acting and following their impulses: will I be any good, will she like me, will I ask a dumb question? All that is getting in the way of acting, because acting is like being a musician: you have to get the person to allow his or her instrument to swing with everything.

The first thing I do in class is ask everyone what they hope to get out of this class, what their expectations are. Then I say to them, "As you try to answer this question, what I want you all to do is try to catch a whisper of something in your response, catch your first impulse, and try to bring it up." And I have a conversation with each person at the beginning, and tell that person that if there is a part he or she has always wanted to play, to play it, or if he or she has always wanted to juggle, to do that. It's the students' time; they can do whatever they want.

Then I tell them a story, which is true, about an actor who studied with me in New York who said he really wanted to be Fred Astaire. So I said, "Why don't you do a scene in class from one of his movies?" He said, "Well, I'm not a trained dancer." I said "I don't care. If you can bring to me what it is that you love about Fred Astaire, then I think it will be very valuable for you." He was shaken by the thought. He came to class and by the third session did a scene that started in his kitchen, where he turned on the record player and began to dance as Fred Astaire. And it was one of the most magical moments I've ever seen in a class. In addition, it unlocked all of his creativity. He really began to be an actor.

And that's exactly like the first exercise I mentioned before when I ask students to catch the first impulse they have when they answer the question, "What would you like to get out of this class?" It's being able to be in touch with yourself that makes the difference between being a good journeyman actor and a star. It's being able to hear your own whispers and go with them. So I'm training all the time on an unconscious basis.

If you don't teach in sequence or through a series of steps, how do you start when a student presents something in class for the first time?

I teach in blocks of four weekends—all day Saturday and Sunday for four weekends. I divide classes up into a morning and afternoon class. Students can attend both. And everyone works each week.

The first thing I do is support everything they are doing right, which can be considerable. Sometimes all people need is to be shown that they already know how to act. That's very different from what other teachers do because most of them get anxious and feel that they have to "teach" something. But if it isn't broken, don't fix it.

Sometime during the first weekend I tell every new person, "I am going to give you your lecture now. This is called the 'Given circumstances, sense memory, personalization lecture'. This is how you go about working on material if you don't know how."

First, you discern the given circumstances of the play. If you are doing A *Streetcar Named Desire*, what are the given circumstances? You see, the only thing that distinguishes Joan or Eva from Blanche Dubois is our given circumstances. I was raised in Massachusetts, I come from a middle-class Jewish family, I went to college, and so forth. Blanche Dubois was raised in the South, she's an alcoholic, she's lost the plantation, etc. All of those given circumstances add up to what Stanislavsky calls the "big if." If I were an alcoholic, and if I had been raised in the South, and if I had lost all my money and been kicked out of town, and if I had been drinking for ten years and was a mess . . . if I can create all those things, all I have to do is walk on stage and it is "as if" I were Blanche Dubois. Now there are physical given circumstances and psychological ones. I am obligated to make all of these given circumstances personal to me. How do I do that? I think the best way to do that is by Sense Memory Exercises and Personalizations.

First, I abstract the situation: i.e., I'm an alcoholic. Since I like to make everything as dramatic as possible, it's not enough for me, Joan, that I'm an alcoholic. Let's say I just spent twenty-four hours on a train where they don't serve liquor, and I've been without a drink. Now I arrive in New Orleans and it's 112 degrees and I can't afford a cab and I have to walk five miles to this address in thin, spikey heels. How am I going to accomplish that? I've never been an alcoholic, but I have had the flu, so I have a few ideas about how bad I can feel. Then I will do Sense Memory work to get at that. The way I teach Sense Memory is that I have an actor do it on the stage while he or she is in a scene. It's not a preparation. Sense memory for the flu means that I will let my body remember specifically all the physical aspects of the flu.

I used to do relaxation work and exercises for half of my class. I would say to students, "Find a chair, not a comfortable chair, in which you think you might be able to go to sleep. The words *think* and *might* are very important. You don't have to be right. Then try to find a position in which you think this will be possible. Then try to find five places on your body you think might be tense and relax them by letting gravity control the weight of your body. Then, if you have a desire to move, rather than moving, make a sound.

The reasoning is that an actor needs to learn to connect his impulses, his feelings, to language because that's what our theater is—language. Any movement in a relaxation exercise is an attempt to get rid of his feelings. I also stress that this exercise is not to calm yourself down; it's not yoga. When you are doing it right, you are making an effort to let your body relax and it usually releases the flow of emotion that we use our body to control because it may be inappropriate to cry at the stocking counter at Macy's when you are twenty-five years old because your mother was mean to you when you were three. As an actor what you want is a body and an instrument that will be so available that the unconscious connections are made and will supply the material that your unconscious mind has told you the play needs. Relaxation is vital because if you don't have it, any information that comes to you is short-circuited before you can respond and react. So I tell students about these exercises and tell them to do them at home.

I also tell the class why I believe in the Sense Memory Exercises. Every actor knows that he has to personalize the material and a lot of them use mental images consciously or unconsciously. The problem with mental images is they wear out. You know that if someone in the play dies, you might think about a time when your father died and get close to those feelings of loss. If you just think about it, what happens is you get one great rehearsal and you are left high and dry trying desperately to dredge up the feeling again. Some actors consider Sense Memory only a rehearsal technique to find behavior they can imitate later. What I want is an actor to be alive on stage.

The way I teach Sense Memory, if it is done properly it works 100% of the time *for the audience.* In the same way that an actor makes a consistent effort to let his body relax, he must make a consistent effort to let his fingers remember, his nose remember, every part of his body remember. Since the way human beings get information is through their five senses, every feeling is received that way. It is a scientific fact that by allowing yourself to remember the sensory stimuli surrounding any event, the memory of that event will come back to you.

The mistake a lot of teachers make with Sense Memory Exercises is that they think the feelings come back consistently and they encourage the student to try to remember feelings. Then the student is all balled up trying to get results as opposed to sticking with the process. Sense Memory Exercises will bring back those feelings. You simply have to make the effort to remember, never the effort to feel. If you do that, the material is always available to the unconscious and, even though you sometimes feel it and sometimes don't, your unconscious is communicating directly to the audience's unconscious because those two are identical. So if I can remember what I could see, touch, smell, taste, and hear when my father died, I'm going to wake those memories up on a physiological basis and the audience will recognize them because they will be the same as the audience's experience of grief and loss. In addition, if you just use your brain, you've already censored the memories. You may think, "Oh, I was so sad when my father died." Then you do a Sense Memory Exercise and you may find out you were thrilled. You got to be an orphan, you could go to school the next day and say you were an orphan. You were furious. You were frightened. You get the whole ball of wax if you do the Sense Memory Exercise properly. This exercise is a way of waking up past experiences that are appropriate for the given circumstances.

Now I come back to my character's given circumstances. I'll substitute the flu for Blanche's physical state. Unlike Blanche, I don't have a problem with heat; so for the 112 degrees in New Orleans, I'm going to do an overall sensation to let my body remember the cold, which I hate. I walk on the stage as Blanche. I'm feeling sick and I'm shaking. I'm not trying to shake. My body is shaking in response to the memory of cold and the audience says, "My God, is she a mess."

Now I decide I need a Place Exercise. What does this place, her sister Stella's house, mean to Blanche? I need to abstract that for myself. This is where the actor's brain works on what he's going to do, not on how he is going to do it. If an actor plans what, but not how, he's a dangerous actor—dangerous in the good sense—because then he doesn't know what is going to happen to him and you, as the audience, don't know what is going to happen to him. And that's exciting to watch.

I feel that the most dramatic way for me to deal with this place is to choose to make it the worst place imaginable, a real place from my past where I felt helpless and trapped. So I walk on the stage and open the door. On Monday night in the theater I open the door and start to cry. Tuesday night I open the door and start to laugh. Wednesday night I open the door, close it, then come back on (because I want to do the play and get my reviews). Thursday night I open the door and want a drink.

These behaviors occur as a result of my Sense Memory work. None of that behavior is better or worse for Blanche Dubois. All of them are Blanche Dubois and they vary as our own behavior varies in life. A really good actor will insist on that freedom and a really good director will allow it. Being a director as well as a teacher, I know that this style of acting will "cut together" because the life created is consistent. And that's the way life really is. The outcome of this interview depends on what we had for lunch today. If we had this interview tomorrow, it would be different. That's what being alive is like, and what I want my actors to be able to accomplish is to act as if they were alive in the given circumstances of the play.

So on with Blanche. Now, as the actress, you have the problem of your sister, Stella, and the lost Belle Rive. That's where you begin to personalize. The way I teach that is as follows: I get the class up as a group and say, "I want you to pick the person that you would most like to be with at this moment. If I had a magic wand, who would you most like to be with? I want you to turn to the person on your right and deal with him or her as if you were dealing with that person. For some of you the person on your right will be exactly like the person you chose. For others, that person will bear no resemblance to the one you chose. Whatever he or she does that is completely different, I want you to believe simply that that person is behaving oddly today." Then I have everyone sit in a circle and relate to each other as their personalization or chosen person. People start learning how to act very quickly this way.

And all your choices as an actor should be fun. Don't pick a glass of wine because that's what the script says you are going to drink in a scene. Pick a 1966 Lafitte because if you do, when you walk on stage, instead of asking youself what you are going to do you're thinking, "I can't wait to sit down at that table and let myself remember that '66 Lafitte." That's a different appetite for the stage and I consciously incorporate that aspect in my training.

Let's say that as the actress I decide that Blanche is jealous and angry at her sister and I pick someone to personalize with whom I would like to get even. So I tell my personalized fellow actress that I lost something of hers, using the words of the play as a code. Suppose the director says to me, "No, no, no. Blanche loves her sister." Then I say, "Okay. Different choice." I don't say I better act loving. Instead I pick someone to personalize about whom I care a great deal and whom I have to betray. Then I simply sit down and tell her about the betrayal, again using the words of the play as a code. Using the words of the play as a code is something I learned from Michael Howard, and it is very valuable. That's about as much information as I would be willing to give a new student. Actually it's more.

One other thing. I tell new students, as things progress, that along with Sense Memory, it is also necessary to stay true to the actor's here and now. Let's say I'm on the stage and playing a love scene and I've done all my personalization work, but I'm not feeling anything. Really what I'm thiking is, why is that jerk in the second row coughing? A bad actor will throw out that thought. A good actor will welcome that thought because in real life, at the moments of high romance you are wondering whether you unplugged the iron. If you will allow yourself the fullness of thought that you have as a human being, the people sitting in the audience will know, on an unconscious level, that you are not lying to them and that they are getting a full moment that is identical to their experience. And then they get really interested in you.

How do you help new students develop a character?

Character is a costume. If your person is old, you go and observe old people. You should make the work specific sensorially, and figure out what kind of pain they experience that makes them move the way they do. Do that as a Sense Memory Exercise. Do not try to feel old. If you do that, you are phony. So part of it is to concoct a costume that adds up to the externals of the old person.

The other half of character is the given circumstances. If I alter my given circumstances to those of Blanche Dubois by doing specific work, I will come out with my Blanche Dubois, without question.

What about body movement in character work?

That's a costume too. You don't try to feel it. That's a mistake that people make, believing they should *feel* old. All of that is a costume and it's all right. Hats, shoes, strange rings, anything that wakes up the actor's imagination.

By the way, I believe that there is no one on a stage but the actor. But what you do is fall in love with the heightened experience of yourself, and that replaces the sense of being somebody else. Think about it logically. It's always you.

The highest level of acting is where the actor is relaxed enough so he can read the play and walk on the stage as himself. As he starts to move through the play, his instrument is so well adjusted and in tune that it simply starts throwing up the information from the actor's being that he needs at that moment to fulfill the demands of the part. The Sense Memory work begins to drop away from the expert actor. The work is a transition period, but you can't drop it until you have a highly trained instrument. Then something else comes into it that is hard to explain.

Acting was originally a religious experience. People went to the theater in Greece and they all spent a week seeing the same plays. It reminded people in the audience of the highest form of being alive. What I try to get an actor to do is walk on stage in the highest form of aliveness, which automatically makes him a star. You see what I mean? That's why you can't leave out the here and now, because any lie in your system shuts you down. When an actor can contact himself in the here and now he or she becomes, as Salinger has said, "God's actress," or, as John Hendricks put it, "We are like musicians with the heavenly music playing up there all the time and we are the instruments for the heavenly music—and sometimes we are able to let it play through us." Well, I think that's what an actor really is: a conduit that allows the spirit of the universe or being human or whatever he wants to call it to pass through him.

That's why my actors are willing to give up trying to be someone else—because they find the experience of being themselves the highest experience that they can have. (Not that they don't convey a specific character to the audience. They do.) Then they lose their concern about the audience because what they are after is that experience. That's what they come to the theater for. And that's what the audience comes to the theater for, and the actor wakes up the audience and connects with it and allows it to experience itself on that high level too. That's what great actors do for an audience. And that can be taught. The key is to teach an actor to allow himself to exist in the here and now.

I don't believe in fourth-wall acting. There is a huge lie in that. Actors don't want to create a wall between themselves and the audience. The reason we all became actors and actresses is that we wanted people to pay money to sit in a seat in a dark place and watch us do something. If we lie when we get on stage and say, "I don't want this," the whole system starts to shut down.

Since we want the audience there, it is only the bad actor who will focus on his acting partner and try to pretend that the audience isn't there. When the good actor is playing a love scene, for example, he is saying, "Everybody out there—you want to know what love is like? You want to know everything about it? Well, here it comes."

I forget who said this, but I believe it. The difference between a good actor and a bad actor is this: a bad actor playing a waiter at a party will glue the glasses to the tray, paint the inside of them so they look as if they have water in them, and walk around the outside of the crowd. The good actor puts more glasses on the tray than he can handle, fills them to the brim with water, and tries to walk through the middle of the crowd.

Getting back to technique: let's say in a scene you're supposed to be a mean person who is going to do something mean to me. What I would do is personalize you as somebody who has never done anything bad to me and whom I trust completely. Then when I walk on stage and you are mean, the effect is much more profound than if I had personalized you as someone who would be mean to me.

I began to notice that as actors got into the highest level of acting they often wanted to laugh in the middle of serious scenes. I picked this up viscerally, not in a conscious way. I picked it up in my body. Incidentally, this is why most teachers are going to want to talk theory to you. After they have been teaching for a long time, they begin to connect with their actors in a way that is not verbal and they get hungry to talk. I'll say to someone who is acting, "Let yourself laugh." At first I get a lot of resistance, but then the actor sees what happens to other people, he sees another actor let himself laugh in a serious moment. The minute he lets himself do that, he suddenly looks as if something has lit him up from the inside—he becomes beautiful or sexy or leaps into that star category. What also happens is the minute he lets himself laugh, very strong emotion comes up that is right for the scene.

Laughing seems to be the way that people have of breaking through a barrier when they are acting. So I become like a coach, and I'll say, "You are at a place where what you need is ring time," and I'll get the actor to do a lot of scenes. Usually we can get his muscle up so that, as someone once said, "My voice will go with you." They hear me say, "Let yourself laugh," and they start to be able to do it for themselves and they grow up and go away. That's getting into the right high level of acting. That's where you are really getting into releasing the spirit. And then you become compelling. I've never had a student who stuck with it who didn't become special in that way.

Are there any approaches to the teaching of acting of which you disapprove?

Yes. In general I disapprove of punitive teachers. They are antithetical to anything artistic or creative. What can anyone learn from being yelled at? Being yelled at is not information and the reason I am so adamant about it is that I get the wreckage of other people's classes and it infuriates me to see a student who spent his money and never got any information. It enrages me that there are teachers around who think that yelling at somebody is information.

What about teachers who encourage actors to reveal their personal lives as part of their approach to training?

My tendency is to believe when they do that that they usually have ulterior motives because you don't need personal information to teach someone to act.

Anyway, the actor does his best work by keeping his own secrets. If he starts to tell people what he was using at a specific moment, it will dissipate, it will be left on the locker room floor. I tell them that they can't tell anybody what they were using. They die to tell, of course, but they can't because then they will turn it into another event.

What is your approach to Shakespeare?

After a student brings in Shakespeare and deals with it by answering all the questions he would for any piece of work, I tell him that he has to take on the burden of the verse. You see, Shakespeare is an opera, not a play. And this is how you go about it.

First, you scan the piece of material you are going to work on for iambic pentameter. You type it up on a large piece of paper with spaces in between. You learn what iambic pentameter is and mark it out. Then you drill the speech with no acting in mind at all. You drill it so much that it is set in your heart and soul, and you can do it without thinking—even while you take a shower.

Then you paraphrase the entire monologue you are working on into modern English. Then you need to start playing with short sounds and long sounds, and you do that until you are totally familiar with the language and can sing the song without any acting.

Next, you have to start picking sensory work that is so passionate that you can do his plays without pausing—because there are no pauses in Shakespeare. Everything is in the writing. All the transitions are in words.

Then you start building up your voice and breath capacity to be able to take an entire speech of Shakespeare's and start at the begininng and go all the way to the end. That's basically how you begin to work on Shakespeare.

Also, I feel that an actor who works on Shakespeare can never accomplish it without good speech. Working on Shakespeare gives an actor a muscle because he has to make big choices. It's like a stage muscle that he develops.

Do you have a favorite exercise?

Yes. It's called the Allyn Ann McLeary Star Time Theater. I tell a student he is going to do an exercise and I tell him to go on stage. When he gets there, I don't way a word. I let him do whatever he wants until he comes to understand that simply *being* on stage is fun and the most attractive to the audience. And I will let him stand on the stage for as long as it takes him to understand that his honestly "being" in front of an audience is interesting. It's a lot of fun. The students often go bananas and the people who watch them have a good time. I like anything that is playful.

A nice thing that happens in my class is that because it's a benevolent atmosphere, actors begin to help each other. A community spirit emerges in the class. I'm not explaining the phenomenon well. What happens is the class becomes one organism of learning. The beginners see the experts and the experts see the beginners and everybody sees everybody else struggling and the problems become very basic. After you've learned all the technique, you have to come back to the problem of how to walk on the stage as if you were alive. That's what all of this technique is aiming toward, simply to create the experience of experience. That's why teaching acting is so wonderful—because you really are dealing with the nature of being.

How do you help students work on comedy?

With my attitude in class. If a piece of material is written well and the actor does the work, it will be funny. If it's not written well . . . how to make it funny past that? Drop your pants. Slip on a banana peel. Talk in a funny voice. The real answer to that is that if the material really isn't funny, anything you do to it is going to be bad. That's one thing. The other thing is that some people are funnier than others because their perspective on life is funny. I think a funnier perspective is a more mature perspective and that I do encourage.

What advice would you give to an actor just starting out on his or her career?

If you really want to act well, you can learn to do it. Find a benevolent situation, a teacher whose work you like. I think an actor today has to develop a relationship to himself as an artist whereby his own experience is the most meaningful part of the acting. Because that's the only thing he will have to sustain him.

Also, actors should think of auditions as opportunities to perform and they have to distinguish between what they can control and what they can't. You can only control how good you are in a particular performance. If you give up the idea that you have control over whether or not you will get the job, you can have a good time when you get an audition. The people who are going to like you will like you. They will find you and like you and give you work.

Clinton Bond

Jeff Corey

Jeff Corey has been training actors for more than thirty-five years. His Professional Actors Workshop in Los Angeles has been described by the National Observer as "a major influence in the motion picture industry." He was appointed professor of drama at California State University and has served on the board of directors of the Screen Actors Guild. Mr. Corey has also had a distinguished acting career and appeared in more than a hundred feature films and on the professional stage in New York and California. He co-starred in True Grit, Butch Cassidy and the Sundance Kid, *and* In Cold Blood. *Most recently he appeared on TV with Vanessa Redgrave in* Second Serve. *His directing credits for TV include* Night Gallery, Alias Smith and Jones, Anna and the King, *and the PBS TV* Meeting of Minds.

Mr. Corey thinks of himself as a conservative when it comes to acting training because he likes to "conserve all that is rich from the past." He also places great emphasis on the necessity for "the actor's body to be alive" and he believes that is "just as important as the psychological ramifications of a play. . . . It seems to me that one of the marvelous paradoxes in acting is that when the nonverbal, physical life of the character is most explicitly and richly defined, the verbal life of the character becomes most meaningful."

How did you get started in teaching acting?

In 1951 I taught a class at the Stage Society, which was a group that Arthur Kennedy and Akim Tamiroff were involved with and I taught in tandem with Michael Chekhov. I never thought of myself as a teacher and I never consciously wanted to teach, but there was one kid there who had a patent lack of talent and when he was asked to leave the Stage Society, he asked me if I would start a class. So I told him to get some people together to start one and he did. And I've been teaching ever since. I never consciously set out to start a class—my phone number is not even listed—but I've never been indifferent to it. I find the whole acting process quite exciting and absorbing and it makes my life a much richer one. I sometimes think what a pity it is that acting is not available to "civilians." On several occasions I've been asked by the California Association of English Teachers to do seminars on Shakespeare for schoolchildren and I have found that I could get them excited about the possibilities of making Shakespeare relevant to their lives. There are ways of doing that if you use your imagination.

Do you work on Shakespeare in your classes?

Yes. I don't think we do Shakespeare out of some arbitrary reverence. I think we do him because there is an element of recognition in his plays. If you see *As You Like It* done well, and I have, with Vanessa Redgrave at the Royal Shakespeare in 1962, you see a theme that is still relevant. I must say that when I worked with her recently on *Second Serve* for TV she was thrilled that I had seen the Shakespeare production because she was so proud of it. In my life I've been in two productions of *Hamlet*, one with Leslie Howard. I played Rosencrantz and decades later I played Polonius at the Mark Taper Forum. There is no end to the exhilaration of hearing and being involved in this play. It feeds me. I don't just do it because it's a beautiful play and you are supposed to do Shakespeare.

How are your classes divided?

I don't use terms like "advanced class" because they are meaningless to me. I've found people who were just marvelously gifted primitives who act so beautifully the first time they try it. I'm not a great one for telling students they have to do this first and this second. I like to generate the excitement of it, like Bottom in *Midsummer Night's Dream*, who says, "I can play a wall. I can play the moon." When I start a new class, students bring in a monologue, and in the third or fourth week they bring in a scene. If it's lousy, we'll just laugh at how lousy it was and what obvious choices they made and fool around with it and not talk it to death. We redo all the work in class. Students get the rehearsal experience and an idea of how exciting it is to get another idea through some metaphoric suggestion. I personally see great value in the sensory exercises, but they bore the hell out of me. I'm not denouncing them, I just don't like doing them. I'd rather the actors grappled with the scenes.

Obviously, if the entrance to a scene is mechanical—if they didn't come in from anywhere and aren't going anywhere—we will talk about where they were, what this place smells like, what they expect to find here, who moved the furniture, etc. These are all sensory elements that they can get through wrestling with the role, rather than feeling as if they are children in school and have to learn this first and this second. I don't like actors to sit and stew. I like them to be active.

If some students are doing a scene and they are only doing the plot and making stage crosses and it's pretty bloody empty, I will say, "For God's sake, what is this scene about? What is its relevance? Stanislavsky said the function of the artist is to reveal the human condition. What aspect of the human condition are we dealing with? What is this scene really about?" Then I will get other students in class up on stage, five on one side and five on the other, and tell them to take sides and argue back and forth about the thematic aspects of the play. A play is a "for instance," the embodiment of an idea. If there is no idea, the play will be static. The students on either side will appeal to the actors who are doing the scene to explain or support their side. Then I will tell them to incorporate the dialogue and try to convince each other that their side is right.

I'm a little leery about what is glibly referred to as technique. There are certain things I believe in, like thematic clarity. I also strongly believe it is necessary for the actor's body to be alive and that it is just as important as all the psychological ramifications of the play. You have to be as specific as you can about what the body is doing. People talk about subtext. I do an exercise to show that subtext is largely the physical impulses that occur to you that you do not enact. You may want to hit somebody or undress someone while you are asking him or her to pass the salt or saying whatever the *text* is. You have to be aware of the aliveness of the body and the potential of the body. Berthold Brecht said a marvelous thing: "The decision to do something is involved with the decision not to do something else." If I elect not to put my hands in my pocket, it's because I *choose* not to for a reason. It's a decision. The *potential* for movement can be embodied in a performance where there is no movement.

Do you have any exercises to encourage the use of the body?

I have an exercise whereby a student does several specific and unrelated physical tasks in sequence: the first might be something like kneeling and crossing himself; the next going up to the window and saying good-bye to someone; the next doing a somersault; the last picking up a book and reading a line on page 32. The student keeps doing those physical tasks, each with a beginning, a middle and an end, so that each is a rhythmic unit. The actor starts with the impulse to move and goes to the completion of each task. Then he goes to the next physical task. These tasks have no relationship to one another except to note how each is done for its own sake.

Then I tell the student to do a poem, a speech from a play, or a song while he concentrates on the specific physical task done to completion without any deviation. And there is so much irony in it because the body is consistently in opposition to and contradicting what he says. You might say this task isn't consistent with what he or she is thinking, but there is a marvelous juxtaposition of the words with the actions. So an actor must choreograph the physical design of his part. Going back to sensory work, it's infinitely richer this way than to do what has become a mechanical act, although it probably was inspiring at one time.

I have many friends who were in The Group Theatre. Some of the sensory exercises that they were able to do were because they knew each other and had a feel for each other. You take that same good sensory exercise and give it to students who come from disparate backgrounds and they don't know what they are doing. It is like people who play chamber music together: they know each other and all have something in common. Otherwise, it becomes just a mechanical device.

How has your approach to teaching been influenced by your own training as an actor?

Anyone who puts out a sign saying that he or she teaches the Stanislavsky method is disrespectful to himself or herself. Stanislavsky is dead; peace to his ashes. I've been an actor for more than fifty years and I'm not slavishly following anyone. I've been excited by many, many things, including a college education I got rather late in life. I've been a speech therapist at UCLA and I had a full professorship at Cal State, Northridge, so I've been part of academia. What I tell my own classes is that you have to be the head of your own academy. Matisse said there are no rules outside of the artist. When people come here, they are not learning a Jeff Corey method. They are watching a guy who has a lot of experience, and demonstrable insight, and a caring and affection for the process and for people—who kind of gooses them and surprises them, gets them going. And it excites them. I must emphasize that I am not condemning other people's approaches. But I'm quite content with what I do.

On occasions I have sat in at The Actors Studio in both New York and Los Angeles and liked a lot of it. I thought there was too much talk, but a lot of good work. Good talk, but too much. I like to keep talk at a minimum and put our energies into reworking the scenes.

Where did you train as an actor?

When I was eighteen I knew the Delsart chart. Just last week I spoke to Harriet Quiggly, who was my teacher at the Fagin School. She's eighty and I still have a crush on her. She saw me recently in *Morning Star, Evening Star*. I asked her, "When you saw me do a love scene with Beatrice Straight, did you see the eighteen-year-old?" She said, "Yes, that interesting young man was in that performance." You see, we don't change that much.

I'm so grateful, since I do teach, that I learned all the academic aspects of theater as well. Then I went to Method classes as far back as 1934 with Bret Warren and Mary Virginia Farmer of The Group Theatre in New York. I worked in the theater in New York for eight years. I came to California because I was going to give up acting. But I thought, I'll do here what I do in New York. I made the rounds and got an agent and work immediately.

So I saw the principal productions of The Group Theatre and knew the people. They thrilled me. When the Actor's Lab started, Roman Bohnen and Jules Dessin taught there. We had wonderful classes.

I've never consciously wanted to be a pathfinder. People start saying, "Well, I'm into Grotowski." I've heard him speak. His ideas are somewhat exciting, but not new. I've lived long enough to say there is nothing new. The experiments in epic theater in this country were exciting forty, fifty years ago. Guthrie McClintock's production of *Yellow Jackets* with Jimmy Stewart and Sam Levine was glorious epic theater. People who don't know the history of theater and movements in theater every now and then get gaga about so-called innovators or pathfinders. Every now and then they say I'm into this or that. I saw Thadeus Kantor's thrilling Polish Theatre recently, but what was exciting about it was that it was, at the root, what Benno Schneider had been doing in the Artef in the 1930s. I thought, good. It is possible for this kind of theater to be reinstated. Benno's epic devices preceded the Berliner Ensemble.

I am a conservative in that I like to conserve all that is rich in the past. I know that I'm not ready to throw it away, to say this or that is old-fashioned. It's like people saying Freud is passé when they don't even know his work.

Do you have any exercises to help students learn to play the reality of the moment?

Every exercise is involved with that. But sometimes moment-to-moment acting can be very tedious because it is devoid of any idea. I would be much more interested in having students understand what a play is about, what the relationships are. I'm tired of actors who are skillfully playing the role, but have nothing happening between them and the other actors. They are doing their sensory exercises and experiencing the reality of the moment, but it stays within the confines of their own skin and doesn't generate any excitement on the stage with other people, the environment, or the audience.

Let's say you have a new student. How do you advise him or her to approach a script?

First, I like people to know that there is no mystique about subtext. It's another way of describing the affect of your imagination. Subtext comes unbidden; inner monologue comes unbidden. So I will give students a piece of fiction and tell them, "You are in such and such a circumstance. What are you thinking at this particular moment?" It's like free association out loud. If they go blank, I tell them to describe the blank and cherish it because some of the greatest scenes in dramatic literature have occurred when people went blank, when the impact of the circumstance was so great that the feeling of no feeling sheerly anesthetized. Lear says, "I will do such things / what they are I know not yet / but they shall be the terrors of the earth." That's a powerful thing.

Later I will have students do this when they work on a part. I verbalize what is happening for myself when I work on a part and I have students do it too. There is a quote from Strindberg that I am fond of: "The author has attempted in this dream play to imitate the disconnected but apparently logical form of a dream. Anything is possible and probable. Space and time do not exist. Based on a slight foundation of reality, imagination wanders far afield and leaves new patterns, mixtures, recollections, experiences, unconstrained fantasies, absurdities. . . ." That's what subtext is. That's what goes on constantly during a performance. So while you and I are talking about something, it's what I am *thinking* that the audience will perceive.

Under what conditions do you have students do that exercise?

I will ask them to improvise to make clear the idea of subtext. Or, if students are doing a scene and the plot seems to contradict what the scene is about, I'll say to one of the characters, "All right, I want to put words in your mouth. Character A tell character B 'I know how distressed you are about what happened, but part of me is so happy it happened. I'm almost gleeful. I am so happily distracted by this disaster that I don't have to face the things that I'm afraid of.' " Then these actors will do an improvisation based on that idea. When it gets going, I tell them to go back to the scene and to use the dialogue.

There was a scene from *Amadeus* in class yesterday, the seduction scene. I told the actress playing Mozart's wife that she should think of Salieri as an appealing man, that she wanted to have an affair with him, and that there was a bonus in it for her. She did the scene using that subtext. I told the actor playing Salieri to think of these Austrians, including Mozart's wife, as sausage eaters who couldn't hold a candle to the sophisticated Italians. Well, with these two subtexts, the scene became very interesting to watch.

How do you help students create a character?

It depends on the character. A well-known actor was very worried when he went to play his first serious role. He had to play a drunkard who winds up a fiasco even though he starts out as a big advertising executive. I told him to make certain assumptions: the character's wife is not really his wife; these are not really his children; this is not really his office or his car; this character never had the feeling that anything belonged to him or that he deserved it. The other thing I told him was to keep a parallax image of his character's father, who died drunk on a park bench near the ocean. I told him that his character desperately wanted to merge and become one with his father's cadaver. Throughout the whole performance there was this marginal preoccupation.

I did a characterization for a film I was in, *Lady in a Cage*. I tried to get a walk for the wino I was playing, so Ann Sothern and I went down to skid row. We talked to some of those folks and she got an idea: everything I own is in this shopping bag. She got so excited about the things she would have in the shopping bag! I wasn't happy with any particular walk that I observed. I had an idea. All of the winos had trousers that were frayed around one hip because they sleep on rough surfaces. Then I thought of diaper rash and how it makes you walk and sit trying to keep the trouser fabric away from the rash—and this affected my voice and face.

There was a woman in class who did a rather sexy role in an adaptation of a Peter Shaffer move. For her particular role I told her to assume that the top of her cranium is removed and if she makes quick moves, her brains will spill out. In several sequences men tried to grab her breasts and she had to hold them off. The character element I gave her produced an "all right I'll let you, but . . ." attitude to her character. These are all kinds of little metaphoric things I use.

When Paul Burke did *Naked City* I worked with him on the first two sequences. He wanted something to carry him through (it did and served him well for eleven years). I told him that (1) whenever you are given a policing problem, don't have any idea of how to start. This gave him a charming bemused look. His assumption became, "Anyone in the precinct can do this better than me. Why did they come to me with the problem?" (2) In the last reel, when someone with a gun is after you, know exactly where the bullet is going to hit you—in the back of the head. Whenever you start the scene, you are waiting for the bullet to hit. By the way, people in The Group Theatre used to love doing these kinds of things. When I give students these kinds of adjustments to metaphors, I'm priming the pump. Then they start thinking along these lines for themselves.

How do you help your students work on characters who are very different from themselves?

My immediate assumption is that we are all so much like each other. Michael Chekhov once said that we are 99% Iago and 99% Othello. I tell students not to try to play the character, but to invest themselves in the circumstances of the character. You cannot play the part until the specifics of that scene are as familiar to you as the everyday events of your own life. Emerson said, "The purpose of poetry is the poet telling you how it was with him and we are all made richer by it." I do what I can to convince students that they know what it's like to have all the experiences of the character they are playing. I always assume that they are more like me than otherwise.

Do you have any exercises for helping students become more expressive?

As I mentioned, I've done a lot of speech work. Sometimes actors don't talk loudly, and in many cases I've confronted them and said, "It's not a vocal problem. It's because you don't know what you are doing, so naturally you don't want to make it big. When you get excited about the decisions that you make, we will hear you and see you and you'll be expressive." That's happened to so many actors in class who were timid. When they got excited about their choices, they were heard.

The reason I put so much stress on physical tasks is to get students to be more emotionally expressive. I think one of the bad aspects of training in the Stanislavsky system was the gross misunderstanding of him. I don't talk about emotion at all. I think the brain is the most emotional organ we have. Our sexuality, our passion, is in the brain. If actors know what they are doing, I've found very few incapable of expressing emotion—when they've thought it through. There is too much so-called work on "getting it all out." Gertrude Stein was generous in her comments to Thomas Wolfe (she liked the galleys of his first novel), "But you must remember, Thomas, that catharsis is not necessarily revelation."

I know a lot of teachers goad people into being more emotional, into "getting it all out." I hate that. I've seen the results of it in my class. I jolly them out of it and say, "I know you like to yell, and I know that an actor can't resist a tirade, but what is the scene *about*? Who is this other person? What problem does he or she present? What do you want to happen? How do you advance action?" If the action is pursued, the appropriate emotion can be evoked.

Let's say you have a new student who comes in to work on Nina in the last act of The Sea Gull. *It's a very emotional scene, but you don't see it. The actress is not communicating anything approaching the complexity of what Nina must be experiencing. What do you do?*

You can't set it out in a technique. I'll give you an example. I worked with an actress, a beautiful young child, Merrie Spaeth, who was in *The World of Henry Orient*. She played a child dying of leukemia and I played her teacher at the hospital. We had a long scene together in which I was to tell her that I know about her illness. The actress said to me, "I can't cry. How do I do it?" Actors do this to me when I am working because they know I teach. I said, "Don't worry. Just before the take I'll say something to you." A few minutes before they were ready to shoot, I put my arms around her and said, "What are you doing when I knock at the door?" "I'm packing my suitcase," she said, "to go on a trip." I said, "Sweetheart, while you are packing your suitcase, pick your shroud." She stood in front of this open suitcase and it became a coffin to her and she couldn't reach for a dress without dissolving in tears. That's a way to get tears, by using your imagination. If you play Nina, think of one thing, maybe how, after you lost your baby, you were ill, and it was a cold night and you knew that Trigorin would reject you again, but you were going to make a fool of yourself and go to him anyway.

Do you use exercises in which students use their personal lives as a way to help them become more expressive?

Very rarely, because anything you imagine is really an echo of your own experience. I think it's much better to use your imagination and not to intrude in this area. I know there are actors who do it. There is a teacher who has taught for me who does the Affective Memory Exercise very well, and I encourage him to do it when he subs for me, so I am not opposed to it. It's just that I think people's imaginations are amazing, and they don't have to deal with personal recall.

I love what we call "character acting." When I was thirty-seven I played Maureen O'Hara's grandfather in a movie called *Bagdad*. But it was still *me* playing the part. At the core of every great performance is an interesting actor. When Laurence Olivier played Archie in *The Entertainer*, you just adored the man who could incorporate that part of himself. When he is not good, as when he played Big Daddy in *Cat on a Hot Tin Roof*, there was no Big Daddy because there was no part of Olivier in the character. In other words, he didn't find a way of engaging his essential self in that role. That is what an actor must do.

Aren't you also saying that part of our experience as human beings comes from our observations of other people, so when we play a character we use that information?

I must assume that I have things in common with everyone, King Lear, for example. I must take what I know about the human experience and say, "It is like me." Otherwise I can't do the part.

Yes, I encourage students to observe other people, but you don't have to be clinical about it. If I had to play a homosexual I wouldn't go to bed with a man. I could *imagine* it.

What are some of your favorite exercises?

The *Los Angeles Times* has excerpts called "The News of the Day." It has short articles about things like Mayor Bradley storming out of meetings. I tear these excerpts into separate scraps and tell students to pick one and incorporate it into a scene they are working on. They will put whatever information is in that news item into the context of the scene. Or I will ask them to pick up a thesaurus, and I will give them a number to look up. That number can have as many as thirty synonyms, and then I tell them to use those words as the text for the scene. They will use them to amplify their attitude in a conflict. They have to use a word from the book that is usually unrelated to what is happening, and try to make it fit by the attitude they bring to it. It shows the dominance of subtext over text.

I do exercises with scripts. Two students have a scene they are going to read. Then I ask other students in class to invent a conflict between two people that has nothing to do with the scene about to be read. The dialogue in the script may be about one thing, the invented conflict about something totally unrelated. The two actors then read the dialogue of their scene using the invented, unrelated circumstances and try to make it work.

Another exercise is to take two copies of the same play anthology.

I pick a line of dialogue at random from a play. I read the line to a student and when I finish, I direct the student to turn to page 54 and respond with a line from another play. The student has been listening to my monologue and while thinking *only* of his response to my speech reads another, totally unrelated line back to me, keeping in mind only that response. And we go back and forth like that with material that is overtly unrelated. But by investing it with subtext, we make a new sense of the material we are reading. This encourages actors to believe that they are in charge of cold readings, that they have to look and listen to the other person and go with their reactions and make their lines fit their reactions, not the other way around.

I never tell an actor that he has to listen to other actors. The most exciting kind of conversation is when you don't listen to what the other person is saying, but you attend to all the things that you are listening to *inside yourself* while the other person is talking. You are listening to the nonverbal messages as well as what is being said.

How would you turn that into an instruction to students?

With the scripts in front of them I say, "Allow yourself to wonder about this person and these circumstances. It's part of our capacity as human beings to perceive and register these things, so it would be pretty dumb to listen only to what people are saying. What's really important is listening to what's being said inside yourself."

Sometimes when two students are doing a scene I'll send up an "alter ego," another student to clarify the importance of a message for an actor by having the alter ego speak for him. One actor assumes the other won't listen to him so he has to have an intermediary. He'll say, "Will you (the alter ego) please tell her that I really care about her?" or "Tell her I'm getting a little ticked off." The actors working on the scene incorporate this dialogue into the scene. Then the alter ego redefines it and says, "What Jeff is trying to say is . . ." Then the other actor tells his alter ego what to say. It becomes a kind of telescopic and pointed speech.

Another exercise is having actors do an improvisation based on a play. In the middle of the improvisation I will ask, "What do you feel like doing right now?" Someone might say, "I'd like to thumb my nose." Sometimes I'll tell the actor to do it. Sometimes I'll say, "Stand up back to back with your partner and join your heads to make a pyramid." And they will do that as the scene continues. "Now what do you feel like doing?" And they can act on any feeling that comes up. Then the scene goes on and I'll ask again, "What do you feel like doing?" Then I may say, "Why don't you get on all fours and ride him around the room?" So the scene will continue with this bizarre behavior, but the actors will get a great sense of how graphic the possibilities are. As I mentioned before, I want them to become aware of the things that they want to do physically but elect not to do. All of us live in harnesses; we put on ridiculous fabrics to hide our beautiful bodies. I try to help students appreciate the kind of extraordinarily beautiful and expressive animals we were before we were put into little stalls.

There are exercises I do where I will play twentieth-century music, Boulez or Stravinsky, and I say, "You are all little slivers of soap in a gym and are used by lots of people. You are almost translucent and you know your fate is to get thinner and thinner. The thing you dread most is going down that shower drain." As the music plays they struggle not to be delivered into that little hole. How does a cake of soap end? It's about death and termination, but it excites their imagination and I know that some of the enchantment of childhood has its source in this kind of imagination. Without being childish I have to instill in them the creative kid—not the brat or the whiner, but the imaginative one. After all, the child is father to the man.

What advice would you give to someone just starting out on his or her career in acting?

There is a syndrome. You go for a part and they turn you down and you feel worthless. You have to have the guts to say, "That was a good reading. I don't know what variables existed in that room, who's scared of whom, but they made a big fat mistake and I know it." Hold on to your stuff and don't fall apart. If you get an opportunity to get in there and read, be in charge of that reading.

That means you are excited by doing the reading and you are going to make that very clear in doing it. Don't worry at the outset what other people are looking for. Don't try to be agreeable and obsequious. Go in as you are, dressed as you are, not trying to ingratiate. If you have to play a hillbilly, you can do it even in your Brooks Brothers suit.

AT THE
UNIVERSITIES

Phoebe Max

Andrei Belgrader

Andrei Belgrader teaches acting at the Yale School of Drama. A director as well as a teacher, Mr. Belgrader has had productions at the American Repertory Theatre, the Yale Repertory Theatre, The Goodman Theatre, etc. He is a graduate of the renowned Bucharest School for the Performing Arts in Romania and was director for several state theaters in his native land before coming to the United States in 1978.

Equally comfortable with Shakespeare and Beckett, he shares with his countrymen, Liviu Ciulei and Andrei Serban, a commitment to integrating new forms and using innovative approaches to the interpretation of classical as well as contemporary texts.

With his third-year acting students at Yale, Mr. Belgrader tries to "remove obstacles to acting" so students can develop "uncontrolled reactions" onstage. He believes that "when we call an actor a genius, that's what it is—uncontrolled reactions, however controlled the whole performance is."

*   *   *

How did you get started teaching acting?

I've been teaching at Yale for the past seven years. I did a play at Yale Repertory in 1979 and they asked me to teach and I've been teaching ever since.

What was your own training like in Romania?

I studied at the Bucharest School for the Performing Arts in Romania, which is known in Europe as being one of the best. It is a four- to five-year drama school, being both graduate and undergraduate together. About 80% of what you study there is theater and theater-related subjects and 20% general subjects. I studied directing there and I was an actor just for pleasure, but the way the school is organized students continuously worked with the actors from the very beginning, so it sort of tied together the directors and the acting process.

What was the acting approach of the Bucharest School?

There was a solid training of realistic theater based on the Stanislavsky method, some Meyerhold, some Grotowski. A lot depended on who the teacher was and we had lots of hands-on experience.

What is the system of study at Yale?

I always teach the third-year students right before they graduate, so by the time they come to me they have gone through two years of study and already have basic training in realistic theater and, in their second year, verse, which consists mostly of Shakespeare. Theoretically, the third year is about acting in postmodern drama, if there is such a thing. We work on a variety of scenes that jump from commedia del l'arte to Beckett to Shepard, but I wouldn't hesitate to go back to Shakespeare. I generally try to avoid doing a lot of realistic scenes because students already have had the opportunity to do that.

As the third-year acting teacher it is up to me to decide with them what we do—which varies from year to year, depending on what the group is like.

What have you done this year?

We did some Beckett, some Shepard, some commedia del l'arte, and many other things. I am not a scientific teacher. I'm sort of grabbing and pushing and trying more or less to adapt to the individual needs of the particular class and even more to the individual students. A lot of their training at Yale doesn't come from teaching directly, but from the projects they do and all the things they get exposed to through those projects. They are also directed by outside directors and student directors. This makes my position very special, because what I am trying to do is complete their training, knowing what is happening already.

Do you feel that what you do primarily is direct individual scenes as opposed to working on technique?

I work on technique as well as direct scenes and it's usually very elementary technique because I think that's the only important kind. I sort of jump back and forth between that and directing and letting the students develop a scene as professional actors would do.

What do you mean by elementary techniques?

Just as a point of departure, have you ever noticed that when an animal is onstage with an actor, the animal wins? There is no way the audience can take its eyes off the animal. I always wondered what they are doing that is so wonderful and why we, actors, can't do it. I call it the child–dog technique. My observation is that both children and animals never interrupt their lives while they are onstage; their lives continue no matter what happens. So what I do is try to develop techniques so that students do not interrupt their lives while they are working, no matter what the style of theater is. That means having all the senses open all the time. Sounds elementary, doesn't it?

Do you have any specific exercises to help them achieve this?

I have a series of exercises I use, but rather than doing them as exercises, I prefer to wait until the need arises in a scene. Then from there I will jump to an exercise. For example, when we start with a scene if I notice that the actors in it are working only from their mouths, that they are basically talking heads, I will ask them to translate the whole scene into body exchange. I'm trying to get the equivalent of a verbal exchange in the scene in pure body exchange. It sounds simple but it's quite complicated.

Take the scene from *Waiting for Godot* where there is an exchange between two actors in which one has to change in about ten seconds from having an enormous need for the other person to stay close by to an enormous need to have that person go away. Those are intense feelings and there isn't much time for a transition. It's very hard for naturalistic actors to do this because they would need a lot of time and there just isn't any. But the whole body could conjure up that feeling a lot more easily. So I go to an exercise where I put the two actors in contact through movement, through desire, through a task given to the body. It's what I call going outside instead of inside. I ask the actor who is having the difficulty to start isolating parts of his body. I say, "Take your right arm and express affection with it, express need with it, and direct that feeling to the other actor's chest, for instance." I tell this to just one actor, not the one who will receive the feeling.

Afterward I do the same type of exercise with words. For example, words can caress, so instead of using the sense of the word, we use the physical force of the word. I alternate between body and words, and I use the text, although sometimes it's more helpful to use the actors' own words, which have the same thrust. What happens is that all of a sudden, when we do get to the actual words, they forget what they did with their bodies. Their bodies are still involved, but not under control. I think the problem with most actors is that their techniques end up controlling them rather than freeing them. Children and animals control nothing.

I have a deep respect for the Stanislavsky method, but one of its traps is that it tells you that acting is fair. And it is not fair. The Method seems to say, "If you do this and this and this, you will be a wonderful actor, just like Marlon Brando." This is not true because even if you do steps four, five, six, and seven you might still be a lousy actor and Marlon Brando would be a genius forever anyway. Only after a certain level of technique does genius come into the work, and I think that the triggers for what we call genius come from someplace other than technique. It's the simplest thing: the ability to make believe as a whole, to completely believe something and just do it. I think that whatever it is that makes one able to strip oneself of whatever keeps one from reacting like an animal or a child is worth learning. So I think that a lot of what I'm doing with my students is giving them a negative lesson. Instead of teaching them technique, I try to remove obstacles that prevent them from being able to react uncontrollably at any time.

When you say "uncontrollably" do you mean something more than just being spontaneous?

Yes, because spontaneity relates to one action or one reaction. There is a paradox with acting. By definition it is a controlled activity; actors use a script they didn't write; they are not the characters they play. And that's the side the Method is working with—how to get into character and react as the character. What I have the luxury of doing at Yale is starting with students who have already been taught technique. My next task is to help them remove what's in their way so they can, while doing a controlled, organized task, have uncontrolled reactions. When we call an actor a genius, that's what it is, uncontrolled reactions, no matter how controlled the whole performance is. While much of the Stanislavsky method talks about the subconscious, as a matter of fact, it is about the conscious, and that's the paradox. I am just trying to shift the balance as much as possible toward the uncontrolled, making sure that the controlled part is assimilated first.

Do you have other exercises in this category?

Basically I go in two ways. It's hard to simplify, but I will try. I am going outside in and inside out. I believe that both are necessary. If someone uses only one way and completely rejects the other, you will get a cliché instead of a live moment. There was wonderful acting during periods in the history of theater when acting was completely external, or so they say. But it's not true. When you look at Chaplin or Buster Keaton your first reaction would be to say that those actors are external; they are shamelessly working on elaborate gags with the purpose of making people laugh. But when you look closely at Chaplin you can see he is also completely authentic and backed by real feelings, whereas there are other comics who work the same way who are completely external and terrible. I do commedia del l'arte with my students as often as possible. Again, basically it is a method of acting from the outside in, in which certain positions of the body are a must, in which certain ways of moving are a must.

What exercises do you do to stimulate internal technique?

I choose certain scenes from, for example, *Woyzeck*, and I will refuse to talk about or let the student think about the character. We go simply for the exchange between two characters, basing it totally on who the actors are, doing nothing but developing reactions back and forth between them. Miraculously, a character arises out of that although we never even touch the subject of the character nor do students think about it. Certain scripts allow you to take that route.

How do you help students learn to work on the moment-to-moment life of a character?

I usually don't say anything directly to them about how to do it, but we do keep going back and forth through a scene and I ask them to perform certain tasks to try to get something from each other. Let's say one character is trying to get her child to sleep. I will ask the student to use her body, her voice, whatever, to make the child sleep. Now, anything outside of this simple task has to be eliminated, so all I do is every time I notice her trying anything else, I stop the actress and point her back to the task. I would say that the core of all I do as a teacher is to help students work moment to moment. Every time we work on a scene, all exercises boil down to that. It's an obsession with me and I try to make it an obsession with them.

How do you help actors learn to respond to each other?

I do the same thing that I do when I work as a director. At a certain stage, I do everything possible to focus all their attention *off* themselves so they are available for the give-and-take happening at that particular moment.

Method acting is so often misunderstood because actors feel they have to do something *well*, focusing the actors on their technique and how to better it. One of the major things that makes an actor brilliant as opposed to mediocre is for him or her to be able to give that up. It's a complete paradox. There is no way to work on both bettering yourself and performing moment to moment. There simply is not enough energy in someone to do both. This is the crux of the matter.

Sometimes you can only get to the immediacy of a moment by stripping away the actor's need to control. For instance, one thing that is hard for actors to do is to use their voices naturally, to believe that the voice adapts itself naturally, which it does. The voice varies with a person's state of mind, with the person he is talking to, with distance, and with many other things. A lot of the attempts to control that, a lot of voice techniques, make it sound louder and clearer, but completely cut off that natural instinct that everyone has to adjust the voice. Again, it's stripping rather than building that is needed, it is forgetting the techniques in order to open up those channels that are completely natural to any human being. The actor needs voice technique, but he has to know how not to get trapped in it; how, at a certain moment of the rehearsal process, he can let go of his preoccupation with it.

There are a series of voice exercises from Grotowski that are very helpful. In one exercise the actor imagines that his voice is coming from his belt, and he attempts to "hit" someone on a part of the body, in the stomach or on the cheek. Those kinds of techniques can transform a thought, a feeling, into action.

Do you mean that the actor imagines his voice is coming from his stomach?

Yes. Practically the whole body can be considered a resonator. It's the belief that performs miracles. Besides, the result can be in a completely different place. The result might be that the body completely loosens up or reacts in hundreds of fresh ways because the actor's concentration is on one place. As a matter of fact, this technique, this singular focus, frees the body to react to other stimuli.

What are the basic exercises you mentioned before?

I try to choose exercises and scenes that are founded on the most basic human feelings, like sexual desire or hatred. Here is an example.

First, I have the two students do nothing but stay very close to each other for five minutes. They are to do nothing but touch each other's face or hands or shoulders. I tell them to try to memorize each other's bodies. When this is over, I ask them to move apart and say their lines, to do the scene again, but this time to *imagine* that they are still close and touching. They then have a very concrete memory to envision themselves touching. It's amazing how that can change the words, change everything. Let's face it, those two actors are not in love with each other. They are just two actors working on a scene. But instead of drawing on memories of when they might have been in love five years ago, they are now dealing with the real person in front of them, and there are things beyond words that happen between them. In a way, it's creating a history, not through memory, but through an exercise that actually uses the person in front of them.

When we work on hate, for example, I may ask a student to look at his partner's shoulder or some other part of the body, and I tell him to have all sorts of horrible thoughts about that shoulder, like what he would do to make that shoulder disappear, to explode it, or to do whatever kind of harm that stimulates his imagination. I don't let him do it, of course; just envision doing it. I also ask him to use sounds or any words with that intention and to direct them specifically at the shoulder or at whatever part of the body he chooses.

Do you ask students to think about why they might want to do harm?

No, not when I do these exercises. It's very important not to question motivation when you are going moment to moment. There is a time for that, and it should be done then. There is a mania to stop and analyze motivation continuously. It's incredibly harmful and boring. The actors who do that are usually afraid of revealing themselves. It's a lot safer for them to analyze something rationally and then try to imitate the general type of feelings that their brain tells them happens in that situation.

The worst thing in acting to me is imitation. I know an actor who is wonderfully talented, but whenever he gets on stage, no matter what part he plays, he ends up imitating old movies because he has watched them endlessly on TV through long nights and he really wants to be Cary Grant. That's his dream. It's practically impossible for him to act anything else, because subconsciously he will end up imitating Cary Grant, even when he plays a ghetto kid.

Many actors have favorite performers they try to imitate. But the subtlest and most dangerous kind of imitation is the imitation of one's idea of how he or she did or would react in a certain situation. It always lowers the quality of acting. That's where sense memory is dangerous. I'm not denying the value of sense memory, I'm just saying it's dangerous.

For example, ten years ago I remember that my aunt took my cat away. I got very angry at her and threw something at her. Now I may be playing a scene and recalling that moment. The result is wonderful except for one major mistake: that happened ten years ago, not now, and it's not a cat in the scene, but a watch, let's say, and it's a park, not my house. The danger is that when I remember that feeling it doesn't go outside toward the other actor or toward the object that feeling is directed to. I'm supposedly getting in touch with my feelings, but those feelings are not my feelings *now*; they are what they were *then*. I'm not the same person and the feeling is not the same. I'm imitating my idea of what happened to me then. It's a trap a lot of actors fall into and stay in forever. Of course, the exercises of Sense Memory are very useful if one understands that at some point they are complete crap. It's useful to go through them if you can completely abandon them at some point and then react to whatever reality is around you on stage. Obviously, all the energy going into re-creating that memory takes the energy away from going outside and performing with the other people or objects in the scene.

Don't you think it is useful at the beginning of an actor's training to help him feel an emotion authentically in front of other people?

Yes. To feel an emotion authentically, meaning in the here and now, not to imitate an idea of how that emotion was or could be. Wanting to be an actor means that you agree to be looked at and that it gives you pleasure to exist and feel in front of an audience. We should keep that in mind—the thrill, the pleasure of acting. A lot of acting methods plus the toughness of the "real world" of show business make one forget that strong elementary need and pleasure. Unconsciously, the actor uses technique as a shield to prevent people from looking at him. The actor hides while he thinks he is revealing. He is trying to control everything in order not to be vulnerable on stage. Then the real flow of emotion is frozen.

How do you approach comedy?

Comedy is supposed to be my specialty. I think it's the most freeing thing on the stage. I try to convince students that they are natural comics, that they have the need and power to be funny. Basically, I work on removing the layers of belief that a lot of actors have that it is not within their capacity to do comedy. Then we work on the concrete things.

In comedy it is fortunate that people laugh so the actor has immediate feedback, an immediate signal that something is working. What I try to do is prove to them that if they stop working toward being funny, they become funny.

I try to use very well-written comic scenes to start with and the most elementary type of comedy. I also use Shepard plays, which have a lot of comic elements. It's a slow process, but what I am trying to do with the students is show them that people will laugh if they don't work at it.

Do you have any techniques that would help students overcome stage fright?

Confidence is very individual. I've seen actors do the most bizarre things and get incredible results, completely losing their stage fright while getting ready for the next scene. I was in a production of *King Lear* and just before the famous tempest storm scene the actor who was playing Lear cursed all the other actors and kept on cursing until we went on stage. It was a horrible thing to do and we were totally incensed backstage, but the scene started with great intensity. He wasn't tapping on anything related to the scene; he was tapping some strange energy. That might not help another actor, but it helped him.

How do you help actors to develop a character? Do you advise them to observe animals or people?

What a lot of beginners don't understand is that observing is only part of the process. Dustin Hoffman in *Tootsie* went around dressed as a woman and acting as one in real life. It was wonderful, and obviously he observed women a lot. But that's not enough. At some point that tapped his desire to be the other sex, to be someone else. It can be done instantaneously if you awaken that desire to be someone else. But stopping at observation and imitation will never do it. It's not true that if you observe bums in New York City you will be able to play a bum, just as it is not true that if you drink a lot you will be able to play a drunkard.

So what do you do?

That's part of why I do commedia del l'arte, to give strength to the idea that in a very open way one can make choices to define character from the outside in. My point is that doing something concrete and external is not in contradiction with behavior that is motivated from the inside. If you play someone with a certain stiffness in the middle of his back, you will naturally adapt the rest of your body to that, but your reactions won't be less natural. Your back will just be stiff all the time.

Commedia del l'arte has such a tradition that all those positions and fixed character choices are very wise: they already contain a series of movements and feelings and hooks for becoming that character.

Can you describe the techniques that derive from commedia del l'arte?

For instance, there are basically two types of old people. One is very tall and has a back that doesn't move well, is slightly bent from the waist up. This old person walks with small steps. The student discovers this right away when he tries it, because you must walk with small steps if you are bent and then your arms must do certain things as a result of walking that way. There are other musts—for example, the chin comes forward, but it has to, or you wouldn't be able to see in front of you.

The whole philosophy of commedia del l'arte is based on mask. It's amazing how naturally alive actors become when they have a mask. With a mask they are not in danger because they are someone else; therefore, they can reveal their own emotions.

Do you work with masks?

Yes. A little bit. I don't have enough time to do as much as I would like. Actors find out how free they are when they are not exposing themselves.

This is one extreme. I also go to the opposite extreme. For example, if I work on Chekhov I refuse to discuss character. Even with Shakespeare I try to show the students that if they take the actions their character takes, they have a character before they know it.

How do you advise actors to begin working on a scene?

It depends on the scene. It's very dangerous to generalize. I do not believe in a step one, step two, etc., that would work for any scene.

What if you see an actor walking onto a stage and he is not coming from a specific place? What if he is just walking out on stage?

It's a very complicated question. I know what I would *not* do: I would not attempt to integrate any mental history. I might attempt some exercises that would make that scene work.

Like what?

For instance, in the scene between Masha and Vershinin in *The Three Sisters*, if they just walk out on stage, I would work on being cold. I'd say to the actors, "It's very cold, yes? Let's say someone has a piece of ice and puts it on your spine. You feel that? Now, lie down. The piece of ice is moving slowly on your body," etc. I would not tie that directly to the entrance. What I am pointing out to the students—and that's why I hate the whole thing with the history—is that there is no history on stage; there is no time but the present. On the other hand, the present has a history—but I try to find something in the present that stimulates different channels containing that history without working on it directly.

In this scene from *The Three Sisters* a lot of what is happening is conjured up by the action that is in the words. I find it a lot more important to use the exercise I described before, the one about keeping two actors together and having them create a memory of each other's body, for instance.

If one character has a need to talk about his wife, as Vershinin does, and that is in the script, that creates history. But it's not played as history. It's lived now and it's based on the fact that his attraction to Masha makes her the only person he can tell everything to. What I am then interested in is not the history of the character, but his need for her. I try to lead actors toward that through exercises and I avoid working on the specific character or general character needs. With most good playwrights, if you throw yourself right in, the character will emerge.

How would you help that student create that need if it's not there?

What I would probably do is direct everything outside. The tendency in that kind of scene is to direct everything inside and to analyze the character's needs and history. I would do the exact opposite. I would continuously direct the actor's attention to the other person, which is, I think, true to the scene, and assume that eventually other values will come through. And they do. I would work toward removing the blocks to the actor's intuition of who his character is and removing the blocks between the actor and the character of Vershinin.

There is a very funny idea that is popular these days that acting is identical to psychology. I think it's a very simplistic and stupid idea. Then doing Chekhov is sort of like going to a mental hospital. It becomes a workshop in psychotherapy.

What is Yale's particular approach to the training of actors?

The main thing that students get at Yale is a combination of a lot of projects and classes. The balance between those is in favor of the projects. I think that's a wonderful thing. It adds two ways of learning: from a master teacher and from experience. And students go through many experiences with different directors on different projects. That, basically, is the strength of Yale.

In the first year there is a class project that is a realistic play and in the second year there is another one. But students do not have one in the third year, because they wouldn't have the time. At this point the playwriting students and the acting students are working on plays. Student directors are also originating all sorts of projects. And actors among themselves originate projects. Then there is a cabaret in which they do a show every week. So the life of an actor at Yale entails waking up in the morning and working until late at night. It's incredibly demanding.

One of the advantages of all this is that at some point students become so used to acting that it sort of kills stage fright for them. They don't have time to be afraid.

Dawn Murray

Bud Beyer

Bud Beyer is head of acting in the theater department of Northwestern University. He founded the Northwestern Mime Company, and organized the theater school at St. Albans Repertory Theatre in Washington, D.C. He has been artist in residence at Loyola University, where he started the program in movement and voice, and he also created the Loyola Mime Company. During the summer he conducts private classes in an intensive six-week program in New York City.

Mr. Beyer is also a director. His productions at Northwestern include Swansong for a Unicorn, Oh Coward, Brand, The Lark, *and* The Crucible, *among others.*

A professional mime as well as an actor and teacher, Mr. Beyer has performed in films and TV and has conducted numerous workshops across the country in both mime and acting. His approach to the training of actors incorporates techniques from mime and the martial arts as well as from Michael Chekhov and Stanislavsky.

*   *   *

How did you get started teaching acting?

It started with mime actually. When I was in college I had the opportunity to study with Étienne Decroux, who was Marcel Marceau's teacher. I really started off doing mime professionally and toured as a mime and taught in the places where I toured. Then I started to do a lot of professional directing and acting and, little by little, the two gravitated together and I was asked to teach acting as well as mime. And I found that I had some things to say about that from my own training and my own experience. That led to a method of approach, but it was a rather lengthy process.

What was your own training in acting?

Most of my actual acting training came from Alvina Krause, who was my teacher at Northwestern when I was a student there. She believed strongly in Stanislavsky's basic concepts, but she really created her own method of working, which was very active and very athletic. It was not at all intellectual or pedantic, although it was based on the same foundations of self-belief that Stanislavsky advocated. She was also very interested in physical education and at one point she asked herself, while she was watching an acting class, why she was so bored by what she was seeing, why it was so passive and so unexciting. So she decided to approach acting like sports. For instance, she used to say that good comedy was like a good basketball game: everybody gets the ball and everybody passes it, but only one person makes the basket, although everybody is focused on that goal. So she would have actors playing basketball while they were doing lines, or she would have them throw a ball back and forth. I remember that one of her images for *Hedda Gabler* was that the conversation between Hedda and the judge was a chess game, that they were master chess players—and she had actors playing chess while they rehearsed that scene. The scene became very active. It took the pressure off the actors to try to understand what was happening intellectually and put it on a very outward stimulus, which allowed them to respond freely. She was very good at doing that.

She was very influential at Northwestern because she had so many famous students, like Charlton Heston, Richard Benjamin, Paula Prentiss, Tony Roberts. There was a group of actors around the school at that time who were her students. I think her fame grew because her students, within a certain era, did extremely well in the profession. There's also Marshall Mason. In fact, she's the one who suggested to him that perhaps he should think about directing instead of acting, and encouraged him in that area. So she's left her mark on a lot of influential people. She never gained the fame of some of the better-known acting teachers of her time because she never wrote about her method of teaching.

In terms of your own approach, what techniques do you give students to help them cope with stage fright?

Right from the beginning there are things that I do in that area that are a combination of what I learned from Michael Chekhov's work and from mime, things to help students get comfortable on stage. The idea of projection, for instance, of filling up a space that Michael Chekhov created, is something I adhere to and find very valuable. I also borrowed from what I learned in the martial arts and the notion of Ki, which has to do with the extension of energy.

So in class I will do an exercise where I will ask students to focus on a spot as far away as possible, let's say out a window or at the opposite end of the auditorium, and I will tell them to point at it. Then I will explain the difference between simply pointing at something and letting our imagination tell us that the action of pointing starts, not from the shoulder, but from the center of the body, so that the body, in effect, moves toward it, and lifting one's arm is the result of the need to point. Once students feel that connection it's very easy to add the sense of the extension of energy. I will usually ask students to imagine energy in any way they see fit: as light, as particles, as water, so that the center that they have been moving from becomes a source of energy that they draw on as they gesture and the energy moves from their centers and actually goes out from the hand to touch the spot they have chosen.

So the first thing students get is the sense of having something to extend. What I keep doing, in order to keep it from sounding too mystical, is to acquaint them with the idea that what they are doing is what they do in everyday life when they have a strong need or intention or objective: that we extend something, a thought or a command or an idea, and it goes beyond ourselves. Projection is only a mechanical way of looking at an emotional process, but we need to have a mechanical way of reproducing it. By the end of the exercise students are no longer pointing, but are extending energy into the corners of the room and filling the space. It's always quite amazing; you can see the difference between filling a space and simply standing in a space.

I don't think I deal with stage fright directly because I don't think that the problem comes up. What happens by the time students are at the performance stage is that different elements like physical warm-ups, concentrated preparations, exercises in relaxation all come together so that stage fright never seems to be an issue. By performance they seem to have enough ammunition in terms of their work to solve the problem of fear.

I believe more in relaxation that has an energy in it and a readiness for work than in the kind of passive relaxation in which one lets tension drain away. Most of my relaxation exercises are more energizing than passive.

What kinds of exercises do you do for relaxation?

One is very simple. If you take your hand and shake the wrist back and forth and do the same with your fingers, and you do that violently for about thirty seconds and then put your arms down and let them lie there, there will be a great rush of feeling in your hand. Now when you pick your hand up and start to move it around, it is very relaxed but very energized simply because you have increased circulation. And you can do that with the whole body. If you have only ten seconds to get ready for a performance, you can prepare by shaking the different parts of your body. If you shake them very vigorously, when you stop you get a wonderful rush of circulation, which also brings a loss of tension—a kind of energized relaxation.

The other exercise that I do to get the same energized relaxation versus the kind in which one is ready to fall asleep is to differentiate between tension and what I refer to as resistance. Tension is a stoppage of movement and potential. When someone is tense he or she can go neither forward nor backward. Resistance is a constant and fluid motion against a pressure. It is also the seed of drama. In other words, you have one thing moving against another. So students learn that gesture can be strong and have a tremendous power and push to it, but that's not tension. That is a kind of relaxation. It's like lifting a heavy object and throwing it with a kind of energized relaxation while working against a pressure. You are not simply tensing up and releasing in order to feel relaxed.

So I will use the notion of resistance in an exercise I call Molding. Basically, the student is standing on stage and I tell him to imagine that he is standing in an atmosphere that is very heavy and somewhat fluid through which he can move. But it takes tremendous pressure and strength to move, as if he were trying to walk through thick water. As he moves he leaves a shape behind him. That's the important concept. As he begins to move, he thinks about leaving a shape in space, so his concentration isn't on the movement, it's on the shape. I'll let a student do that abstractly for a long time with very heavy resistance and then lighten the resistance until he is moving extremely rapidly, very fluidly, very abstractly, and very largely. Then he will experiment with different kinds of shapes: with his fingers open or closed; moving geometrically in curves, circles; always thinking of the shape he leaves behind, until finally, after about fifteen minutes, he comes to a standstill and then simply takes a normal step forward while he is thinking about the shape he is leaving. This immediately gives a form to the most ordinary movements. There is nothing overly melodramatic about the movement of reaching for a cup, but if instead of just reaching for it the actor thinks about the shape he is leaving with every move, it adds a kind of importance to the movement and tends to focus him. He or she becomes aware that everything done onstage must have a specific reason.

For example, Olga grades papers in the opening scene of *The Three Sisters*. The question is, how does she grade papers? The choice of how an actor performs an action as a way to reveal character is very crucial. Olga is not merely grading papers. What goes on in Olga that allows one to find the way in which she and only she would grade papers sitting at her desk? If an actor becomes aware of the importance of movement, that reaching in a pocket for change or brushing one's hair can create a whole life and a whole aura, it's an easy step to take that movement and make it a specific of character. Then nothing onstage is wasted, nothing is going on that isn't succinctly pointed toward communicating an idea.

Talking about character, what techniques do you give your students to help them in this area?

I find that when students try to play all the information about a character—who says what about whom—when they try to answer all the standard questions, I get a kind of intellectual mush. So early in my work with actors on character development, I will try to get them to work on nonintellectual approaches.

One of the very first things that I will do, because it makes it much easier for students to work later when we study the Greeks, Chekhov, and Shakespeare, is to develop a sense of torso. This is based on a concept that basically comes from Decroux. It states that the hands and face can lie, but the torso always reflects what's true for the character. It's similar to the concept of body language, in which these elements are talked about. Well, the mime has been talking about this for a long time—over a century.

The reason I do a lot of work on the torso is to encourage actors, particularly because they are so embedded in contemporary drama, not to be fearful of the large response that may come from using gesture and torso. A lot of my exercises have to do with using the torso as the foundation of expressiveness. I'll use the terms "spine" and "torso" interchangeably and talk about the spine and torso of the character. Decroux has a wonderful example. He felt that when a character leaves somebody, it's important to note whether he pulls his head away and leaves his heart with the person, or pulls his heart away and leaves his head with them. When actors start to leave, particularly in a warm-up situation, they are encouraged to look very specifically at what they are doing physically because it has such ramifications on the observer. Choices made very specifically about whether one is leaving with one's head or heart become a way of focusing the audience on an emotion without it knowing that or being aware of being told in words. It's a method of reinforcement.

In the area of character work I try to help students develop their imagination. I have what I call Extension Exercises. In these exercises a portion of the body becomes a part of or an entire object. It's similar to what children do when they draw an imaginary gun or turn their fingers into scissors. Students will come up with extraordinarily imaginative ways of turning portions of their body into objects. Although it's a very pantomimic exercise, it's wonderful to see actors open up their imaginations.

Another technique for developing character is through the use of metaphor. That's something more active that creates a conduit through which all the information they have can come to the surface. I will ask students to bring in a character based on a metaphor. The first stages of this work are almost pantomimic, almost like a fantasy assignment in which they are as much an object as they are the character.

For instance, if an actress chooses to play the common interpretation of Laura in *The Glass Menagerie*—that is, she is a fragile piece of hand-blown glass—I will have her create the piece of glass, become the piece of glass by finding the need for delicacy of movement first, and then have her work toward becoming more human, work toward the character. But the metaphor she is working on is a specific piece of fragile glass. If she can, I ask her to bring the object in. So if an actor is working on someone who is like an old tennis shoe, he will talk about the qualities of an old tennis shoe and see if he can bring them into some human form. The main point is for the actor to have a strong image off which to work.

I will do the same work on metaphor with musical instruments. I might suggest that students think about Chekhov's characters as a string quartet or a group of instruments. Then I will ask them to pick any orchestra instrument and use that as a metaphor. That gives them a complete physical and vocal sense. Sometimes an object will suggest or give a student a voice. Let's say Masha in *The Three Sisters* is a violin or viola and that's the melody her voice plays: there is something in the quality of that instrument that is part of her. I tell students that there is no right or wrong. It's what the metaphor does to them. If thinking of Masha as a violin brings you to something that is Masha, then that is a wonderful way to work. If not, we'll find something else as a metaphor.

With music, for example, I'll take a character like Ariel in *The Tempest* and I'll find a piece of experimental music based on tinkling wind chimes. Now it's just the sound that the student is working off, nothing visual. Or someone might look at Ariel and say he's like a puff of wind and he will work off that—just the sound of it, not even the visual image. Or a student may take a sound like the blast of a car horn and he'll create whatever occurs to him from that, perhaps a visual image as well as an auditory one.

Do you use animal exercises to help students create character?

Yes. I do them in three different stages. First, I tell students to go to the zoo and spend three or four hours just walking around looking at the animals. They are asked to find one that they have an affinity for: a monkey, a bird, a reptile, etc. Then they go back to the zoo for careful observation of that particular animal. They take notes and, as much as possible while they are standing there and looking, they begin to play with the movements of that animal's torso and spine, trying to capture its center. They come back to class and present the animal that they have now spent two or three weeks observing. They try to become that animal. They are looking for qualities of spine, fluidity or rigidity, explosiveness of movement, the center of gravity, the breathing rhythms of the animal, the sensory alignment, the primary sense the animal uses. I even encourage them to talk to the zoo keeper to get information. We had one student who was working on a baby chimp. She got to know the keeper very well and he let her handle it. When she presented the animal in class, the keeper came to see her. He liked her interpretation.

When students bring animals in they present them one at a time in class and I work with them. I may poke them or throw them something, just to make sure that they are responding as the animal, not as themselves. It's interesting because it's very easy to see in the actor if there are human thoughts going on in his head or we have the animal responding sensorially. You can see immediately if the actor has managed to transcend his human self and get to the animal's responsiveness. Someone did an iguana last year and everyone in class got up and worked with the actor. He responded with that wonderfully mindless pulling away. There is a mindless repetition of movement in an iguana when it is trying to free itself.

When this exercise works well, it's amazing. Your eye tells you you are looking at an actor, but every other sense tells you you are looking at an animal.

In the next stage I'll bring in groups of four or five students and have them interact as animals. The only ground rule I set is that any altercations must be broken off before there is aggression. Students can get into some fairly strong confrontations and you have to guard against that. Then, without much forewarning, I will ask them to begin to move out of the animal into a human form, carrying with them as many of the qualities of the animal as they can. They have no predetermined character that they are working toward; they are only going to see what happens as they bring a puma, for example, slowly up on its feet and begin to find human activities that suggest the animal. For instance, if someone is doing a squirrel, that actor might turn the nervous eating gestures of the squirrel into nervous little scratches of the character. Usually the characters that are created are interesting because they have these strange idiosyncratic gestures that are very human, but are obviously based on those of an animal. The point of the exercise is to demonstrate the capacity of transformation that is possible by careful work.

Then the class will hold a little interview session with the students who are working onstage; it will ask them questions and they will answer whatever comes to mind. For instance, if they are asked how old they are, the age they give will help define them. So we end up with a very real human being.

After that I will ask students to bring to class the accoutrements of the character they are creating: the right hat, the right clothes, the right accessories. Then we will do some improvisations or talk some more to them as the characters. They are still abstract characters, not specific ones from dramatic literature.

Later on in the semester when we start doing scenes, all of these elements are open to them to use to achieve characterizations.

How do you help students work on different styles of theater?

I'll usually design an acting course to go by periods of theatrical history both because the linear development of dramatic text is interesting when you deal with it that way and because it demands different elements of acting, different elements that all end up in a totality the actor can use for any period. When we are starting with something historical like Shakespeare, the Greeks, Chekhov, or Ibsen, I'll talk about the "period spine"—the Elizabethan spine, for instance. Or I'll talk about something in more nationalistic terms, like a Russian spine, a Polish spine, or a Norwegian spine. By "spine" I mean the way in which the central axis of the body is carried, its degree of fluidity, its degree of expressiveness, its degree of rigidity. Because the Elizabethan era was the "age of astonishment," the spine tends to have an uplift that is always there. Once one keeps that and lifts that, something interesting happens to the way one thinks—one begins to think outward and upward. Then instead of allowing moments in Shakespeare to become inward and contemporary, students have the capacity for a sense of astonishment at having an idea or being in love or wishing to murder someone or questioning one's existence. I'll use that as a strong foundation to begin work on character as well.

It's the same when I talk about nationalistic spines. There is such a thing as an Italian spine. If you walk down through Little Italy in New York City and watch Italians speaking from a distance, you can see, not just the stereotypical gestures, but something in the spine, in the way the central axis is carried, that is nationalistic. Of course, what happens when you stop there is you get a kind of stereotype. Individuality of character has to be built on top of that. But the foundation moves you immediately from your own contemporary upbringing to something large and different, so that you are not carrying your 1987 spine into a moment in Shakespeare—because it doesn't belong there, it doesn't belong to the way of thinking, of speaking, or of having ideas.

What techniques do you give your students to help them become more expressive?

I don't deal with that directly and find I don't have to when I work on stimulating the imagination. Usually, I'll start on the imagination from the first day of the term by teaching students to create an imaginary stimulus and the response to it. To me that's the heart and seed of it all—the capacity to imagine something and be able to respond to it. Exercises like projection, which I mentioned before, in which one begins to imagine that one is sending energy to all corners of the room, to me is also a way of subtly getting students to imagine something—though I won't talk to them directly about imagination; I'll talk to them about projection. What I'm doing is laying the foundation for a lot of the basic acting work they'll be doing all year, work that requires them to imagine something, to see something that isn't there.

When I really begin to hone in on imagination varies from year to year. But I find that students have less and less of a capacity to imagine. It's really kind of frightening. So I spend a lot of time on the imagination, getting them to play as children, because students don't seem to be able to do that anymore. I'll start with exercises that are based on mime, usually within the warm-up session.

For instance, I'll do some mime, and in the guise of doing that, I'll cover all the technical elements of handling objects: seeing them, establishing the space, reaching for them, moving the arm so that the torso is leading and responding to them, establishing something concrete in space, feeling their weight and the weight's effect on you; the difference, for instance, between picking up a water glass from Woolworth's and a Waterford crystal champagne goblet. I'll really focus on that because I want them to learn to be responsive to something that isn't there, some specific thing they are creating.

This sounds very much like classic sensory work.

Yes, in a way it is. But the emphasis is different. I also ask students to allow the object they are creating to find *them*. For instance, I will try to make the point that any object we pick up causes in us a total kind of response. If you pick up a piece of delicate crystal, your whole body takes on the sense of that object as you touch it. It's not just the mechanical handling of the object in space, but its effect on the body that is important to focus on.

I will do the same kind of imagination work using environments. Students learn to establish an environment pantomimically, which means a very definite physical response—including the entrance to and exit from the environment, and some completed action within the environment that establishes it—again, so that they get used to being aware that it's their responsibility to let us, the audience, know where they are, why they are there, and what they are doing. And this too is all imaginary.

What exercises do you use to help them create these environments?

I use what I call the Atmosphere Exercise to help them use their imaginations to create an environment. I will ask a student to enter a room—a dormitory, for instance—remain in it a few moments, and handle any objects he has created. He must create an atmosphere of, for example, forbidding, danger, longing, or regret. Students learn that in a series of simple actions they can create an atmosphere that isn't just on stage, but is also projected out to the audience. The very act of entering a room begins to cause us to feel something. They use very specific elements in order to get to whatever it is they are creating (events or personalizations from their own lives). The point is not whether or not they are feeling something or whether or not they are having a cathartic experience, but whether or not that atmosphere is being communicated to the audience. This leads to some interesting discussions about choices, because something that may seem real to a student may not mean anything to the audience.

This exercise is normally without words, but if they wish to talk to themselves because they actually would in a similar real-life situation, that's fine. It's like a Private Moment, but the focus is on what the audience is getting.

Then I'll send in another student with an "atmosphere" that is in opposition to that of the person who is already in the room.

Someone may play that she has just flunked out of school and is in her dormitory creating an atmosphere of regret or depression when a second person enters with an "atmosphere" that is diametrically opposed to that of her roommate. At this point it becomes an improvisation and the students can talk. Then we see what happens when a war of atmospheres, not just of moods or personalities, takes place. It doesn't really matter which one wins; it's just interesting to see them hang on to their "atmospheres." I will then follow that immediately with text.

Take *Romeo and Juliet*. When Romeo enters the garden by himself, there is an atmosphere of danger and foreboding. When Juliet enters, the atmosphere begins to warm and change. When the two of them are together, it ebbs and flows in the romance of the moment and fear of discovery. Again, if the concentration is on what atmosphere they are creating, it helps the actors to learn to make interesting choices for certain moments in plays.

The next step is to move students from something that is based on reality to something that is based on fantasy. Fantasy is stimulated by going out and looking at any inanimate object and asking the question, "If that object could move and respond to the world around it, what would it do?" Students have to create a three-minute vignette as the object, giving it a personality and allowing it to respond to different events.

Can you give me an example of how this exercise is done?

Students can use just about anything: chairs, tables, lamps, a revolving door, a blackboard. The goal is to have a sense of what kind of chair; for instance, is it a modern or a Victorian chair? Say someone chooses to be a blackboard. Because she has asked the question, "What is this object like?" she immediately imposes a kind of personality on it. She may see the blackboard as superior—it's clean, there is nothing on it, it sort of oversees everything. Then the blackboard will see someone coming up to it and write on it and it may become ticklish. Or someone might write an obscenity on it. What would the blackboard do? Erase it? Or maybe a person is working out a math problem and gets a wrong answer. If the blackboard likes that person, it might take a piece of chalk and correct the problem. It's the same thing we do when we kick the car if it doesn't start. We assume the object has a personality. People work on such a wide variety of things: a shoe, a tube of toothpaste, windshield wipers. Just about anything is fair game.

The next step is to give students a long random list of unrelated objects and ask them to create a vignette in which they can either be or use any three objects. They have to connect them logically in a story that has a beginning, a middle, and an end. Say I give someone a fishing pole, a door, and a sea gull. He may decide to be a sea gull who wakes up, decides it is hungry, goes outside, closes the door, tries to fly but gets airsick, decides it doesn't like to fly, and takes the fishing pole to fish for food instead.

Do you have any specific techniques to help your students learn to play comedy?

I love comedy and I love to teach it. I like to demystify it. Too often we are told at an early age that we are either funny or we are not. That's a terrible thing to do. Anybody can play comedy. I like to approach it from a very technical standpoint: let's look and see what happens in the comic moment, let's look and see how a laugh works and try to understand what constitutes a comic moment.

For me the basis of all comedy is incongruity. Incongruity becomes the foundation for looking at a comic moment: what's incongruous to what? What makes something funny is when two things are wildly out of balance. For me there are six basic kinds of incongruities:

(1) A *simple incongruity*. When Laurel and Hardy stand next to each other they are a simple incongruity; a short round figure next to a skinny taller figure is an incongruous image.

(2) *The collapse of dignity*. Someone in a position of authority or power suffers some collapse of dignity. What's funny about that is the person's attempt to recover dignity. That creates the laugh. It's the denial that it ever happened.

(3) *The character's knowledge versus the audience's knowledge*. This is used in French farce all the time. The audience knows something that the character doesn't.

(4) *Expectation versus fact*. This is another term for surprise. You

are led to expect one thing and another happens. If someone points to stage right and says, "Here comes the king," and the queen enters from stage left, that's funny.

(5) *The pun.* This is a difficult incongruity because everyone has to groan when they hear it.

(6) *Ridicule.* Don Rickles' kind of humor is an example. It walks the fine line between humor and insult.

The only thing important about these categories is that you can look at a piece of material and take the mystery out of it by asking what the incongruities are. If an actor gets a pie in the face, what's the most incongruous thing he can do? Probably nothing. And that's probably the most successful or funniest response. You can always isolate what's going on.

What I will do is help students attack comedy in two directions at the same time. One is the verbal comic technique, like pointing and lifting words or vaudeville routines in which the jokes are bad, but landed with great verve right out to the audience. Students either make up their own routines or find them on their own. I even ask them to do a three-minute comic monologue that they write themselves to help them get over the fear of doing it.

On the physical side I will ask students to make a comic entrance. All I want them to do is make us (the audience) at least smile, if not actually laugh. That's when I start to talk about the comic attitude, which is an aura that a good comedian or comic actor has. It communicates that at any moment something funny is going to take place. That can be an inner melody that the student has in his head, or a secret of some kind. So even at the very entrance to a scene, everyone in the audience should be able to smile.

I will then ask a student to do a simple walk across the stage and create an incongruity. I tell him to practice this by having one part of his body move to one rhythm and another to another rhythm.

I might ask him to construct a simple pantomime in which he creates a specific person in a specific place—someone at the laundromat, for example. He then has to create a comic vignette that is based on physical humor—comic takes, comic responses, arrests, etc. The students learn in all of that that it's not just the movement; it's the authenticity of their responses as well as the technique and clarity of action that makes something funny. It's the knowledge of where they are going and where they want the laugh, of when they will release the laugh.

We will then put this together with scene work. I'll usually start with Neil Simon because that's sort of bread and butter for an actor to be able to do well. I'll be concerned about the believability of the characters and the relationships as well as their ability to construct comic business and the comic interplay between the people in the scene.

Sometimes we will do Molière or Restoration scenes simply because they are a little broader and a little easier to deal with in terms of physical technique. We may also do some Shaw so that we get to practice verbal comic technique by itself.

What is the course of study at Northwestern?

It is a four-year liberal arts university. We all adhere to the fact that we want to develop actors who have a world sense, who have knowledge of a tradition beyond themselves. It's fun to teach theater in a liberal arts institution because you can make everything students study relevant to their work as actors.

The freshman year is almost solely introductory courses, with a little work in movement and voice. The acting training itself doesn't start until the sophomore year and continues for three years.

Sophomore year is basic acting. It starts with the most basic elements and ends up with students beginning to deal with characterization and some elementary scene work. The junior-level class is probably the core of the acting program. The first quarter is Greek drama, the second is Shakespeare, and the third is usually Chekhov. It is a very difficult year because all the techniques are used to illuminate text. That year is a real shaping and performing year.

One reason we start with Greek drama in this year is because the issues in the plays are larger than the individuals. Antigone was concerned with something bigger than herself. That's always a frustrating quarter, teaching Greek drama, particularly in this day and age. Teaching Greek drama in the 1960s was a snap. Everybody understood the issues and everybody understood what it was like to be willing to jump off a building for an ideal. Nowadays Greek drama is very alien to students. They have a hard time seeing things beyond themselves. It's only when you have a tragedy like Sadat's assassination or the Jonestown massacre that students begin to understand the nature of Greek drama.

Senior year tends to deal with styles of drama that can cover anything from Pinter to the most contemporary plays. Students now will bring all their technique into productions.

What advice would you give students who are just starting out on their careers?

Very simply I would say, "Don't lose sight of whatever it was that inspired you to embark on acting in the first place. You will get sidetracked many times by the commerciality of the profession. That's when it's important to remember what you loved about theater in the first place." I am also fond of saying, "Make your career about your *work*, not about getting an agent."

© Martha Swope 1986

Michael Kahn

Michael Kahn is artistic director of The Acting Company and most recently was appointed artistic director of the Shakespeare Theatre at the Folger in Washington, D.C. He is currently chairman of the acting department of The Juilliard School, is on the faculties of the Circle in the Square Theatre School and NYU's Graduate School of the Arts, and is director of the Chautauqua Institution's Theatre School and Conservatory Theatre Company. Mr. Kahn served as the artistic director for ten years of the American Shakespeare Festival, where he directed twenty productions for the Stratford Company.

Mr. Kahn has had an active career as a director. His directorial credits include many productions both on and off Broadway, in regional theaters, and in opera. Some of these include, on Broadway, Show Boat, Cat on a Hot Tin Roof, and Death of Bessie Smith, and off Broadway, A Month in the Country and Hedda Gabler at the Roundabout Theatre, The Rimers of Eldritch and Three by Thornton Wilder, and, most recently, The Acting Company's production of

Ten by Tennessee. *He has also directed productions for the New York Shakespeare Festival, the Texas Opera Theatre, and the Greater Miami Opera.*

Mr. Kahn believes that acting is both visionary and a reflection of its time. "One of the things I am proud of is that I don't teach the same way now that I did ten years ago." However, one aspect of his teaching has remained constant: his belief that "the most important thing you have to do is break down the actor's predecisions about how something should be or what he believes is the correct way to do something." In this way you get "actors to feel that anything that happens to them onstage is useful and usable." When that happens, "the actor no longer feels inappropriate, no longer feels separate from his character."

How did you get started teaching acting?

I have never wanted to do anything but direct plays since I was about four years old. I directed my first play when I was about five or six. So I went to Performing Arts High School, where Michael Howard was my favorite teacher. I studied with him privately when I graduated. My first teaching experience was when he was directing A Thousand Clowns and asked me to take over his class. I taught for a short period of time at his studio. It was a strange experience because the class was filled with people I had been doing scenes with. That probably got me started teaching. I never planned to teach, nor did I ever plan to teach as much as I am now doing.

You seem to be active in several acting schools—NYU, Juilliard, Circle in the Square.

It's a very interesting position to be in because I seem to be teaching in the three major institutions in New York City.

In which of these institutions do you feel you have had the most influence?

I couldn't answer that question in those terms. First of all, I've been at Juilliard since the day it started. John Houseman saw me directing The Merchant of Venice at Stratford, Connecticut, and I think he thought, "What an interesting young man." This was in 1969. And so he asked me if I would be interested in teaching at a school that Michel St. Denis and he were going to start at Juilliard. And I said yes, although I didn't know very much about St. Denis's approach or what that training from the Old Vic was about. We met and had a long talk, and I did indeed become resident acting teacher. I was the only acting teacher at the time, because initially there was only one class.

I was very interested in the idea of Juilliard. Having begun working in the classics, having just directed *Measure for Measure* for Joe Papp, and knowing that I was about to become artistic director at Stratford, I had a vested interest in American actors being able to do classical theater. Acting training in the 1950s taught actors to mistrust words, which certainly got in the way of the actor's ability to do verse and the classics. I felt pretty strongly that there had to be a way for our particular American brand of emotional honesty, physical energy, and realistic temperament to come together with whatever we used to call technique. I was personally interested in that because I was attracted to that kind of theater and therefore interested in the school that was being formed to do that very thing. I have been at Juilliard for about fifteen years, with time off when I was at the McCarter Theatre.

You asked me in what school I think that I personally have had the greatest influence or impact. It's hard to answer because I feel very strongly about the training of actors and I'm passionate about it wherever I teach. When Circle in the Square called me up about eight years ago and said it was starting a school and asked if I was interested in coming in and teaching, I accepted and got involved in reorganizing it. Then when Zelda Fitchandler took over the NYU graduate theater department about two years ago, I was approached by her because she wanted to reorganize that program. And I think that I've had something to do with that. I've been at Juilliard longest, and in a way it's been my home, but I'm very actively involved in the other schools. I think that one thing feeds another and one of the things that has kept my enthusiasm going is that I now have a broad variety of actors with whom I come into contact. The schools attract different kinds of students—and my interest is fueled by that.

I am also the kind of teacher who continues to evolve, because I think that acting is both visionary and a reflection of its time. One of the things I am proud of is that I don't teach the same way now that I did ten years ago. Of course, there are some things that I still believe, but I think I let the students connect with all kinds of things that come up.

In what way has your own training as an actor influenced your teaching?

Very strongly, obviously. I will believe till the day I die that the most important things for an actor to have are a relaxed body and an available instrument. I learned and still believe they are the essential ingredients for an actor.

Who would you say has influenced you the most?

Michael Howard, because he was a wonderful teacher and a genuine mentor and saw me as a protégé. And in another way by Lee Strasberg. I think he was a genius. I learned a lot from Lee during the four or five years that I attended The Actors Studio as a director and was able to observe. I also learned that it is very dangerous for a teacher to create a situation both for himself and his students in which he has to feel omniscient, and that you cannot and must not create an atmosphere of fear. I think I learned that from Lee's inability to say, "I don't know the answer to that." He got himself into trouble with that. I don't think a teacher should be a guru or a god, and I really refuse to accept either of those choices.

I believe that I am good at finding out where an actor is blocked. And I am also able to say, "I don't know the answer to that and I want to think about it for a while." If you demand honesty from your students the only way to get it is to be honest yourself.

The other thing that influenced me was the fact that I have always directed while I was teaching.

How has that influenced your teaching?

For me acting is always practical. How are aspects of training to be used in the play? How is it practical in the work? You must realize that acting is a process and you are basically working with people who come to class and don't want to have any process at all, who want instant answers and results. That's the hardest thing about teaching anything. There is nothing in our society that celebrates process or time taking or thoroughness. But directing is all those things and I was always aware when I was teaching that my students might someday end up in a production with me. So I've always been aware of teaching as a laboratory, but a laboratory that would end up in a rehearsal room.

You mentioned before that your focus as a teacher has changed over the years. In what way?

I do different things with different people at different times *all the time*.

Let's start out with the fact that I think that relaxation is the key to everything. Now, there is muscular relaxation. I like teaching in schools because relaxation is taught in other classes and I can just point out to an actor where he is tense and feel confident that he understands what I'm talking about. What I think causes the most tension in an actor is his expectation of the way something should be. The most important thing for me to do when I start with students is to get them to feel that anything that happens to them onstage is useful and usable. *Anything*. For instance, an actor may say to me, "I didn't feel anything in that scene." I don't believe that there has ever been a human being standing in front of other people who did not feel something. So what he is really saying is, "How do you feel about what I decided I was supposed to be feeling?" Or "Was I feeling the right thing?" Or "I wasn't feeling what I thought I would." The most important thing you have to do is break down the actor's predecisions about how something should be or what he believes is the correct way to do something. And when you break down the actor's desire to be right or correct or to be good or to please, it's the best way to get him to relax.

How do you do that?

First of all, I say, "Use everything that you've got." There is no such thing as an inappropriate feeling. That means that you have to consider every performance a rehearsal. Why is an actor freer in a rehearsal than in a performance? Because a rehearsal is exploring, and when he is "performing" he is no longer exploring. So I will say to an actor, "Whatever is going on right now, use it. I see that something in your body wants to do something. Why are you stopping that and jumping to this?" And he might say, "Because I'm supposed to be happy in this scene." "Don't worry about that. You will get there. Stay in the moment that you are in. See what happens." I don't let actors jump past moments and I stop them when they do. What they will jump to is the next moment they have decided should be there or the next feeling they have decided should be there. You have to get an actor to trust that he will get to where he has to be in a scene, rather than make himself get there.

How do you help your students cope with stage fright?

I had an example of this today. I asked a student, "What are you afraid of? Why does being nervous have to mean being unconcentrated?" It's not being nervous that stops the actor from concentrating. It is the fear that the nervousness is wrong and it is the energy that the actor invests in covering up the nervousness that results in the actor's intention no longer being the character's. The actor's intention then becomes to cover up his nervousness. The actor feels nervousness is inappropriate. I'll ask why. And an actor will usually say because he was unable to do what he wanted to do in the scene. So I'll say, "Start again. You are now Paul in *Loose Ends* or Hamlet or Medea—whatever. Now why are you, as the character, nervous?" There will never not be an answer to that question. If you are feeling nervous or insecure, those are powerful feelings. Put them into the scene. Use them as the character.

When that happens, the actor no longer feels inappropriate, no longer feels separate from his character. The actor begins to ask himself why the character might be nervous. Once the actor accepts what is going on inside him, he no longer fights it; he is no longer unconcentrated. That's a very bad word, "unconcentrated." An actor is never unconcentrated. He's just concentrating on something that he doesn't think he should be concentrating on.

I believe very strongly that an actor cannot be too narrow about his life on stage. He cannot be available to the things he thinks are right if he is not available to everything. He is either available or he isn't.

An actor does all this work to connect with the specific parts of the character, but then he also has to *leave himself alone* and use whatever feelings come up in him. And the minute he refuses to accept for use whatever feelings are there, quite frankly, all the stuff he's worked on won't be available because he's closed off his instrument.

I believe, finally, that the work of the actor is to become the character he is so that he can then leave himself alone. Depending upon where you are in the rehearsal process you are whoever you are. As you begin to take on the given circumstances of a character, begin to believe that you no longer live on West 72nd Street in New York City in 1987, but in the nineteenth century in this particular room, and that your parents were such and such people, etc., as the role becomes more and more yours. You must then go out on stage and leave yourself alone. It's now the character that you are leaving alone.

How do you help students develop a character?

I do a variety of things, but one of the things that most actors don't do is go out and find someone and really try to create that person both physically and psychologically. Most actors work on character by imitating what they have seen in another performance.

I have an exercise in which I ask students to select a photograph or a painting of someone and create that person both physically and psychologically. I ask them to decide what just happened in the picture, who the person is, why he is there, etc. Then the students come out onstage and present that character as completely as possible. This exercise is good for character work and for teaching students about given circumstances. I also ask students to study animals and create people based on those animals.

Do you teach period movement?

In most of the schools I work in there is someone who does that. But I don't think that I believe in period movement per se. What we used to think of as period movement can be taught, probably, in a couple of hours during the rehearsal of a play. You can learn how to bow, how men and women greeted each other, how to use a cane, etc. In this area we are basically talking about clothes and etiquette. An actor can read about that. A person who really knows about period style and movement has an advantage, but I personally think that's easy to get from an actor. What's more important, and harder, is to get the relationships in a scene.

I am working on a lot of Shaw and Wilde right now in schools that have not been known for doing a lot of classical work. I've been struck by how much of the technical work gets achieved when the actor tries to justify what's happening in a scene. For instance, nineteenth-century manners start to appear when the actor starts to justify what's going on in a situation.

Are there any exercises you do that you feel are particularly effective?

I don't think that way. I can tell you what actors should do, but I don't think that I have a Michael Kahn exercise. I do think that the primary thing I do is insist that the actor have more and more facts about the play and his character so that if an actor walks on stage I can tell where he is coming from.

Today a student brought in a scene from *Of Mice and Men*, the one where the woman comes into the barn. And she came in looking sad. So I stopped her and said, "I know this is a big scene and you are going to get murdered in twenty-five minutes, but quite frankly, I'm not going to care if you get murdered later because right now I don't know where you are coming from and I don't think you know either." She said, "Well, I just came from the other house." "That's fine. Tell me about the other house." Then the actress started to invent on the spot. That's fine, but that means that she's not done her homework. Then I asked, "When you left the house, what did you see or do between the house and here? There were ten men playing horseshoes? What did you do? Did you just look at them and go, or what?" Once the actress makes a choice about those kinds of things, she enters the scene entirely differently, and you can see it—not because she is acting or because some big event is happening, but because when she walks into that room she is coming in from a specific place and she now has a reason to be in that room.

Then the actress put the valise down, and I stopped her again because it was clear that she hadn't thought about the barn she had just entered. I asked her what the barn looked like, and she started to invent again. I'm sure that after a while the actress started to think to herself, "Why do I have to do all this work when I really want to get to the part in my monologue about going to Hollywood? Why do I have to do all this work when I haven't even said anything yet?" Because that's the truth, because that's what happened to her character, and unless the actress does that, she is not going to get anywhere. She has to do one thing at a time.

I do a lot of stopping and saying, "No, no. I don't care if the meaty part of the scene is coming up. You didn't come in from anyplace." I don't have an exercise, I'm just rigorous about that until the actress decides that she has all that work to do and starts to do it. Then all of a sudden a year later she will say, "My God, it was easy today." And I will say, "That's because you did your homework and lived off it and left yourself alone." It's a lot of work to get actors to do that. They don't like doing it because they don't do it anywhere else.

What techniques do you use to help actors become more expressive?

The first thing I do is to say that I think everyone is emotional all the time. I think there is a bugaboo about emotion and people should just stop it. People are emotional. It's the things that stop them from being emotional that should be dealt with. I believe that acting is doing, not feeling. I know other teachers say that also, but I mean it. Today I saw a scene from *Top Girls*, a big confrontation scene between two sisters. I could see that the two actresses felt so obligated and responsible to being emotional. It was as if they were saying "I intend to be emotional," and it was getting them into trouble. You could see they had come out on stage to do an emotional scene. So I asked, "What are you coming into this room for: to have a fight or what?" And one actress said, "To make the bed." Then I got really simpleminded. I asked, "Why are you making the bed?" And she said, "I'm getting ready to go to sleep." "Oh, you are? Well, what you did was come in to play the scene from *Top Girls*, not go to sleep. Start again." Well, of course, the emotional life was much easier to get to because the tension created by the obligation to be emotional was removed.

So the first thing I do is get students to decide what to do, rather than what to feel, in order to release them from the obligation to be emotional and allow them to concentrate on something else. That frees the emotional life. Now, what about bigger, more crisislike events? I have found very few actors who can't get an emotional life going once they stop worrying about it.

Second, I say whatever emotion you have, use it. If you are not feeling anything and are in despair, please use that, but put it into the situation. I think where I part company with a lot of people is in this area. I say put it into the situation immediately. Then it's no longer the actor feeling bad, but the character feeling bad. That prevents the actor from feeling that he and his character have different emotions.

Third, I think that Affective Memory Exercises and Personal Objects Exercises are fine if you need them. I will do sensory work also. I believe in them.

How do you use personal objects?

I tell students to use anything—teddy bears from childhood, a bracelet that your boyfriend gave you. It will release an emotion if you just try to re-create that object—but then it must get reconnected to the situation of the play.

How do you instruct students to do this exercise?

First, I would use it as preparation. Then I would find where in a scene I could use the personal object or a task or the heat or the place or shining my shoes. I would try to re-create it—but this is a rehearsal technique. An actor does not do exercises when he is playing the role.

So you have the students work on sensory elements in order to bring on the emotion.

Sometimes. But you can't rely on it. You have to make a bargain with yourself, which is, "I don't care if it works." I think that's the hardest thing for actors to do—do all this work and then not care if it works. That's what I'm probably most successful at getting people to understand. And it's very hard to do because we all believe so strongly that we have our work to do and it *must* pay off and show. When directors say, "Go out there and have fun," they mean "Trust yourself."

I will do anything to get actors to do that. For instance, today actors came in with the most organized scene from *Dylan* that I've ever seen. It was so organized on the basis of the text that I didn't believe a second of it. I didn't believe there was a relationship between the people in the scene. I told the actress this and she was stunned because she had worked very, very hard on it. I said, "Do you understand that you have made all your choices on the basis of the dialogue? That's wrong. You should base your choices on the past, the given circumstances, and what you walk in with. You have to decide those things and then let whatever happens happen. Choices made before you investigate those things are no good because they are obvious; anyone can do something that is based on the text." An actor has to redefine his job as playing the first beat, trusting that he will get to the next one organically, and not stopping until it's over. That's what frees actors. It's hard to get an actor to believe that a beat does not depend on the dialogue and that it ends only when it is really over or it has to change.

How do you define beat?

What you want in a scene and how you go about getting it until you can't get it anymore, and you have to get it another way or get something else because of what someone else has done.

By the way, I don't believe in chopping the script up into beats and finding them *before* you work with your scene partner, because beats are often based on what the other person does. I don't think an action or a want or an objective, or whatever word you want to use, is worth a damn if it doesn't make you totally sensitive to your fellow actor. Anyone can say, "Let me out of here" or "Give me the five dollars." If you don't have an intention or objective that makes you totally sensitive to how the other person reacts—to every detail of how his shoulders move or what you see in his eyes—then you don't have a very good intention. So an actor can't break down the beats until he's worked with his acting partners because he doesn't know what they are going to do. An actor's intention is only valuable when it fuels his need for the other actor.

Our characters have expectations of other people, just as people do in life. Whatever I say to you, I expect you to respond in one way or another. And most often I even know what it is I expect. So, if you respond in the way I expect you to or you don't, it should affect me. I think that the more an actor can have expectations that are not delivered, that are not fulfilled, the more fun it is to act. For instance, if the student who came in to play the scene from *Top Girls* today had come in expecting to go to bed, it would have been much more valuable to her than expecting to come in and have the fight with her sister. She was going to have the fight no matter what, because it's in the dialogue. But if she had come in wanting to go to bed (and sure she would be able to), that fight might have surprised her.

A lot of actors feel that an intention is there to impel them to speak. I think that an intention is not a good one if you aren't affected by what the other person does.

Let's say a student is new to your class. How would you advise him or her to start working on a script?

Reading it to each other and just listening to each other without making any choices is really an important way to begin. Just the experience of hearing each other is important. You have to get the acting out of the actor, which means the student has to see what happens if he says something to his acting partner and to see how that affects him. Then he has to go with that feeling and see what happens. If he can do that, he will be amazed at how many connections he makes to the script just by himself. But if he gets in his own way and says, this is an angry line, this is an emotional line (which is what actors do all the time), he becomes his own obstacle.

An exercise I always do that is helpful for learning how to work on a scene is to take the first scene in *Hamlet* and ask students to read it. Then we talk about it in depth. I ask them to tell me what it says and to describe how cold "bitter" cold is, for instance. What does that mean? Then we go through the whole thing one sentence at a time and I ask, "What do you think your intention is, for example, on the line, 'Stand. Who is there?' " And they always say that the intention is to find out who is there. After we go through the line they begin to see that maybe the intention is to challenge the ghost.

And I do that with all my classes using the first scene of *Hamlet*.

It sounds like a way to teach students how to look for intentions and create an environment.

And also what the text tells you about the circumstances. I use the short scene where Marcellus has been outside for eight hours in a pitch-black, totally quiet environment. Now this man's state must be quite something. And it had better be different from that of the other character who is about to join him and knows there is a ghost about. I always ask students to tell me how this day is different from any other day. How is this night different from any other night? That's how we begin working on script analysis.

Then I ask students to define what they want to do in each rehearsal. I don't care in what order they do it. The average beginning actor's way of rehearsing is aimed at trying to make the scene work. What I want the students to do is explore a specific aspect of the work in each rehearsal. An actor should continue to do that for the rest of his life, including opening night on Broadway. That's all I think an actor *can* do. That's what I meant earlier when I said a performance is just another rehearsal. And each time the actor has to *let* things happen to him rather than try to *make* them happen.

With beginning students I do ask them to decide some basic things about the scene, like what they want and what their overall intention is. I think that the overall intention anchors the scene.

You have a very active career as a director. What advice do you give your students about working with directors?

Of course, they are always asking me that. I tell them to try first to do what the director asks, so that the director feels that they are making that effort. As a director, I always let actors do what they want to first, because I know if I don't they will never get it out of their systems. But I do that because I've been teaching a lot. I tell students that most directors don't know a lot about acting. They know a lot about the play, so actors should try to do what directors want first. Then they can develop a relationship with the director so that he feels they are interested in working with him. It's important that a director feels an actor will try his direction first. After that the actor can ask the director to give him some freedom if he feels he needs it.

If a director won't let actors have that freedom, I tell my students to rent a studio and ask their fellow actors to rehearse without the director. Because of the economics involved no one has enough time any more to explore a play thoroughly.

Before an actor can say to a director that he needs to "get in touch" with something, he had better be very secure in the way he works. And he has to have a good reason to trust himself in that kind of situation. So an actor needs to learn how he is going to work, and then maybe he can start trusting himself.

Do you give your students any advice on how to audition?

I tell them, "Try to remember why you always get the parts that you don't care about." It's usually because they are not under terrible pressure. So I tell them to try not to want a part too much. The only way they can do that is to audition a lot. Once they audition a lot, they begin to see what the percentages of success are, and that takes a certain pressure off them.

I also think an actor should make a choice that he can play—right or wrong. He shouldn't take it for granted that simply *how* he feels is going to get him through his audition. He should decide what he wants, what task he has, what images he can use, etc. Then he should figure on probably not getting the part anyway.

You teach at three major acting schools in New York City. Do you find there are differences among the students at these institutions?

First of all, they are different kinds of schools. NYU has a three-year program for graduates. The Circle in the Square is a two-year program and most of its students have already gone to liberal arts colleges. They don't really want to go through another three- or four-year training program because they feel they do not have the time or the patience. And since there is no financial aid from Circle, these students tend to have significant jobs that they have to maintain. Also, NYU is in transition from having been a sort of radical and successful alternative theater school in the 1960s to training actors to be able to work in the regional theaters—which was the original goal of Juilliard.

And Juilliard was very successful at that.

Yes, although we are now very famous for our movie stars at Juilliard. It's ironic that Bill Hurt, Kevin Klein, Chris Reeves, and Robin Williams trained for the stage and have all become film stars.

The student who comes to Juilliard knows that the training he gets there will focus on meeting the challenges of classical theater. So he has to want that to begin with. And in this day and age the kind of student who wants that probably fits into a certain social and economic level.

The student who goes to NYU has probably been drawn there by the mystique of the 1960s, so he or she is interested in a less conservative and classical approach. Of course, these are generalizations and each school evolves as it continues.

I found it very liberating to work with NYU students. When I walked into class I could see that they were thinking, "Juilliard, Juilliard, O my God"—that sort of misapprehension that the Juilliard actor is a technical actor. In Juilliard, I'm considered a rebellious teacher who makes students feel and do all sorts of crazy things. Then I come to NYU and I can hear them say, "Here he comes, the formal teacher." There are all these odd notions about the kind of teacher I am. I found that I am full of admiration for the amount of physical training that goes on at NYU. It's wonderful. I am also full of admiration for the amount of vocal and text training that goes on at Juilliard.

Encountering different attitudes in different groups of students is fun for me. I've quite enjoyed this particular year—the third at Juilliard and the third at NYU. Third-year students at Juilliard are quite apprehensive about avant-garde theater—Jean Genet and Sam Shepard, about doing *The Maids* and *Cowboy Mouth*. But they are doing very well. Meanwhile the students at NYU are afraid of doing Shaw—*Man and Superman* and *Misalliance*. Since I work on both those styles in exactly the same way (as a director I've done both), I enjoy making the NYU students really comfortable with Shaw or any elevated text. And I enjoy exposing Juilliard students to the darkest parts of themselves and making them comfortable with that.

I asked Tom Hulce to come to speak to my students at Juilliard the other day, and he gave a wonderful description of how he worked on a specific scene in *Amadeus* and how he was able to use whatever happened spontaneously, how once he knew what he was doing, he really wanted the unexpected to happen. You know, at Juilliard some students are afraid of that.

You mean there is very little spontaneity among the students?

No, but every play they do is so important to them that it's hard to feel free. I mean, if a student goes from doing *King Lear* to doing *The Rivals*—that's pressure. Every play is such "great literature," it's like climbing Mt. Everest every time you act. One of the things I do in acting classes is give them other kinds of hills to climb, so that they are not struggling with yet another so-called "great" play all the time.

What advice would you give someone just beginning a career in acting?

The first thing I would say is get some training. I think training makes a difference in an actor's ability to get hired, and it certainly makes a difference in the longevity of a career. It's easy to get kids in movies, kids who look right or have sex appeal. The movies are full of them. But they may not be able to continue their careers because once their looks fade, they are left with very little skill. Training is very important and you have to be careful about where you look for it.

Are there any approaches to training that you disapprove of?

If an actor is looking at a school that basically trains by doing productions, he has to ask himself if he is going to get good training there. He should also ask, "Am I going to be trained in anything but acting? Is there any movement or dance being taught? Or is it just theater history and an acting class?" I wouldn't fool myself into thinking that that's really training. I obviously lean toward conservatory training, and I believe that if an actor can take that kind of discipline, it is more rewarding. There are individual teachers who do wonderful work, but you just can't teach 1950s Method acting and sensory work and then let students go. Of course, they're important, but they don't go very far.

A student has to ask himself what it is that he likes about being an actor (and I don't know if you can answer this when you're young). If he doesn't love doing the work—rehearsing, exploring—and if the process doesn't fill him with joy, I would think again about acting as a life. There are, in the end, no other rewards that count, and there are no other rewards that you can count on. In your heart of hearts if just doing the work doesn't excite you, the fact that you fail more often than you succeed is going to destroy you. You have got to have the kind of personality where failure doesn't send you off the deep end, or you shouldn't be in the profession.

Ron Van Lieu

Ron Van Lieu is head of faculty and master teacher of acting at New York University's Tisch School of the Arts graduate acting program. He was a working actor for many years, performing in major roles in productions at Playwright's Horizons and the New York Shakespeare Festival, and was a member of the Milwaukee Repertory Theatre. He has also directed productions at the Public Theatre, Vassar Experimental Theatre, and Playwright's Horizons.

A graduate of New York University's actor training program, Mr. Van Lieu received his training there during the 1960s, when the faculty represented diverse views and a major focus was on experimental theater. Today the training program stresses the study of text and "creating character actors, not personality actors. I don't see how you can deal with the text unless you go deeply into it and begin to tap the transformation of self into character."

* * *

How did you start teaching acting?

I received my training here at the NYU School of the Arts in 1966. The major influences on me were the teachers I had at the time: Lloyd Richards, Peter Kass, Olympia Dukakis. I think those were the people who gave me important information about acting that I tend to use today. After I left NYU I went to the Milwaukee Repertory Theatre Company for two seasons and when I came back to New York I worked in an improvisational group called Section Ten. I worked at the Public Theatre as well. I began to realize that what really interested me most was the process of acting, even more than the career aspect of it. I was asked by Olympia to teach here for six weeks while she was doing a play and I have been here ever since. Since then I have devoted my time to teaching.

Is there a point of view you received at NYU that you still maintain?

I got different things from different people. It was a very eclectic time when I was here in the 1960s. The belief was that an actor should be exposed to many different philosophies and many different approaches, some of which contradicted each other, and that you could then pick and sort those things that touched you, that informed you the most, that gave you the best basis for the craft. From Lloyd Richards I got a real appreciation of character creation and how important that was. From Olympia I got a strong sense of how to bring yourself onto a stage, create an honesty about yourself, and tap feelings in yourself that are alive and true. From Peter I got a strong sense of what it means to truly play an objective, to really pursue it in a scene with a sense of its personal importance to you through the character. Through Omar Shapli and theater games, because I was really quite stiff when I came here, very rigid and basically terrified of any spontaneous life onstage, I got a sense of what it means to play and to come on a stage ready to deal with the circumstances at hand, feeling confident that I could, so that I wasn't always trying to control every step of the way. Hovey Burgess, in his circus class, gave and still continues to give great physical courage and daring and also incredible concentration. If you are going to learn to juggle, you have to be able to concentrate. So there was no unified system at that time. You did a lot of different things and it was up to you to pick and choose those you found valuable.

Is there a system now?

I think so. There is a clearer sense of progression. We don't begin with a scene class right away. We begin the first semester with an emphasis on circus and theater games, and pay great attention to releasing the body and the voice. There is technical work on speech, basic work on the instrument and freeing the actor's imagination and spontaneity. This is before we begin work on text.

The second semester I start students on the basic scene class, and we do that for two semesters. The emphasis there is on the real fundamentals, which include how to begin working from yourself, how to understand the transformation of self into character, how to study the text in depth in terms of the history of a character, the intentions and objectives in individual scenes, prior circumstances, the emotional life of a character, and how to bring the character's past life into the present without the actor having to leave the circumstances of a scene in order to get at emotion. The character always carries his past around with him, and what he is trying to do is deal with the present moment in time with all that history living. This is very difficult.

What I find problematic is that when actors do certain exercises, like Sense Memory or Emotional Recall, many of them, in order to deal with or re-create personal moments in their own past, seem to leave the present, leave their acting partners, and go into a kind of self-created, isolated reality to get at a particular feeling or memory. I emphasize that the actor needs a sense of bringing the past on in an alive way, trusting that it will be there, and that he can still get on with the scene. He doesn't need to detach himself from his fellow actors.

How do you help actors create a character's past and present emotional life?

The key to that for me is to expand the actor's imagination. If somebody is really an actor, he has the ability to pretend on the deepest level. I feel that if he can't do that, he is not an actor; if he can't believe in a character's circumstances, he doesn't have the imagination an actor needs.

The first thing actors have to do is study the play to try to understand all the factors that have brought the character they are playing to the present moment in time. Through their imagination, not so much their own personal biography, actors must try to take on the circumstances that have molded the character, and believe that the facts in the text are their own, and are the same as the character's. Clearly, when you do that you are going to find parallels from your own life in some instances, and you are going to have emotional reverberations and associative memories. When that happens, I say let those live and exist. Those are coming from you, you understand that, so just leave them alone. They will be right for the character.

When a student says, "I can't relate to my character because I have never been a king" or "I have never murdered anyone" or "I never had any children," he must, at that point, imagine that it is possible for him to have had all those feelings in his life and to yield to his imagination and have what I call "scenic faith" in himself: if he believes in it, an audience will believe in it. When actors don't really believe that they could be that person, when they don't have enough faith in themselves to try to transform themselves into that character, they will only deal with the outside of the character. They will try to "represent" that character to the audience. It's like an actor saying, "The character couldn't show up today, so I'll just stand in. I'm not really this character and you'll never really believe me, but I will represent him."

I think a great deal of it really has to do with belief in self, faith in one's ability to transform oneself into the character, and a lack of skepticism. A lot of actor training fosters skepticism. Teachers try to challenge students, sometimes in a negative way, by constantly saying, "I don't believe this and I don't believe that, and you can't do that, and you are not ready for this or that." They set up a kind of skepticism in the actor and a self-defeating kind of energy that always makes the student actor feel inadequate. Then he develops a negative self-image and becomes defeatist and the kind of imaginative faith that an actor needs to transcend himself doesn't flourish.

We as actors may never have experienced all the things we are called upon to act as the character, that we are required to do in a play, but if we are really actors we have the seeds for all those experiences inside of us. We have to have a kind of courage to open up our imaginations to ourselves and yield rather than control. In that way we can get to our feelings.

Do you have any specific exercises that you use to help students transform themselves?

There is an exercise from theater games called Transformation. If a student can play this game, he can accept and live in the circumstances of a given moment without predetermining what it is.

Transformation is the most sophisticated of the theater games and it is only taught at the very end of the system of theater games. What happens is that two people get up and are given something very simple to deal with, an imaginary object—say, a ball. The only requirement is that they deal with this imaginary object. While they are tossing it about, examining it, or playing with it, they are to be alert, looking toward a point where the reality of the moment seems to be transforming, of its own accord, into a different set of circumstances. Say in dealing with the ball both people lunge toward it at the same time, put their hands together, and end up sort of nose to nose. They may realize at that moment, for example, that they have become two people in love. They accept the change in their circumstances and feelings, they yield completely to it and begin to respond like two people in love. A story, a relationship, may emerge and, after a while, they may be in a set of circumstances in which, for instance, one has now died and the other is mourning that person's death. They accept that transformation.

Who gives them those circumstances to play?

No one. It's sensed by the two actors at that moment, and they are transforming into different characters in different circumstances. Again, they make a leap of faith.

What if they are not in tune with each other?

Ideally, they are tuned in and their sense of collaboration is so strong that they actually can sense the same thing at the same time. When it doesn't work well, it's because one actor is trying to control, is trying to be a playwright, refusing to live in the moment and afraid to accept where his imagination will take him. It takes great courage to play this game, but it also takes great courage to act.

Do you have any techniques for helping students learn to respond to each other on a moment-to-moment basis?

For instance, I will say, "On such and such line you didn't see your partner's reaction because you went to the next moment and you made it all up by yourself. Your partner, in fact, was giving you everything that you needed but you didn't take it."

Or I will say, "You are skeptical of the fact that you are married in this scene. You refuse to believe that you could possibly be married to your partner. Why is that? Is it your personal feelings about this actress that are in your way? Is it your skepticism about yourself that's in your way? Why can't you accept the fact that you and she, for this period of time, are married? Then when you're saying these things, you're saying them to your wife, not to your scene partner." It's my constant effort to get them to believe in who they say they are in the scene. If they really heard what was said to them, their next line would be true. Some students are terrified of eye-to-eye contact or of having a strong emotional response. Ironically, if I can say to them, "It's not you. It's the character who's doing that," that allows them to go deeper into themselves.

I will go through a scene with a student for a painfully long time, moment to moment, to find out why something didn't happen. It's either a lack of understanding of the play or scene or it's a block within himself.

Do you use other exercises from theater games?

They are not really helpful in solving problems in scene work. I don't think you can incorporate them into solving the problems of text, for instance. What I think you can do is use theater games exercises to give the actor a greater sense of spontaneity and, sometimes, to get at certain aspects of character.

For instance, there is a theater games exercise called Chatty in which one character needs to come into a room with a very strong objective and try to achieve it. Let's say he's locked out of his apartment, he needs the key, and he goes to the superintendent. The superintendent has been given the task of concentrating on being chatty—which means he talks constantly, he loves to talk, and everything is of interest to him. So the actor trying to get his key has to deal with a particular kind of character who is incessantly chatty. This provides a clear obstacle to the accomplishment of the objective and creates a particular personality for the character of the person who is chatty.

When an actor deals with text in a plodding, pedantic, unspontaneous way, learning to do Chatty, to be that character and then going back to text, can help in a very playful way to break up boring and predictable line readings and get at a kind of energy. But that's a game. It's not a technique. I think that theater games' greatest asset is in teaching an actor to be spontaneous and to have what I call "scenic faith," which means that you accept and believe in all the circumstances that surround you in a scene or play.

Is there a more unified approach to the teaching of acting at NYU now than there was when you were a student here?

When I came to NYU to study in 1966 New York was just ablaze with experimental theater: Grotowski was here, and Joe Chaikin was here, Andre Gregory's first company came out of our first graduating class, Richard Schechner was working here. There was clearly at that time a disdain of and a lack of interest on the part of students for anything that might have been called traditional theater. So everybody was interested in reinventing everything, or deconstructing it, and, like most students then, I was very attracted to that. As a result, we didn't pay much attention to studying text or trying to understand what the playwright really wanted or what his intention was. I think we were very arrogant and silly in a lot of ways, because we were trying to reinvent things that we didn't understand. We were trying to uncover new interpretations of things when we really didn't understand the fundamentals, the tradition from which a play or writer came.

I now feel differently. I still think it's legitimate to try new interpretations of a play, but first you have to know what it is you are revising, you have to understand everything about that play: when it was written, why it was written, what personal view came out of the playwright, what the social fabric of the times was. I think that in order for a student to create character he has to understand these things first.

Also, in the 1960s character acting had a bad name. There was a great emphasis on personality or just being yourself and getting everything from your own biography and self. The idea of creating a character was held in disdain at that time as though that were not good acting. I think it's the highest form of acting.

Do you think that The Actors Studio approach contributed to that feeling?

Perhaps. I think that any studio training that never got beyond the self, never got into character, contributed to that. There were many teachers who didn't get beyond dealing with self, who didn't take actors into real character work. Also, a lot of character work at that time tended to be stock, clichéd, and simply bad. Students didn't even have good role models for character actors then. It may have been the province of the English, but not the American, actor.

Much of what we do now, especially since Zelda Fichandler joined the faculty, is geared toward creating character actors, not personality actors. I don't see how you can feel with the text unless you go deeply into it and begin to tap the transformation of self into character.

Your primary focus seems to be working with text. How do you begin? What's the first thing you tell students when they start scene work?

The first thing they must do is read the entire play—thoroughly. That sounds obvious, but many students simply pick a scene and bring it in. Then they need to understand how the central event in a particular scene relates to the whole play. In other words, *why* is this scene in the play, and *what* takes place here that makes it significant in terms of the whole play? Let's say that the important event in a scene is the discovery of the husband's infidelity. Perhaps what happens in this scene is that the wife realizes she loves her husband. That is the central event in this scene. Next, the student has to break the scene down into beats, knowing where one begins and another ends. He then has to understand what objectives he is pursuing in the scene and what events occurred before the scene began. Next he must be willing to create those incidents imaginatively, bringing them into the scene, and then proceed with playing the objective while experiencing the emotional, psychological, or physical effects of these prior circumstances. This is a lot to juggle. It doesn't happen the first time a student brings in a scene.

The first time a student does work on a scene I'm basically interested in two things: is he willing to play the scene moment to moment, willing to come into the circumstances of the scene without trying to control either himself or the other actor, and does he seem committed to the pursuit of the objective? We don't even talk about whether he is credible as a character at this point. Basically, we are trying to find out how much of the character's life he can find from himself and how much he has to use his imagination. When he brings the scene back we usually try to add layers. That means dealing concretely with the preceding incidents, the environment in which the scene takes place, and whether that lives for him. Is he living in a specific place or is he on a stage?

If you sense that a student isn't pursuing his objective, how do you help him?

It depends on the student. When something is awry in that respect, it's usually because the student is tense, highly controlled, or fearful. After the scene is over, I'll simply say what I observed without criticism, without saying it's good or bad. I'll try to be as objective as possible and say, "What I didn't believe was . . ." and then try to get him to articulate for himself what got in his way. I think, for instance, when a student can't really commit to the pursuit of an objective in a scene, it may be because he or she finds it personally very difficult to do what the character is doing in the scene. He may find it embarrassing or humiliating, or feel that he lacks the inner conviction that the character has in order to do that. It's usually about a fear or a personal inadequacy. All I can do at that point is try to liberate him into an imaginative world that gets him beyond his own self-consciousness.

Each person has a different way of pursuing the various aspects of acting and I have to take the person in front of me, his gifts and his liabilities, into consideration. If someone says, "I really understand what this character is going through, but I just can't seem to do it," all I try to do is give him permission to do it. If he does understand and is not lying to himself, all he usually needs is a kind of permission to go ahead. So I will repeat, "Commit to doing. Go ahead. It's all right. Take a chance." Rather than try to give the student an exercise, I try to feed his own sense of courage and risk taking.

Often when we are talking about problems in a scene we are talking about these kinds of issues. So we talk about what blocks the students might have had in the scene. Was it a block about their understanding of the play or was it something in them—a rigidity, for example? But I don't do psychotherapy. I don't deal on that level at all. In fact, I rarely, if ever, ask a student to reveal personal information. Where I can be of help without becoming a therapist is by telling him or her objectively what I observe about that person, about his or her behavior and where that behavior might be coming from.

In a university setting students sometimes get more rigid than they might in studio classes because they know that they are being evaluated. That can lead to the kind of fear that kills creativity. You have to be very careful then to think of them not as students, but as actors.

Do you encourage students to comment on their classmates' work?

Yes, but not in a judgmental way. I like students to talk to each other objectively, to say, "This is precisely what I saw," without saying this was wrong and that was right. I want them to look at the work honestly.

How does text analysis proceed?

Students work with other teachers on text as well as with me. Nora Dunfee is a wonderful text teacher and she feeds into my work. For instance, she feels, as I do, that you can't really speak the text until you are the character because it was written to be spoken by the character—not just spoken beautifully or right, but from the energy and inner life of the character. The meaning of the text is found in the character and his or her wishes and wants. You get that through a study of the play, a gradual building up from self into character. That's a gradual evolution. As students get closer and closer to feeling themselves in the character's life, being in his or her shoes, living through this person's biography, when they finally speak the text it starts to change and alter in ways that have nothing to do with predetermined ideas. They start to find the right rhythms, the right meanings, without asking themselves. "What's the right way to do this?"

If an actor is having trouble finding a particular character, how would you help him or her?

· There was recently a scene done in class from *The Gingham Dog*. It was about the breakup of the relationship between a white man and a black woman. The actor in this scene was quite full emotionally, quite believable in his choices, and quite uncompromising in the pain the situation caused him. The actress in the scene had completely shut herself off from receiving anything that was coming from the actor. As as result, she was not credible as the character. There was no conflict, she was making passive choices, she was pulling away and retreating. And she is a very talented actress. When the scene ended we talked, not about her problems as an actress, but why her character wasn't believable in this situation. She eventually came to realize that the problem was with herself in *that* situation, that certain acting problems of hers got in the way of the character. For instance, she simply lacked the courage to look at the other actor, to take him in, to hear what he had to say, mainly because her feelings were so strong and so alive that she was afraid of the size of them and the purity of them. But they were precisely what would have made her character alive and believable.

In order to solve the problem for that particular actress, all one needed to do was, first, to feed her courage, and, second, to let her know that she has to do these things on the stage, that she does not have the option not to do them. In the name of being true to herself, she walked out on the character; hence she walked out on the life of the scene, hence she walked out on the experience that the audience could have if she unlocked that part of herself that was so beautiful and useful in the scene.

A young actress might say, "Well, that's me. I'm defensive. I'm self-protected." Sure you can say, "I'm being myself." But I have to say that that part of you is not useful as an actress. That's not your gift as an artist. So rather than give an exercise to overcome that, I will directly challenge an actress on her choice and try to give her permission to unlock her feelings, because that's what will bring the circumstances of the scene alive on stage. It's a more direct route. As soon as this actress did that, the character emerged.

Do you encourage students to observe people or work on animals to help them develop specific characters?

Both. New York is the greatest character center in the world. I love to watch people and daydream about what they do, who they are, and what got them to where they are now. When actors do that, they stop rummaging around in self and put their thoughts into the world of imagination. It's very expansive. It's great when somebody sees a person on the street and says, "Oh, God. Someday I would love to do that on the stage."

How do you work with students on developing the physical aspects of character?

Students need to find the physical life of the character on their own from the inside. But many students work better if they begin to develop the physical aspects of a character, the walk and gestures, externally first, and then internalize those things later on. I never say one way is better than another. It's all individual. Each student needs to discover if his behavior as a character is going to grow from the outside in or the inside out. A student has to know himself in order to know what works best for him; either approach is legitimate. Some students get very timid physically and need to force themselves into bold physicality that will become organic later on. I sometimes have students do character improvisations modeled on people they know and observe to help them develop character.

Could you describe that?

I ask them to pick someone they know, anyone they have known long enough to have some idea about what he or she is like inside, what that person thinks and feels. I tell them to try to get inside the person's skin, to put on his clothes, to begin to walk like him, to take on his speech rhythms. I encourage them to do this around their apartments, while they are washing the dishes, to do everything like the character would—answer the phone, read the paper, brush their teeth, the ongoing things of everyday life. Again, I'm always after this feeling of transformation rather than representation, so they do this in the privacy of their own rooms, not in front of an audience, trying to impress it. They are simply trying to feel like the person they have chosen. Then each student comes into class dressed like the character and I put the students into different situations. They meet one another as strangers. They do improvisations around meeting, including a physical activity that I give them. At this point I'm trying to get them to think of character as an ongoing living experience and help them realize that they could feel the same way in a play. They could have the same sense of authenticity and relaxation with the character when they portray one in a play.

Do you have any techniques to help students play comedy?

Of course there are technical concerns such as timing and a sense of rhythm. But also in comedy an actor has to be open to being laughed at. I love comedy. In the 1960s, comedy, like character acting, had a bad name. We had to believe we were serious actors; that meant we didn't do comedy. I think that comedy that grows out of character, where we recognize the human condition and what we all are, is marvelous.

I ask students to bring in comic material, but I don't ask them to go at it in any way that is different from drama.

Do you have any techniques to help students cope with stage fright?

We have recently put a great deal of emphasis on Alexander technique in our program. We try to approach everything from a sense of release, from a sense that feelings and sound come from a release, not from pushing out; that the body needs to begin by being relaxed if it's going to go anywhere. From Alexander technique students learn to begin to work free of tension so that they can escape their own flesh if they are trapped by tension or terror. I always emphasize beginning with relaxation. The students are taught to relax in other classes in the program.

In their first semester here students are taught to be emotionally available through their work with Zelda Fichandler. She teaches improvisational work that is personal and revealing of self in public. Then with Paul Walker in games class, they are taught to be spontaneous, live moment to moment, not to try to control themselves or one another, to speak out of a spontaneous sense of self. Hopefully, students come to understand that they need to stay emotionally alive in their day-to-day life because it's required of them in their craft.

I feel that if a person doesn't understand these things, no exercise you give him will make him an actor. If he doesn't know that he has to be emotionally alive, if he doesn't want to be emotionally alive, if he doesn't want to be someone other than himself, if he has to be forced to do that or if he needs constant exercises to do it, he really isn't right for acting.

How do you prepare students to work on different styles of theater from Shakespeare to contemporary plays?

We do Shakespeare here in our first year, when students start performing. We try to see if the fundamentals that we are talking about seep in and support them when they do scenes from Shakespeare. The students' first crack at Shakespeare is simply to taste it and see what it's like and to see if they can apply what they are being taught. The same challenges apply to Shakespeare that apply to any drama. But the great thing about Shakespeare is that it teaches students how to sustain something, how to concentrate for long periods of time on a thought, a feeling. You don't often find that kind of energy in contemporary plays.

When you were talking about observing people, you mentioned that daydreaming was a good way to start character work. How do you encourage that in students?

It's a good way to get to the imagination. Students in an academic environment don't usually allow themselves to do enough daydreaming, enough imaginative work, to take pleasure in yielding to imaginary circumstances or wanting to be somebody else. They can get very pedantic.

Things are different for this generation of young actors. When I began teaching everyone was wildly emotional, experimenting with all sorts of things, and the last thing one wanted to be was conservative and conventional. So part of my job as a teacher at that time was to give students some craft to put on top of all their impulses and feelings, to make them look like regular human beings so they could be realistic in plays. Now I find, because times seem to be a little more repressive and conservative, that what I have to do is help students break up their need to be right all the time, to be correct. They want to do everything the right way. It's harder to get to their own desires and wishes, to their own feelings, and to help them be daring.

Students are not rebelling any longer. They are desperately trying to "make it" within the conventional mold, and they try to figure out what that is rather than focus on what they are experiencing. The shame is that they have wonderful things to contribute. I find this generation of students more intelligent, and when that intelligence gets tapped, the students are emotionally richer than I or any of my peers were. I don't know why that is, but it is harder to give students a sense of freedom now. Young actors are very worried, like everybody else is, about "making it." They are even suspicious of the training they get—wondering whether it will help them to "make it" or get in the way. Many students come here having already acquired techniques they know are commercially attractive, and they fear that those will be taken away from them.

Are NYU students still interested in experimental theater?

Not many, but what I find wonderful are the number of students who are again forming their own companies and finding their own places to work. This year two of our graduates have founded 44 Walker Street, where they are producing plays and backing performance artists. They are creating a home not only for themselves, but for different kinds of artists. They are not waiting for somebody to give them a job.

What advice would you give someone starting a career in acting?

To be an actor you have to have a sense of mission, not profession. The bottom line has to be your need to illuminate the human condition in all its forms, in all the various styles of theater. Careerism is a big, big impairment to that sense of mission. I try to impart to students how much joy and pleasure can be found in a profession when they have a sense of mission, when the rewards come from the process itself and from their collaboration with other artists. They need to be reminded of the wonderful freedom they feel when they transform themselves from the narrowness of their own biography into another person. These are the things they can count on and that will sustain them—not the reviews, the salaries, or the stories about them in the newspapers.

Dale Moffitt

Dale Moffitt is head of the undergraduate acting curriculum at Southern Methodist University. Before entering academia, he was an actor, and he maintains an intimate contact with the performance aspect of acting by continuing to study a wide range of approaches from theater games to British classical techniques to mime. He believes that teaching, like actor training, is an ongoing process.

Dr. Moffitt is involved in every level of undergraduate teaching from the freshman preparation year to the improvisation course in senior year. He aims at providing new students with a strong core of self-confidence and self-esteem that will "strengthen them so that when they are out working in the world they will have a central sense of self to which they can return." He is concerned with helping students acquire integrity and a sense of purpose in their art. This, he believes, can come about when an actor "is willing to give up the self and go for the character," when he is willing to stretch his craft beyond "the limits of his own personality" and create a new life.

361

How has your own training as an actor influenced your teaching?

After Stanislavsky's last tour to the United States some of his group remained to teach in this country. An American actress, Mary Harris, studied under and subsequently taught with the Russian actress Maria Ouspenskaya. Mary subsequently married a man who became head of the University of California at Berkeley drama department, but because there was a nepotism law, she could not teach there. However, they were a team and she coached unofficially. She remains the single most brilliant acting coach I have ever encountered. Although at this point I have reconsidered some aspects of her approach, it has clearly been the basis for my own work. It was a pure Stanislavsky method that she used and it was very straightforward: objective, superobjective, through line of action, unit of action, Sense Memory, Affective Memory. I have pulled back a bit from Affective Memory Exercises because I feel it is an area better suited to professional therapists than to acting teachers.

Mary also had the genuine conviction that as actors we must be a part of something bigger than ourselves, and that has stayed with me and informs my teaching more than anything else—that what we do is important. To this end, I look for a way to transmit a kind of theater ethic to my students.

Would you describe what you teach?

I teach 360 hours of programmed training as one of nine teachers in the undergraduate program at Southern Methodist University. By "programmed" I mean the use of specific exercises at specific times as opposed to simple scene study classes. It's essentially a lesson plan. It's an academic program in that students are responsible to a liberal arts degree program that also includes courses such as rhetoric and anthropology. What makes this program unique, I feel, is that members of the graduate acting faculty also teach in the undergraduate program. We offer the undergraduate university liberal arts student a degree of specialization in acting that I have never encountered in a university program. And what I like is that the program has that degree of specialization without losing the broader education that I firmly believe is essential to an actor. The more an actor is, the better he or she is. Purely professional programs can lead to a kind of tunnel vision.

What is the course of study for the drama student at SMU?

The first year is not conventional actor training. It is a preparation to go into actor training. I find this unique. We audition nationally. A student cannot just come to SMU and enroll in the theater program. We auditioned 580 students this year and we selected twenty-seven of them to enter the program. During their first year they spend up to six hours a week with me and I attempt to establish a common vocabulary for them before they go into the intensive training. There are great differences between students' backgrounds. SAG members may be sitting on the floor next to students who don't even know what those initials stand for. To plunge all of them into the same level of training without trying to reconcile them in some way is not healthy. The first year's training is geared toward setting them up to be a unit, a social and artistic unit that will go forward into the intensive training of the third semester in a healthy, productive manner.

How is the "pretraining" course structured?

First, let me tell you what I want for the students in general: health. I am increasingly convinced that we in the teaching profession can affect their subsequent degree of well-being in an incredibly difficult field. I think we can also affect the students' state of happiness, their self-image, their self-esteem. I want us to invest them with power. That informs the choices I make about teaching. I do not want to drain their power, I do not want teaching to be about the teacher's need. I want us to feed into their independence so that when they are out in the working world they have a central sense of self to which they can return when directors fail, when God is not with them, so to speak. This is of great concern to me. I really want us to teach students to be their own people.

In the first year I try to teach them how to sense the things they have within them that will sustain them. Basically I want them to believe that they have what they need within them and can call on it when they need to. For example, I use Joe Chaikin's sound and movement exercise in the first year's pretraining course, but perhaps a bit differently from the way he set it up.

This exercise does a number of things. It teaches the actor how to sustain. It also creates a group dynamic. Specifically, I take my class of sixteen people and I line them up in two rows of eight each facing each other across the room. One person will move into the center of the room making any repetitive sound and movement. That student moves across to a partner who will begin to receive the pattern and replicate what he or she sees and hears. Those two students will share what they are expressing until it becomes a mirror exercise. When these students sense a connection within that movement and sound, they have found a meeting place.

And they duplicate the sound and movement?

One begins to sense, to absorb, and to join what he sees coming from his partner. What I do is work the exercise there for a while and then I have students consider a dimension other than simple replication of what they see and hear. I want them to pick up on how their partner is feeling about what he is doing. Is he happy or sad? Can I also absorb and meet him within his feeling even momentarily?

So you ask a student to be aware of his partner's intention?

In a sense. An argument can be made that Stanislavsky started with the belief that content dictates form and he wound up believing that form dictates content. This is a "form dictates content" exercise. Movements and sounds that are intuitively chosen inevitably create an internal state. It may come out as hostility. Can the partner feel that hostility? Will he open up, not just to see and hear, but to what his partner is feeling inside. And will he meet his partner there, then try on the feeling and see where it leads? The two students meet, and they exchange, and one takes it over, draws it in while the other relinquishes it so that the original movement and sound and feeling are transferred.

Then you are left with one student again.

The one who started moves back to his place in line and sits down. The new student, the one who has been transformed, so to speak, moves into the center and allows what he took from the first student to become something out of himself, yet based on what was given him. Students are not consciously to change the initial movement and sound. That's part of the learning. One of the reasons for doing this exercise is to teach them that the sound, movement, and feeling will change if they leave them alone and let them go. Again, whatever they need is within them and will come forth to support their work. We go through the entire group in this way.

In a variation by H. Wesley Balk, when the last member of the group completes the change of his pattern, all move to join him with complementary sound and motion patterns. In our version, the group is charged collectively with finding an end to the exercise. What this exercise does is force them to work creatively as a group. And that's an important part of the first year. In some years the group is so together from the beginning that these exercises are joyous, but sometimes the exercises are like having root canal work because it's so hard for the group to find its sense of ensemble.

What other exercises do you use during this first year?

I use a passage from T. S. Eliot that is incredibly evocative. It's the last stanza of "Four Quartets," which starts, "We shall not cease from exploration. . . ." I wanted a piece of material that affects simply by virtue of its words. This piece of material is a meeting place for the freshmen, it is theirs and it becomes a creative arena for them. Of course, it changes every year because it stimulates different things in different groups.

I ask the group to sit in a circle with its eyes closed and I tell one person from the group to sit in front of another student and offer him the first line, touching the seated student as he speaks. The seated student, still with eyes closed, allows whatever he is feeling to color the way he says the next line of the poem. Then the seated student will get up and go to someone else and say the third line. That student will respond with the next line, expressing what he is feeling. We work our way through the entire poem in this way. Students also allow themselves to express the impulse to return the touch they have received.

The other day when we were doing this, we wound up with one

student left over, and he had his back turned. So we began to play with what would happen if someone offered a line behind someone's back. Could he sense whether the line was directed to him or to someone else? If he sensed that it was to him, he would turn to respond with the next line. The reaction was extraordinary. When a line was offered and the student sensed that it wasn't offered to him, he felt abandoned and disconnected. At the same time, he was suffused with joy when he correctly sensed that the line was offered to him—when he made the connection. We could take this exercise and analyze it for the many aspects of acting that it taps: the reality of the moment, being in touch with your impulses, and so on. Over the years, I've developed a range of exercises using the Eliot piece.

Another exercise I use with freshmen is called Christmas in September. The students are told that they are going to give gifts to each other, and that gift will be their own creativity. They are all strangers and they don't understand each other's creativity. The assignment is for each student to find a picture, any picture, that is vivid to them for any reason—it can be evocative of any feeling, positive or negative. It can be a picture from an art book or a magazine, just so long as it generates a strong feeling. The student will then take his response to it and create a five-minute presentation out of that response. So when the student finds a picture that moves him, he must ask himself, "What can my response become? What can I do with that?" And he gives it form. There are no bounds to what he can do except that he can't hurt himself or anyone else or damage the building.

What kind of presentations do students come up with?

I've seen everything. Each student presents his or her creation to the group. Once a student used four folding chairs. She lined up three on one side of the stage and put the other one across the room. She sat in the single chair and proceeded to execute a variety of movements across the space in the direction of the other three chairs. Her movements looked like swimming, then canoeing. She moved between the chairs in various ways. It's difficult to describe what she did, but when she showed us her picture at the end of the exercise, it was of a log cabin. I asked her if she could explain how she constructed her exercise from that picture. She then described a series of events in her life—her parent's broken marriage, divorce, remarriage, stepbrothers, etc., all of which she had incorporated into her five-minute exercise.

I've had lights turned out and poems read in the dark. I've seen gorillas doing Emmett Kelly–type routines. Last year a girl came in wearing overalls and spread a canvas sheet on stage, put a cinder block down, and proceeded to smash it to pieces with a sledgehammer. When she had reduced two blocks to rubble, her exercise was over and she showed us her picture. It was Dürer's *Man's Hands Joined in Prayer.* She then said to the class, "Some of you have BMWs and money. My family are laborers and I got to thinking that what I am about is hands. Everything about me is hands." So you see, the picture can go anywhere.

What instruction do you give students before they prepare this exercise?

I tell them to use their imaginations in a way that reflects their feelings, whatever feelings a particular picture has evoked in them.

What I want them to do is create. It's about them taking the time to do some thinking about themselves and making choices and creating something—something that is for someone else. It's not for their own indulgence. It's a way to share, but not their history or their unhappy childhood. It's a way to share their creativity with the people with whom, theoretically, they are going to create. What happens is that they begin to sense the realities and humanities in each other and they begin to sense a common thread of fear and joy. Then the group dynamic begins to move. What also happens is that they've conquered the fear of taking responsibility for creating something on their own, and they gain a kind of strength. That's important in the first year of training.

At the same time, freshmen read Chapters 3, 7, and 15 in *An Actor Prepares.* I lay in the notions of superobjective, through line, unit of action tactic. We beat the hell out of them. They go to shows and then write out what the superobjective was, what the through line was, etc. They begin to exercise those concepts that I will build on when we study characterization. We all go to the symphony.

Some students have done this all their lives; others have never been to a concert. They are also obligated to read the Arts and Leisure section of the *New York Times* every Sunday; we have a pop quiz on it. I've told them that when they can convince me that they'll do that on their own, the pop quiz goes. They must begin to acquaint themselves with what is happening in the theater because they don't know very much. To them there was no history before their birth. All this occurs in the freshman year.

I focus on the concept that behind everything an actor does is something he wants. I bring in the notions of subtext and inner monologue. We do monologues and scene work.

How do you work with monologues in the first year?

What I do is ask students to write their own monologues. I want the monologues to be about affecting human behavior; that is, about changing something in someone else. That gives them just enough form. Their work here helps me to get to know them a little bit and gain some knowledge of their individual process. Once again, it is about a wanting that causes people to do what they do.

Their final project in freshman year is scene work, but not scene work toward a product. It's about learning to work on *Fool for Love* (or whatever play the scene is from), not about doing *Fool for Love* well.

How do you help students learn to develop a character?

First of all, character work has to be both internal and external, and it's different for everyone. An actor can work on the externals, the outside, and never deal with the inside. But you can't do the opposite successfully because there is no way not to have the audience see and hear you. I prefer to teach working from the inside out, because I like having the security of knowing that the work will have both an inside and an outside. I try to teach them that content will generate form, and, conversely, that form can generate content when they haven't been able to go to it directly.

We start off with a lecture series to help them gain control of their craft. "Let's say you have been cast in a play and rehearsals start in two weeks. What is the actor's homework? What should you have done during the two weeks before you arrive at the first rehearsal?"

We discuss what they should have done, but they can change the order or the vocabulary.

The first thing the actor has to do is establish a superobjective. He must ask, "What am I, as a character, a part of?" Then we read the play with five categories in mind: what do the people in the play say about my character; what do I do; what does the playwright say about me; what actions are implied in what I say; what are the units of action in the text?

Then I ask them to look for a motivating desire, what we called the "through line," and then to name it actively so that it generates activity. I use much of Charles McGraw's work in this section.

Then we work on externals. What external choices will I explore actively in this piece? These are all things actors can do on their own before they even meet with the director.

Now we start to use Studs Terkel's *Working*. A student picks a monologue, but he won't work with it for a while. What he does first is answer a set of questions about his character. Arthur Miller wrote a set of questions that I like to use for this. So did John Osborne. I give the students both sets of questions and tell them to answer them for the character they chose from *Working*.

Let me digress for a moment. I think that we don't adequately teach an actor how to monitor his own work. Part of keeping the actor independent is teaching him to know the difference between the lie and the truth of his own work, to *feel* the difference. I think sense memory work is the way to teach that. It's old-fashioned, in a way, but I think we have thrown it out too soon. You can teach the actor the experience of what something *feels* like versus the experience of indicating a feeling. Either an actor is capable of having an authentic experience or he is phoning it in, sending out intellectual signals to the audience. So what I do in my characterization class is go back and do a little basic sense memory work to give students a sense of the truth and lie in themselves, and remind them of how absurd it is, for instance, to act from intellectual clichés when experiences are so readily available. I try to make them aware that sensory work is specific and individual, that it doesn't consist of generalities. It's the truth of your experience *in* that moment. If an actor can find truth for himself, he can create reality for the audience. I think that's what acting is.

When we do basic Sense Memory Exercises I often use an exercise developed by McGraw. I give each student a slip of paper that has things written on it. It might say, "a bowl of hot soup filled to the brim" or "a worm" or "an ice cube" or "two bags of groceries with a hole on the bottom." Then I tell the students to go home and prepare, from direct observation, an event that has a beginning, middle, and end that uses that object. I want them to develop a conflict with the object they are using and I want it resolved in some way. They present the exercise in class, without the object, and then they do the same exercise again, as their character from *Working*. In this way they become aware of the difference between the way they respond to sensory events and the way their character responds.

I start to work on character by telling students to apply Arthur Miller's questions to the character they have chosen from *Working*. These are really very conventional questions: where do you live, what kinds of relationships do you have, what do you want out of life.

After that students will go into a series of exercises based on their character. They will develop a five-minute exercise on their character from *Working*, presenting material that isn't in the monologue. In one version they must present five minutes out of that character's life as a child. It's their creation. It's not in the monologue. In the same way they will develop a five-minute scene from information suggested by the monologue in which the character is attempting to persuade someone to do something. We will do another exercise that focuses on that character's relationship to props, the kinds of things he works with or carries in his pockets. We will do all of this before we ever begin to work on the monologue.

I thought characterization was going to be about moving from the self to someone different from the self. What I discovered is that at this point in our training the student really needs to synthesize that training toward presenting the self effectively. If one believes that you learn to act the self first and only then are able to work with the differences from the self, then at this point our student works on that first step. I have just finished organizing another semester to work on the next step: the use of the self to create characters.

In the second year students take all theater courses. They take acting, voice and speech, movement, theater history and literature, and two technical practicums. All majors in their first two years are also required to take technical practicum courses, including set construction, lighting, costume, and front-of-house publicity. The other years we balance three-fifths theater courses with two-fifths general outside requirements. By the junior and senior year courses become more specialized, such as classes in styles (usually Shakespeare), combat, audition training, film acting technique, Alexander, characterization, and improvisations.

Are the exercise and scene classes separate?

No. Acting classes embrace both.

The sophomore faculty takes over the full year of specialization. The sixteen students in the upper division acting track rejoin me at the beginning of their junior semester and I then have them six hours a week for a semester of characterization. After they leave me, they go to a technique course. At the beginning of their senior year they join me again for a year of improvisational work. Right now I feel strongly that the improvisational work should be moved to the beginning of the second year.

You mentioned earlier that you were concerned about developing a "theater ethic."

The question is: how do we teach our students to have integrity or purpose in the theater? I think one way is to help them experience the importance of a script so they can begin to sense the potential purpose of acting. Smaller scripts, ones that don't deal with the larger issues of humanity, won't do it. They need, literally, to be able to experience the size of the script.

I have tried to get students to consider that to be an actor is to make choices. They have to be taught to sense the kinds of choices that are available because basically, at seventeen, acting is about your parents loving you and giving you standing ovations. At seventeen, acting is the good feeling of applause. Can we begin to lead these young people beyond that? I think that in the larger terms of health and happiness we must. One way is to define what acting is, so we spend time discussing the different kinds of acting. We discuss the different types of actors there are—the commercially successful ones, the ones who are always stretching themselves in their craft, and the ones who are both.

We talk about freedom, about being in a self-actualization age, and although each of us is "free to be me," an actor who is only himself is limited to his own size. The point is to go beyond the limits of our own personalities, like the Oliviers and Hoffmans, who can create a new life. I want students to sense that an actor is more himself by his willingness to give up the self and go for the character. That's a kind of freedom. That's the way I've been working with students—getting them to think about these issues and find their own values. I worry that I brainwash rather than teach; it's very important to me not to impose my own values, but rather to help them find their own.

How do I define acting? Do I do it for me? Is it for my own satisfaction in the moment of performance or can it be something more? I would suggest that the real satisfaction comes from learning that one's dedication to the craft of acting gives one an extraordinary power: the power to create reality for other people. Acting then becomes about helping others experience themselves through one's work.

Ken Andreyo

Mel Shapiro

Mel Shapiro was the head of the drama department and is currently Professor of Drama at Carnegie–Mellon University. A professional director as well as a teacher, he has directed many acclaimed productions, including Two Gentlemen of Verona *and* Bosoms and Neglect *on Broadway,* Richard III *and* Stop the World, I Want to Get Off *at Lincoln Center, the American premiere of* Accidental Death of an Anarchist *at the Mark Taper, and John Guare's* Rich and Famous *and* Marco Polo Sings a Solo *for the New York Shakespeare Festival, as well as the original off-Broadway production of* The House of Blue Leaves. *He has also directed numerous productions in regional theaters such as the Arena Stage, the Mark Taper Forum, the Old Globe Theatre, the Tyrone Guthrie Theatre, and the Stratford Ontario Shakespeare Festival.*

Mr. Shapiro helped develop the concept for the theater program, School of the Arts, at New York University and was a member of the original faculty. He also conducted an ongoing acting workshop for

373

professional actors in New York City that focused on developing skills in playing both Shakespeare and contemporary plays.

How did you get started teaching acting?

I was a director. In fact, I studied directing at Carnegie Tech. In 1971 I came back to New York from the Tyrone Guthrie Theatre, where I had been directing, and I was asked to help develop the theater program at the School of the Arts at New York University. I was a founding member of that, and have been teaching ever since.

Has your approach to actor training changed since then?

When I started teaching, I was very concerned with making things happen for the actor by creating events for him around the text. I used to focus on getting actors to relax and then having them do exercises like playing basketball or tennis while they worked on text material. I used exercises that were always about doing something other than creating the author's event. This was very interesting because many people opened up and freed themselves, and I used to say, "Oh, this is wonderful. Now they can act." But I learned that they weren't acting the *text*. This became a crisis for me. What is the point of teaching acting if, in the end, you are not acting the text?

My whole approach has changed. I don't do any of those exercises anymore. I deal with language, I deal with Shakespeare, I deal with how to make the language your own. The basic reason for this is because we are now dealing with mass illiteracy in this country. Just getting kids to read the repertoire is more important to me now than teaching acting, because students don't know the plays from the past, they don't know what a play is, they don't know about the important artistic contributions to their culture.

I have become aware that the teaching of acting is a cultural problem. In other words, the way acting was taught twenty years ago was related to the culture. At that time we were into a very nonverbal approach—the metaphor was the thing, the persona was the thing. We didn't want to use words because we believed that the words were a means of lying.

I am now faced with teaching acting to students who haven't read Plato or Shakespeare. They haven't even read Neil Simon. They never heard of Clifford Odets or George S. Kaufman. This is an awesome problem. How does one deal with training illiterate people to perform? Where do you begin? How can you teach acting without a student's awareness or knowledge of literature?

How do you begin?

You get them to a certain level of awareness of the history of art and civilization first. Then you inject them with the idea of theater, because they don't have one.

I recently gave a talk to some students with Steve Bochco, the creator of *Hill Street Blues*. He asked them which episode was their favorite. They all raised their hands. They all had seen four years of episodes! I'm sitting there thinking, why aren't they reading books? Are they only media literate? How do we begin to teach them and *where?* It's a monstrous problem.

The first thing I do is have my teachers get students to read. They take Dramatic Literature. They used to take it for one year, but now they have to take it for two. Next year they will have it for three years. I really think the problem is that the 1960s dismantled everything that was important in our educational system and we're paying the price for it.

What kind of exercises do you have students do now?

I have one exercise I call an Autodrama. I ask a student to do a one-man show that is the story of his life. He has fifteen minutes to do it. He can bring in props or costumes or music—whatever. The Autodrama has two qualifications: it has to be entertaining, and it has to be revealing—but only if it gives the student pleasure to reveal. This is not psychotherapy. It's an interesting exercise because a lot of things come up and are displayed, and you learn a lot about the student.

The best way to describe it is by giving an example of one. In one of the best Autodramas, a student asked the class to leave so that he could set up. When we came back into class there were a dozen outfits laid out across the room and he was at one end of the room naked. He said, "When I think about my life I always think of the clothes I wore at different periods of my life." He started dressing and transforming—he became a baby, a boy with knickers, a boy with his first pair of long pants—and he got the feeling of being each one of his different selves by wearing those different clothes. He also had something he wore the first time he made love. The exercise was extremely useful because it brought back a lot of memories that he could use in his work, memories that he could tap. If he is playing a scene in which he's making love for the first time, he can think of the costume. His feelings will come back and may be of use to the character he's playing—if the character's experience is at all analogous.

When the students and I get to know each other we do two other exercises: one is to present a story, an autobiographical event from their lives, and the other, right after that, is to present a piece of fiction. It's then up to the class to detect which is true and which isn't, which actually happened to the student and which didn't. The stories are told through words and actions. The actor has to be so convincing that the class won't be able to tell the difference. I always liked the title, "Lies Like Truth." The actor has to lie like truth. Half the time I can't discern which story is real and which isn't. This exercise addresses the actor's ability to believe in what he or she is saying and to play it truthfully. It also addresses the actor's imagination. Some students get extremely emotional over their fictional story and wind up believing it themselves.

These exercises also help students find courage. The ability to be brave has become a crisis in our society. Most of the kids at Carnegie come from upper-middle-class families. Everybody wants to be conventional. Nobody wants to rock the boat. Everybody wants to conform to either Jerry Falwell or GQ magazine. I always thought that wanting to be an artist meant wanting to have your own voice heard, wanting to be individual, wanting to say, "I am different and I want you to love me for it." The problem today is that students start conforming at such a young age.

By the time students are seniors, their one-man shows are very different. They are much more willing to expose themselves emotionally and they are braver. Also, as freshmen, students are still very connected to their parents, so a lot of their first exercises, their first one-man shows, have a lot to do with parents. By the time they are seniors, students are much more connected to their own anxieties about going out into the world.

One very good-looking student did an Autodrama about a job he had had the previous summer. He did it extremely well, but what he revealed was how much he didn't like himself, how much he disliked his body. I mean, this kid was as handsome as a movie star, and he lifted weights! He was a very commercial type. In the exercise he went on a bender about his self-hatred, how he thought he wasn't attractive. In this case the exercise was somewhat therapeutic, because this boy, who always had to be charming on stage, almost cute, was able to release his rage. I told him that he was very angry about a lot of things and that I would like to see some of his rage in a role. Then he played the lead in a play that required him to be selfish, needy, and manipulative, and I must say that he was so in tune with those things that he scared the hell out of the audience. It was exactly what the part called for. I think that before he did this exercise he would never have confronted that rage and been able to use it in front of the audience.

Do you have any specific techniques for arousing emotion?

No. I hate that. I did that fifteen years ago to engineer students around the Shakespeare text—I had them tie their shoes or tap-dance—whatever—while they were doing lines. I don't believe that is fruitful. I now have students work on the language directly.

One of the great things about Shakespeare is that he says what he means. It's all in the words. I have students work on the "Gallop apace" speech from *Romeo and Juliet*. I will ask a student to tell me what the text means, breaking it down into sentences. What happens is that each image becomes personalized and comes into focus. Then I ask the students to focus on the first four beats, and to note what the words sound like—that the rhythm is like that of a horse galloping. No exercise work can ever be as productive as simply dealing with the text. The American Method approach to acting has done everything *but* deal with the text. The acting of the 1950s and 1960s ignored the playwright.

Why does Broadway love English actors? Come on, let's admit it; we do. Because we like hearing how they say what they're saying—

how they "read" the damned lines—which is a lost art in our country. "Line readings? Please, I'm dealing with my inner life."

Do you believe that students can arouse their emotions by dealing purely with the text?

Absolutely. When an actress deals with great language like "Gallop apace . . . ," if she concentrates on what she is saying, things will happen to her organically. She doesn't have to substitute a lot of things or put in a subtext. It's there. When Juliet says, "Take him and cut him out in little stars/ And he will make the face of heaven so fine/ That all the world will be in love with night/ And pay no worship to the garish sun"—what an image! The actress only has to realize what she is talking about. And that's the hard part. It means dealing with the obvious, not looking for something psychological. It's right there in the language and she doesn't have to go any further. Juliet wants her lover. She is desperately impatient, burning up for him and invoking night to come. I could do all kinds of sensory work with the actress, but if she has never desired someone that much, all the sensory work in the world isn't going to help her.

Do you have any techniques for helping students develop a character?

Character work is very important in the third and fourth year of training. We do a lot of real-life studies where students observe people carefully and then present them in class. First I ask them to present the person in the situation in which they observed them, and then they do various improvisations as that person.

I also do a lot of rhythm work to help students find a character. It's the equivalent of a quick sketch in drawing. For example, I will tell an actor to bring in four different characters. After he presents them I might say, "In this character you were getting back to your old rhythm problems." Or "That character was a little slow in gestures, or a little too intellectual. Tomorrow bring in a character that has a faster rhythm." I try to break an actors's habitual rhythm so that it doesn't permeate every character he plays. One of the things to learn about Shakespeare is that his characters talked and thought quickly. Most beginning actors believe that everybody speaks slowly. Variation of rhythm is as important in acting as it is in music.

Animal studies also help in character work. I ask students to decide what animal a character is most like in terms of energy, power, the form his or her aggression takes, etc. One of the best books on acting that I know of is Michael Chekhov's *To the Actor*, especially the chapter on psychological gestures. It's what today we call body language. I do a lot of work on that.

So studying acting is a combination of the actor getting down into himself through the Autodramas and getting out of himself by working on his character through the requirements of the text. It's always a two-way stretch: inside and out, feelings and imagination, heart and mind.

Do you teach students auditioning techniques?

We do it, but I'm tacitly opposed to it. I don't think the department should turn into a finishing school. And that's what's happening in many places. I think students in theater programs have so much to do and learn that it isn't worth wasting six months on that. As I say, we do it, but with the minimum amount of anxiety for us all. When the marketplace invades the conservatory, we have to strike a very delicate balance between the realities of the world outside and our integrity to what training is all about. Training is not about getting students jobs. It's about how you teach young people to teach themselves to become artists.

What is the course of study at Carnegie–Mellon?

Actor training is on the undergraduate level. Students audition for the theater department as freshmen and we accept about forty into the program. Only about half of these graduate because we evaluate students each semester to see if they are suited to our program and if our program is suited to them.

In the junior and senior years the students are members of a company that continually performs in front of audiences. There is four years of voice and speech, movement, and dance, as well as theater history, dramatic literature, and required departmental and nondepartmental electives.

Do you believe that learning to scan the meter is important in performing Shakespeare?

Yes and no. Theoretically yes, but in actuality I think young

American actors have to be careful because they have to find their own meter and scan it differently. Also, I don't like rhymed couplets. I feel like I'm sitting through *'Twas the Night Before Christmas*. I find it much more exciting and unpredictable when actors break the rhythm. In the best English acting today the audience is not aware of the rhythm because it sounds natural. That's what we have to do here when teaching Shakespeare: try to get Shakespeare's words to sound like the language of the person who is speaking. That doesn't mean the actors naturalize the speech (I hate that)—it's still heightened, elevated speech—but actors have to make it seem their own. If you overstress meter scansion, it never becomes the actor's own language; instead, it becomes a very provincial, post-Victorian idea of doing the classics.

Do you use relaxation exercises in training actors?

It depends on what you mean by relaxation. I don't want students to discharge or release their tension, I want them to keep it. They need it to get revved up for what they want. Relaxation exercises make actors look and act anesthetized. Or like the lobotomized victims of some psychic rape. No. This business of relaxing is rubbish. I want actors to learn how to concentrate, not relax. All this business of making the actor comfortable is nonsense. The world is not a Simmons mattress. Whenever an actor tells me he's not "comfortable," I know we're on the right track. Otherwise he's comfortable, the character's comfortable, the audience is comfortable. Let's all go to sleep.

Do you have any approaches for working on comedy?

Comedy is the ability to be very real. I don't like camp or artifice. Fundamentally, I try to help students understand *what* is funny about a basic situation. If they can understand that and deal with the realities of their character through the *language*, and through what is usually terribly painful for that character, what that character wants to the point of absurdity, they can begin to work. Of course, some actors just can't get a laugh if they try. Comedy is a special gift.

How has being a director influenced you as an acting teacher?

When I work with professionals they generally want me to tell them what to do—not *how* to do it. I have to tell students both. But as students progress, I stop telling them how because I believe the actor needs to be free to discover that on his or her own.

As a director, I don't look at things just from moment to moment, but in the context of the overall play—what the play is about and how a character fits into that context.

What advice would you give an actor starting out?

Two things. First, courage! Hang in there and try to believe in yourself. I loved it when Ruth Gordon in her seventies said, "The secret of my success is I hung in there as long as I could."

Second, reality. Don't let your ego stand in the way of your artistic development. Assess what your weaknesses are, know what you need to work on, and go about solving those problems.

Glossary

Affective Memory: A term first used by Stanislavsky. The actor re-creates the stimuli that were present during an emotional experience in his or her own life. He or she tries to re-experience the specific stimuli of the past event instead of simply recalling the event or remembering the emotion.

Beats: A term employed primarily by Method actors to describe how a scene is broken down into a series of intentions or objectives; a beat is a unit of a scene that starts when an intention begins and ends with its completion.

Emotional Memory: This term is used interchangeably with "affective memory."

Endowment: The process of attributing properties or qualities to an object or person so that it affects the actor emotionally or stimulates him to take an action.

Fourth Wall: The side of the stage facing the audience. The fourth wall is an imaginary wall or area between the actor and the audience, used to contain the actor in the environment of his character and to help the actor's concentration.

Given Circumstances: Any event or fact about a character's background that will affect how the actor plays a scene. These events may take place during the time period depicted in the play or may have occurred before the play begins. (Often used interchangeably with "prior circumstances.")

Indicating: Often used as a derogatory term to describe behavior that is not a response to stimuli or is performed without an intention. Often contrasted with "organic behavior."

Inner Monologue: The actor's thoughts underlying the dialogue; what the actor is thinking as the character.

Method, The: An American school of acting that stresses the need for actors to use experiences from their own lives in order to motivate their acting properly. Its chief proponent in the United States was Lee Strasberg.

Moment to Moment: An aspect of acting that focuses on the actor's ability to become aware of and respond to momentary impulses; responding spontaneously to other actors or events as they occur.

Objective: Often used synonymously with "intention." The reason for performing an action; what the character wants or desires in a scene or play.

Obstacle: What stands in the way of a character achieving his or her goal; what makes it difficult for a character to accomplish his or her objective or fulfill an intention.

Particularization: To make something particular and specific. The actor makes all details of place, relationship, objects, the character's needs, and obstacles specific.

Private Moment: An exercise in which actors carry out an activity that they ordinarily would only engage in when alone. The goal of this exercise is to help an actor learn to concentrate so that he can reveal ordinarily private behavior in public.

Sense Memory: The use of the five senses to recall or re-create an object or physical sensation—i.e., heat, cold.

Song and Dance Exercise: An exercise developed by Lee Strasberg intended to interrupt the habitual connection between the patterns of sound and movement in order to release inhibitions and promote expressiveness in the actor; also used to help the actor become aware of his momentary impulses.

Spine: The main idea or theme that permeates the entire play. Every character has his or her own objectives, which are derived from the main theme of the play.

Stanislavsky System: A theory of acting and set of techniques that promote a naturalistic style of acting that stresses "inner truth" as opposed to conventional theatricality.

Substitution: The process whereby an actor uses a person or object from his own life in place of the person or object on stage.

Subtext: The actor's thoughts behind the words, not just their literal meaning. Similar to "inner monologue."

Superobjective: The primary motivation or desire that underlies a character's various actions in a play.